中国当代书画名家作品收藏指南（第二辑）

孟云飞 著
孙琦彦 译

中央编译出版社

《中国当代书画名家作品收藏指南》编辑委员会

名誉主任：高占祥
名誉副主任：王琦　沈鹏　刘艺
执行主任：陈红伟
副　主　任：吕立新　刘金富　田爱生
艺术顾问：廖静文　赵长青　李铎　姚治华　米景扬　张旭光
　　　　　邹德忠　田伯平　梅墨生　李洪海　李涵　李元茂
　　　　　史希光　董辰生　石晓玲
编　　委：张铜彦　张瑞祥　张金卫　夏国珠　顾莹　鲁闽
　　　　　韩振刚　张敢　李家骝　吴守峰　缪法宝　翟品善
　　　　　何学斌　郭利杰　杨军　袁睿　朱清　周佳洁
　　　　　程宇　周钊
主　　编：孟云飞
副　主　编：杨文国　张天文
摄　　影：薛立强
特约编辑：王静
责任校对：谷嫚

序 言

中华民族文明的历程，于今已达数千年之久了。中国书画作为民族文化艺术的重要部分，为促进人类文明和社会进步发挥了巨大的历史作用。独特的中国书画艺术，造就了许许多多伟大的艺术巨匠，他们为我们留下了极其丰富的艺术瑰宝。

胡锦涛总书记在中国文联第八次全国代表大会、中国作协第七次全国代表大会上指出："全面建设小康社会、开创中国特色社会主义新局面的历史进程必将推动我国文艺事业全面发展繁荣，中华民族的伟大复兴必将伴随着中华文化的伟大复兴。" 建国后，尤其是改革开放三十年来，社会稳定，国民经济飞速发展，党和政府对文化建设的高度重视，促使了文化艺术产业的大力发展。人民群众生活水平随着经济的发展，得到了很大的提高，收藏书画艺术作品已经成为很多人尤其是企业家、收藏家重要的文化生活内容。艺术品市场已经成为不可或缺的投资市场之一。

为了让广大书画爱好者及企业家、收藏家更好更准确地了解把握书画艺术品市场，了解书画家的艺术风格、特点、市场认知度及收藏价值，提高书画收藏的水平，我们特邀请了全国著名书画艺术家、文化部文化艺术评估委员会的专家以及拍卖行业的专家，组织编撰了《当代中国书画名家作品收藏指南》一书，供社会广大书画艺术品投资者、企业家、收藏家参考。

高占祥

Preface

Chinese civilization has a history of thousands of years, and being an indispensible part of national culture and art, Chinese painting and calligraphy have been playing an important role in the promotion of human civilization and social progress in history. Numerous great art masters have contributed to the unique art of Chinese painting and calligraphy, leaving later generations with art treasures of extremely abundance.

President Hu Jintao, General Secretary of CPC, said in the Eighth National Congress of China Federation of Literary and Art Circles and the Seventh National Congress of the China Writers Association, "The historical process of building well-off society in an all-round way and creating a new situation in building socialism with Chinese characteristics is bound to promote the overall development and prosperity of our literature and art, and the great rejuvenation of the Chinese nation will be accompanied by the same great rejuvenation of the Chinese culture." Since the People's Republic of China was founded, especially the three decades after China's reform and opening up, China has been enjoying a long-term social stability and rapid development of national economy; meanwhile, our Party and governments have attached great importance to the cultural construction, which has vastly promoted the development of arts and culture industry. With the great improvement of people's living standard benefited from the economic development, it has become the primary culture life for people, especially for entrepreneurs and collectors, to collect calligraphy and painting works; consequently, the art market has also turned to be indispensable for investment.

With the aim of benefiting all the painting and calligraphy enthusiasts, entrepreneurs and collectors and providing with professional information on painting and calligraphy art market, the artistic style, characteristics and market awareness of the artists and the collection value of their works to ensure high-level painting and calligraphy collections, national renowned artists and experts from Arts Assessment Committee of Ministry of Culture and from the auction industry as well are invited to compile Collection Guide to Contemporary Chinese Painting and Calligraphy Works for the reference of art investors, entrepreneurs and collectors.

Zhanxiang Gao

刘岳林	三五
张天文	三六
夏方明	三七
刘德君	三八
严海砚	四〇
刘德君	四〇
汤禄仕	四二
李智民	四三
丁卓辉	四四
沈忠信	四五
耿协生	四六
张天文	四七
冯步明	四八
谢天成	四九
高菲	五〇
李云光	五一
汤锋	五二
陈宏光	五四
槐芳	五六
孔德馨	五八
刘心敏	六〇
米占芳	六二
张文贵	六四
王铁中	六六
常福清	六八
王斌	六九
李欣雨	七〇
辛晋瑛	七一
唐栓怀	七二
陈明逊	一〇六
邓承敏	一〇七
李鸿超	一〇八
李兴建	一〇九
陈维国	一一〇
姜立法	一一一
党正	一一二
张传文	一一三
苟中元	一一四
王丽荣	一一五
郭瑞	一一六
童威尧	一一七
霍炬	一一八
刘武宏	一二〇
柯明	一二二
陈福圣	一二四
况路生	一二六
刘从善	一二八
梁涛	一三〇
梅国庆	一三一
李鹏飞	一三二
杨长喜	一三四
李新斌	一三六
宋学亮	一三八
李赞集	一四〇
王春林	一四二
刘军	一四四
史文青	一四六
王宽中	一八六
陈鸿娟	一八七
王程	一八八
魏仕龙	一八八
王德凯	一九〇
陈昭华	一九二
王高宣	一九三
栾谨魁	一九四
王更新	一九五
梁鹫	一九六
王金光	一九八
王根顺	二〇〇
王珂	二〇二
李增雪	二〇四
王长金	二〇六
李家洪	二〇八
王桢杰	二〇九
马福友	二一〇
卫效卿	二一二
李景春	二一四
文永图	二一六
吴启祥	二一八
沈忠信	二二〇
邓枫	二二一
阎继臣	二二二
吴福田	二二四
尹维忠	二二六
张良田	二二八

目录

姓名	页码	姓名	页码	姓名	页码
张海	一	刘峰	七三	刘万杰	一四八
吴雅明	二	高丽华	七四	唐智东	一五〇
尉天池	三	刘远景	七五	刘希舜	一五二
邢子一	四	张春生	七六	刘希波	一五三
黄惇	五	侯延峰	七七	毛明强	一五四
赵玉林	六	邢顺华	七八	何伟生	一五六
宋华平	八	刘金锡	七九	潘庆五	一五八
张天霖	一〇	刘景堂	八〇	尉迟纪平	一六〇
孙晓云	一二	潘电凤	八二	任仲德	一六二
张立佳	一四	蒋光前	八四	李贵生	一六三
杨京豫	一五	沈勤邦	八六	沈桂林	一六四
郭利杰	一六	冯玉霞	八八	耿协生	一六五
苏茂智	一七	马双彦	八九	史德辉	一六六
张元吉	一八	贺祖荣	九〇	刘谦	一六七
杨燕豫	一九	李政贤	九二	王彤富	一六八
宋传中	二〇	吕能华	九四	刘占起	一六九
骆云	二二	邵建刚	九六	苏世忠	一七〇
胡向麟	二四	郝英辉	九八	崔洪良	一七二
王永峰	二六	张弓强	九九	孙乃恭	一七四
郝志国	二八	李光泉	一〇〇	林汉国	一七六
张寿石	三〇	张传森	一〇一	唐芳卿	一七八
刘振洲	三一	贺书元	一〇二	徐声才	一七九
古凤林	三二	闫道辉	一〇三	谭英群	一八〇
陈立刚	三三	白银禄	一〇四	赵贺庭	一八二
刘远景	三四	黄国建	一〇五	童兆炉	一八四

袁胜聪	二三〇
陈叔铭	二三二
张伯周	二三四
丁连兴	二三六
张 坤	二三八
潘国祥	二三九
张连德	二四〇
余展武	二四一
张明康	二四二
胡德保	二四四
张善贵	二四六
李雅鑫	二四八
张铁成	二五〇
顾林祥	二五一
张耀宗	二五二
刘绍斌	二五三
张 维	二五四
朱国俊	二五六
赵国鸿	二五八
张映文	二六〇
周元蛟	二六二
宋存哲	二六三
朱长明	二六四
王明亮	二六五
李智民	二六六
张宝珍	二六七
刘中方	二六八
张荣华	二六九
江太生	二七〇
张文健	二七一
路建军	二七二
金威昕	二七四
栾传益	二七六
张 馨	二七七
罗少模	二七八
甄春明	二七九
马东山	二八〇
吴俊祥	二八二
马 杰	二八四
李恒才	二八五
毛明强	二八六
樊春华	二八七
彭国远	二八八
于 宏	二九〇
陈伯龙	二九一
郭学忠	二九二
蒋徐风	二九三
解长河	二九四
李兴建	二九五
王 军	二九六
吴庆瑞	二九七
潘振德	二九八
徐 茂	二九九
玄 一	三〇〇

张海　　*Zhang Hai*

张海，男，1941年9月生于河南省偃师市。现任中国书法家协会主席，郑州大学美术学院院长。全国政协常委，曾任第八、九、十届全国人大代表，河南省文联主席，河南省书法家协会主席，河南省书画院院长等。

润笔价格：50000/平尺

Zhang Hai, male, born in Yanshi, Henan Province, in the September of 1941, is President of China Calligraphers Association, and of Fine Arts Department of Zhengzhou University. He is also President of Henan Federation of Literary and Art Circles, of Henan Calligraphers Association, and of Henan Painting and Calligraphy Academy.

Reference price: RMB50000 per square feet

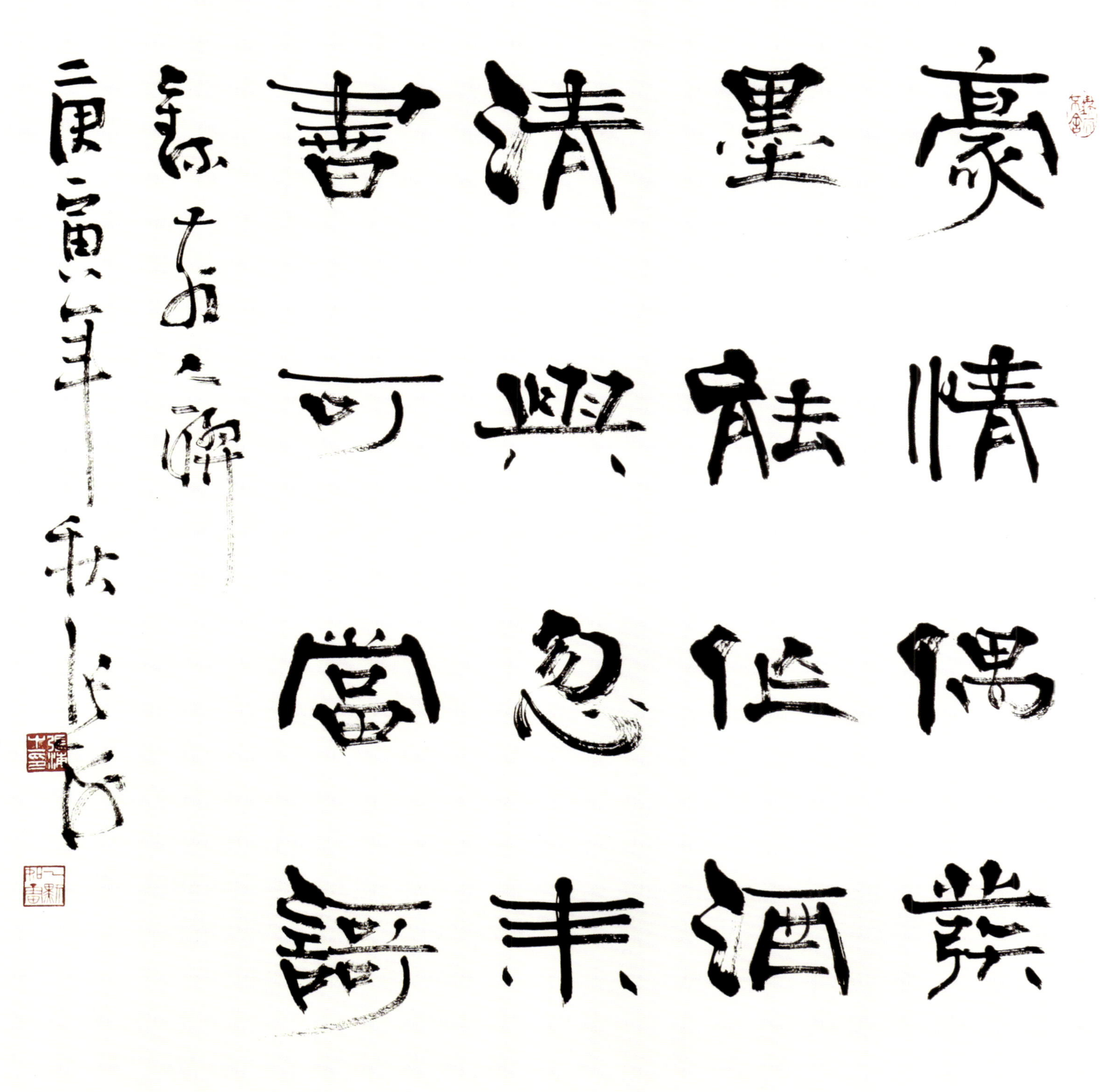

《豪情偶发墨》　　68cm×68cm　　*Lofty Sentiments*

吴雅明　*Wu Yaming*

吴雅明，男，号称三江蜀人，1947年出生于四川洪雅。中国书画界联合会副主席，中国禅学艺术研究会会长。

润笔价格：16000/平尺

Wu Yaming, male, born in Hongya, Sichuan Province, in1947, and with Sanjiang Shuren as his literary name, is Vice President of Federation of Chinese Calligraphy and Painting Circles, and Director of Zen Art Research Institute of China.
Reference price: RMB 16000 per square feet

《花溪河畔》　98cm×90cm　　*Huaxi Riverside*

尉天池　*Yu Tianchi*

尉天池，男，1936年4月生，安徽省砀山县人。中共党员，1960年7月毕业于南京师范学院中文系，江苏省书法家协会主席，曾任中国书法家协会副主席。

润笔价格：25000/平尺

Yu Tianchi, male, born in Dangshan County, Anhui Province, in the April of 1936, is a Party member. He majored in Chinese and graduated at Nanjing Normal University. Yu is Vice President of China Calligraphers Association, and President of Jiangsu Calligraphers Association.

Reference price: RMB25000 per square feet

《舍得》　35cm×70cm　　*Giving and Gaining*

邢子一 *Xing Ziyi*

邢子一，男，1949年出生于吉林省榆树县，现为中国美术家协会会员、中国国画家协会理事、中国文联书画中心画家。1987年拜北京画院著名画家张步为师，主攻山水、多次赴名山大川写生。

润笔价格：10000/平尺

Xing Ziyi, male, born in Yulin County, Jilin Province, in 1949, is a member of China Artists Association, council member of China Association of Traditional Chinese Painting, and painter with Calligraphy and Painting Center of China Federation of Literary and Art Circles. Xing learned about landscape painting with Zhang Bu, a celebrated painter with Beijing Art Academy, and went to many famous mountains and rivers for sketching.

Reference price: 10000 per square feet

《清居图》　68cm×138cm　　*A Comely Residence*

黄惇 *Huang Dun*

黄惇，男，别署风斋，南京艺术学院美术系教授，博士生导师，1947年3月生于江苏太仓，现为中国书法家协会学术委员会委员、中国书法家协会篆刻艺术委员会委员、全国中青年书法篆刻展评审委员、全国篆刻艺术展评委、江苏省美术馆艺术鉴定顾问、中国美术家协会会员、西泠印社理事、中国沧浪书社成员等。

润笔价格：20000/平尺

Huang Dun, male, born in Taicang, Jiangsu Province, in the March of 1947, and also by the name of Fengzhai, is a doctorate supervisor, and professor with Department of Fine Arts of Nanjing Arts University. He is a member of Academic Committee and Seal Cutting Committee of China Calligraphers Association, and of Appraisal Committee of National Calligraphy and Seal Cutting Exhibition and National Seal Cutting Art Exhibition. Huang is also a consultant of art appraisal with Jiangsu Art Museum, member of China Artists Association, council member of Xileng Society of Seal Arts, and member of China Canglang Book Society, etc.

Reference price: RMB 20000per square feet

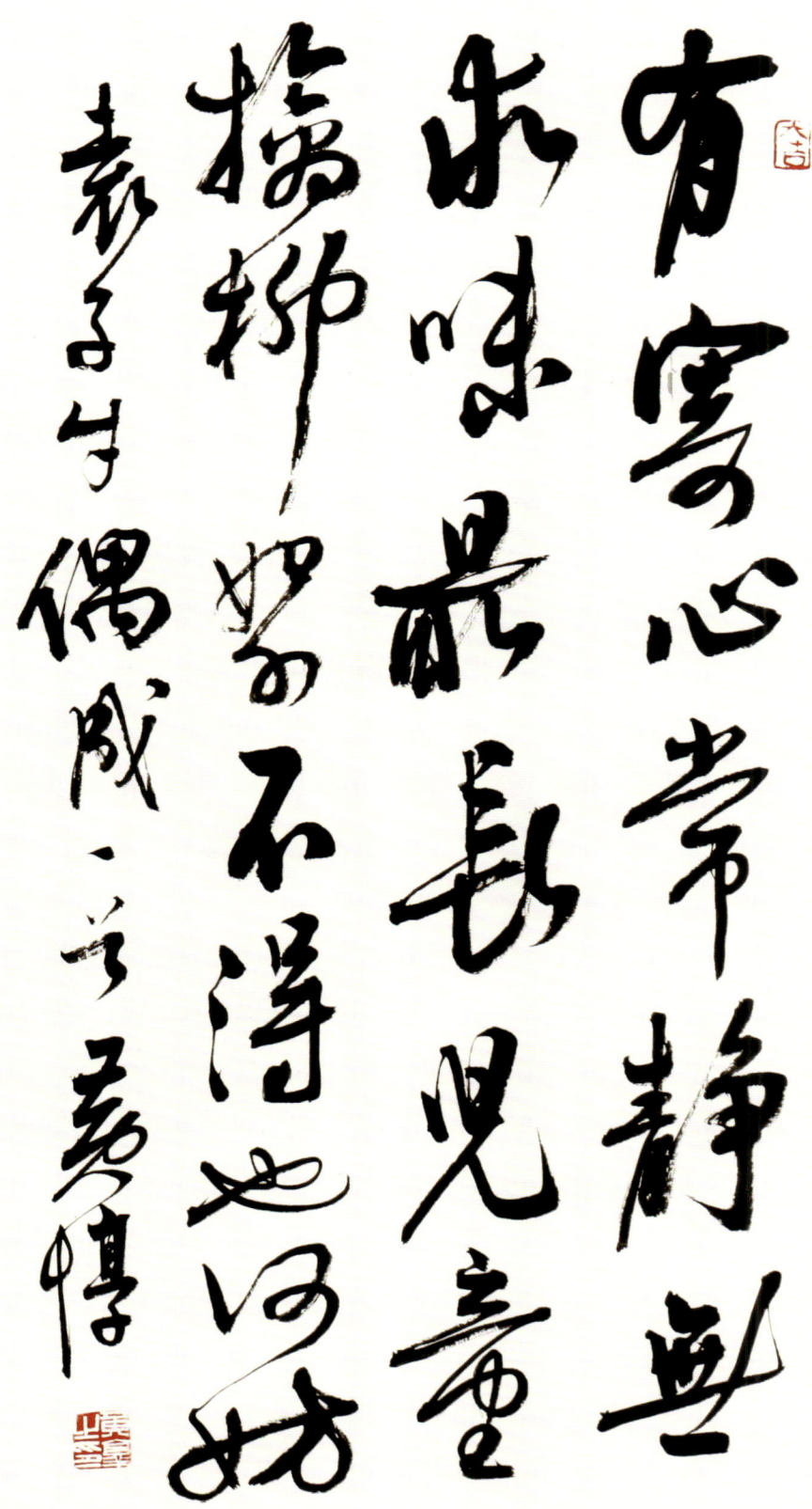

《书法一幅》 70cm×35cm *A Calligraphy Scroll*

赵玉林 *Zhao Yulin*

赵玉林，男，笔名三友，包头市美协副主席、内蒙古草原书画院院长、中国书画家联谊会会员、新加坡神州画院院士、泰山书画研究院客座教授、画家杂志社编辑、国家博物馆特邀书画家。

润笔价格：16000/平尺

Zhao Yulin, male, with Sanyou as his literary name, is Vice President of Baotou Artists Association, President of Grassland Calligraphy and Painting Gallery of Inner Mongolia, and member of Chinese Calligrapher and Painter Federation. Zhao is also a painter with Singapore Shenzhou Painting Art Gallery, visiting professor of Mount Tai Calligraphy and Painting Research Institute, editor of Painters, and distinguished calligrapher and painter with National Museum.

Reference price: RMB 16000 per square feet

《太行福地》 97cm×180cm *Auspicious Places in Taihang Mountains*

《胡杨礼赞》　180cm×97cm　　*A Psalm of Huyang*

宋华平　*Song Huaping*

宋华平，男，1955年1月出生于河南确山县，祖籍山东泰安，1984年调入河南省书法家协会，现任河南省书法家协会主席，河南省文联副主席，河南省政协常委，中国书法家协会行书委员会副主任，郑州大学书画名誉教授。

润笔价格：25000/平尺

Song Huaping, male, though his family were originally from Tai'an, Shandong Province, was born in Queshan County, Henan Province, in the January of 1955. Song joined Henan Calligraphers Association in 1984, and now is its President. He is a CPPCC member of Henan, Vice President of Henan Federation of Literary and Art Circles, Deputy Director of Semi-Cursive Committee of China Calligraphers Association, and honorary professor of calligraphy and painting with Zhengzhou University.

Reference price: RMB25000 per square feet

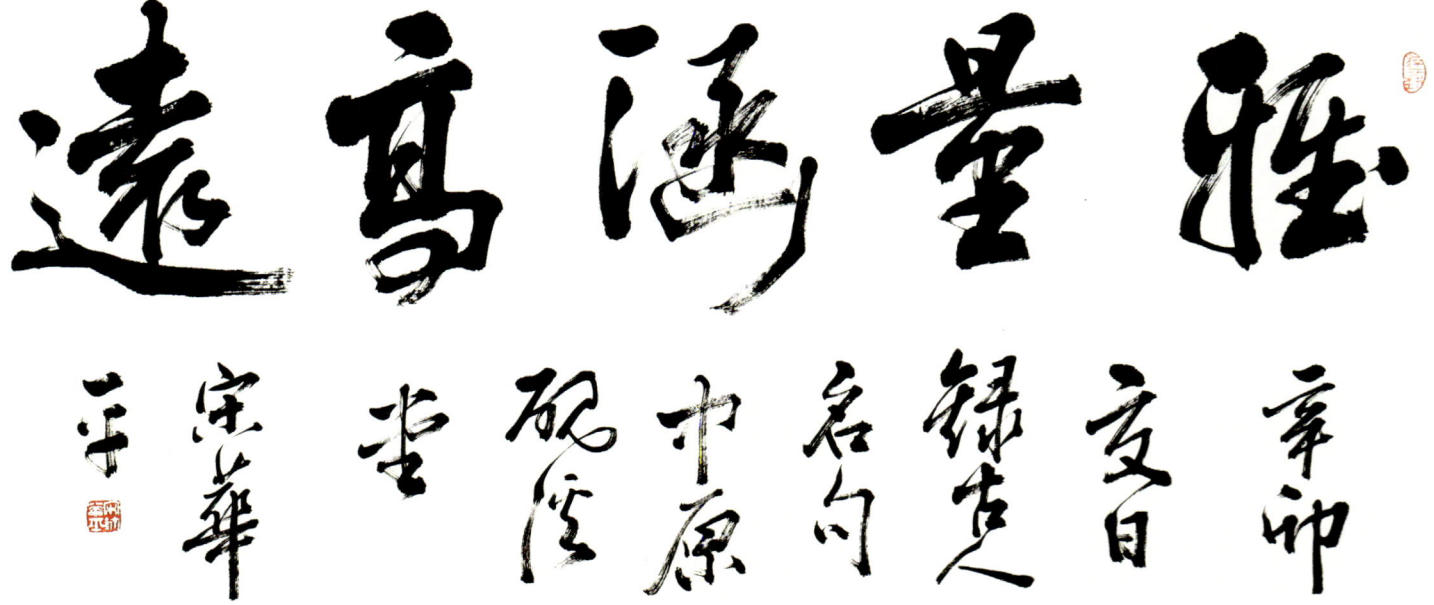

《雅量涵高远》　　138cm×69cm　　*Lofty Magnanimity*

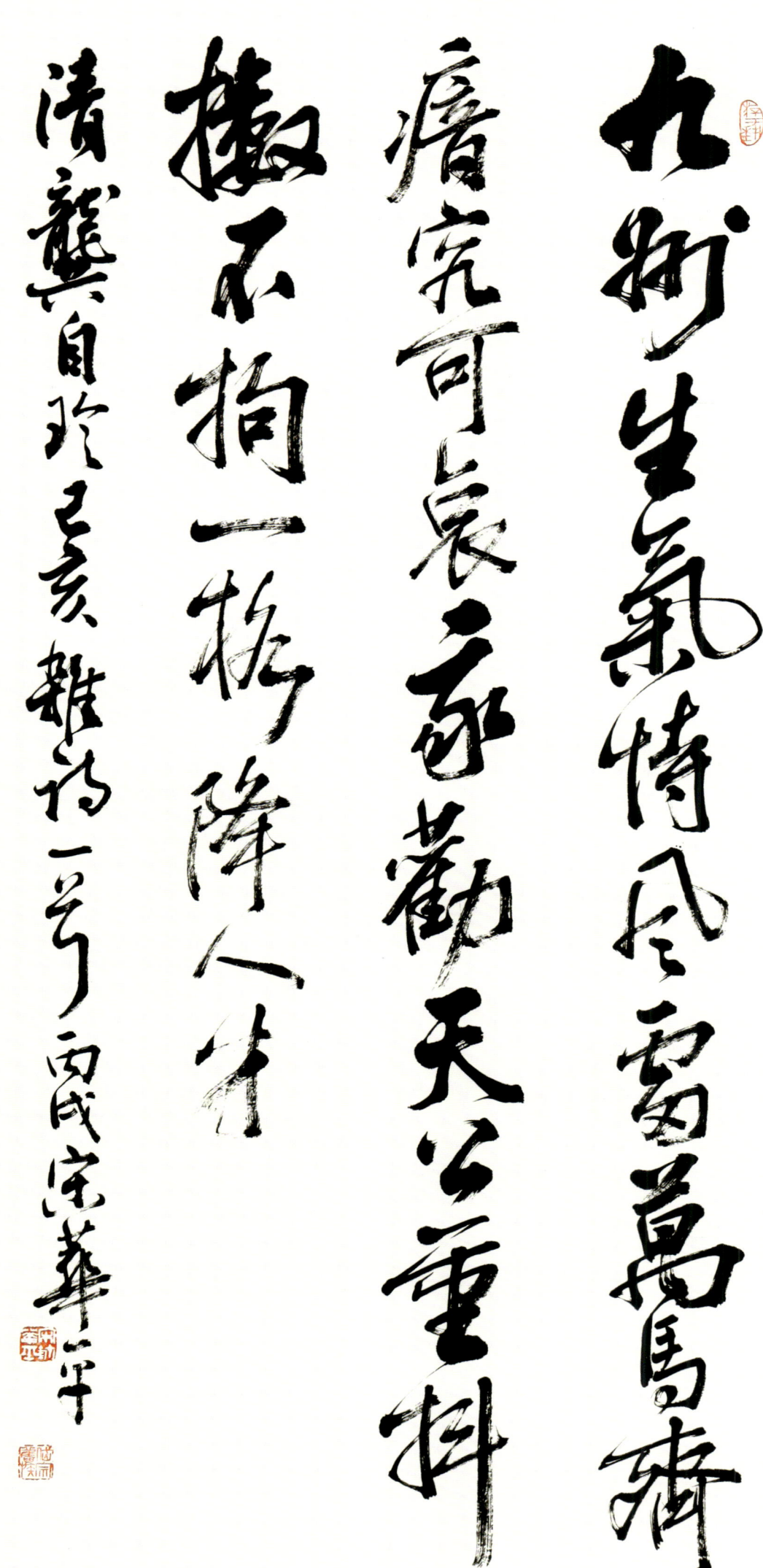

《清龚自珍诗一首》　138cm×69cm　　*A Poem by Gong Zizhen*

张天霖 *Zhang Tianlin*

张天霖,男,浙江湖州人,南京军区文艺创作室美术创作员,国家高级美术师。1953年4月生,曾先后结业于江苏省国画院、解放军艺术学院,受教于宋玉麟、刘大为等老师。1990年加入中国美协。

润笔价格:12000/平尺

Zhang Tianlin, male, born in Huzhou, Zhejiang Province, in the April of 1953, graduated from Jiangsu Traditional Painting Institute and then from PLA Academy of Arts, during which he learned with Mr. Song Yulin, Mr. Liu Dawei and other masters. He now is a National senior artist, and painter with Creative Studio of Nanjing Military Region, who joined China Artists Association in 1990.
Reference price: RMB 12000 per square feet

《天风海涛》　97cm×180cm　*The Winds and the Waves*

孙晓云 Sun Xiaoyun

孙晓云，女，1955年8月生，现为国家一级美术师，南京书画院副院长，中国书法家协会理事，江苏省书法家协会副主席，中国书法家协会评审委员会委员，南京大学兼职教授、研究员。

润笔价格:25000/平尺

Sun Xiaoyun, female, born in August, 1955, is a National Class A artist, Vice President of Nanjing Painting and Calligraphy Academy, and council member of China Calligraphers Association. She is also Vice President of Jiangsu Calligraphers Association, member of Appraisal Committee of CCA, and researcher and part-time professor with Nanjing University.

Reference price: RMB25000 per square feet

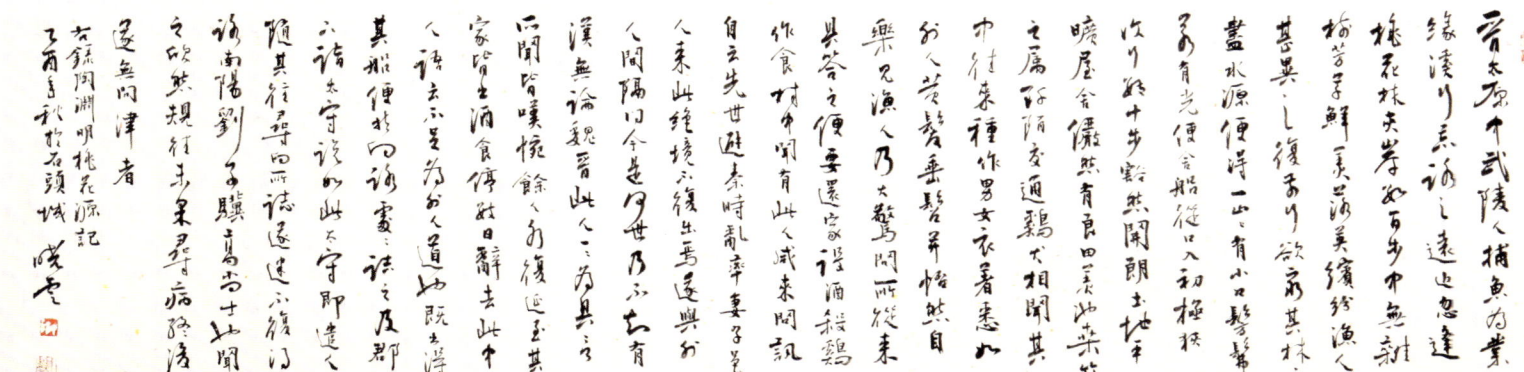

《桃花源记》　　34cm×128cm　　*Notes of the Land of Peach Blossoms*

张立佳 *Zhang Lijia*

张立佳，男，1949年生，河北雄县人，自幼师从胡荫樟先生学习传统山水画，后拜中央美术学院教授梁树年先生为师，现为河北省美协会员。多次参加省级全国大型美术展览，部分作品被有关单位收藏，出版多部个人专集。

润笔价格：12000/平尺

Zhang Lijia, male, born in Xiong County, Hebei Province, in 1949, learned about traditional landscape painting with Mr. Hu Yinzhang in his childhood, and later with Mr. Liang Shunian, professor of Central Academy of Fine Arts. Zhang is now a member of Hebei Artists Association, whose works have been exhibited in national and provincial large-scale art exhibitions. He has published several personal collections and some of his works have also been collected.

Reference price: RMB 12000 per square feet

《峰峦叠翠》 97cm×180cm *Running Mountain Ridges*

《青山牧归》　69cm×138cm　*Herding Returns*

杨京豫 *Yang Jingyu*

杨京豫，女，1964年3月出生，大学学历，副教授，国家二级美术师，中国书法家协会会员，河南省美术家协会会员，河南省女子书画家协会理事，新乡市女子书法家协会副主席。

润笔价格：8000/平尺

Yang Jingyu, female, born in the March of 1964, is an associate professor and National Class B artist. She is a member of China Calligraphers Association, of Henan Artists Association, council member of Henan Women Artists Association, and Vice President of Xinxiang Women Calligraphers Association.

Reference price: RMB 8000 per square feet

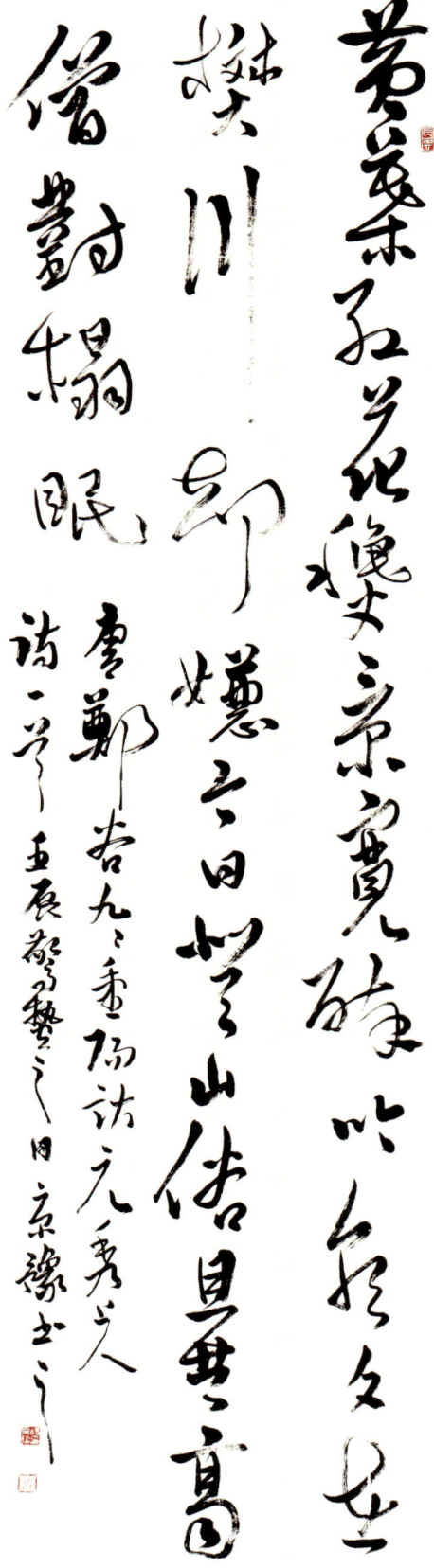

《唐诗一首》   180cm×53cm   *A Poem*

郭利杰 *Guo Lijie*

郭利杰，男，中国书画家联谊会画家、陕西西北书画研究院副院长、陕西太白书画院名誉院长、陕西书画培训学院国画教授。

润笔价格：16000/平尺

Guo Lijie, male, is a painter with Chinese Calligrapher and Painter Federation, Vice President of Northwest China Calligraphy and Painting Research Institute of Shaanxi, Honorary President of Shaanxi Taibai Art Gallery, and professor of Traditional Chinese Painting with Shaanxi Calligraphy and Painting Training College.

Reference price: RMB 16000 per square feet

《春风得意》　68cm×68cm　*Vigorous Spring Breeze*

苏茂智 *Su Maozhi*

苏茂智，男，字道生，1951年12月生，河南省长垣县人，中国书法家协会会员，中国艺术研究院特聘研究员，中国书法艺术研究院学术委员，嵩晖印社理事长，新乡市书法家协会副主席。

润笔价格：7000/平尺

Su Maozhi, male, with Daosheng as his courtesy name, born in Changyuan County, Henan Province, in the December of 1951, is a member of China Calligraphers Association, especially employed researcher with Chinese National Academy of Arts, and member of Academic Committee of China Calligraphy Research Institute. Su is also President of Songhui Society of Seal Arts, and Vice President of Xinxiang Calligraphers Association.

Reference price: RMB 7000 per square feet

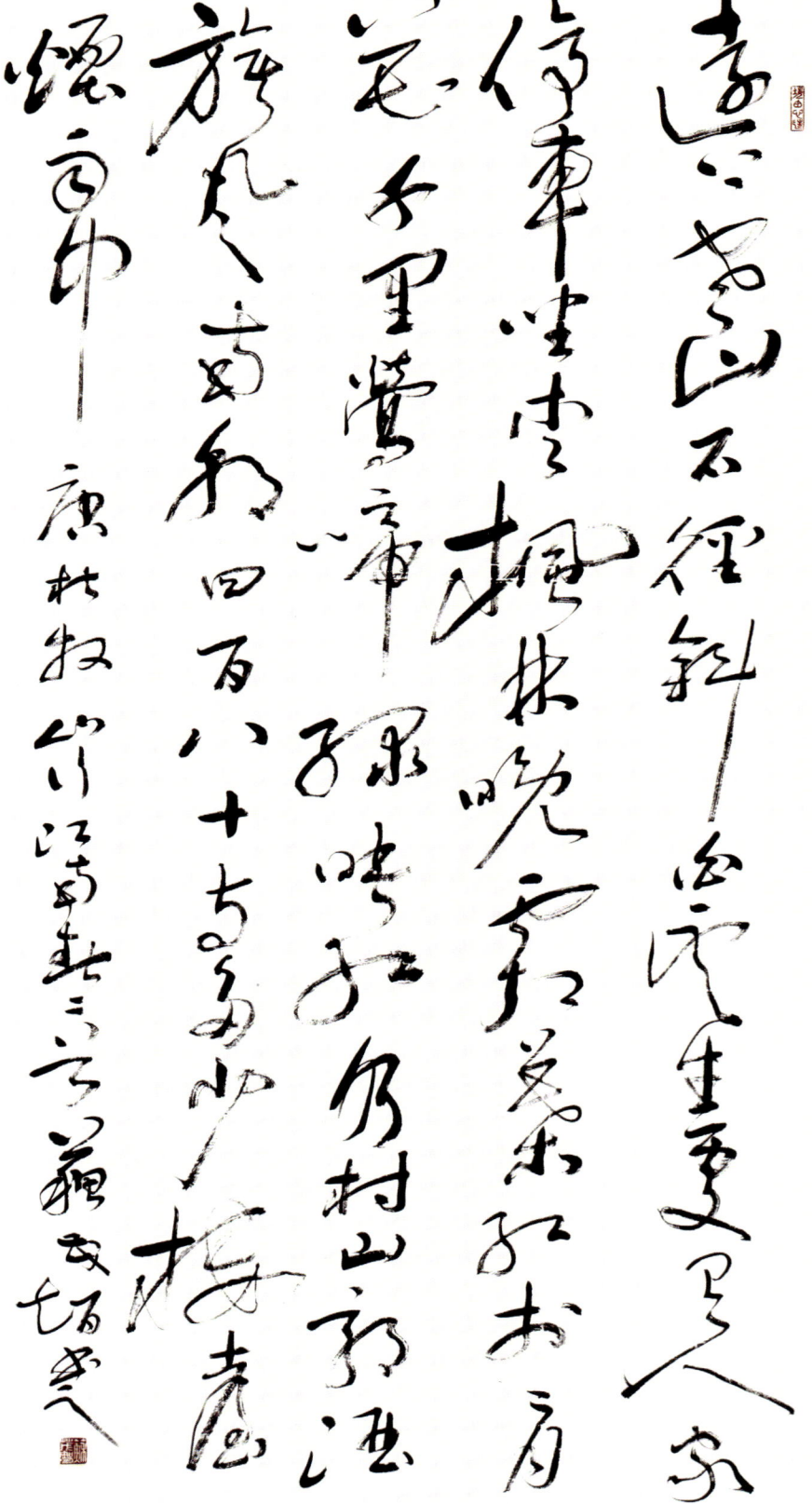

《唐杜牧—山行》　180cm×98cm　　Trip to Mountain by Du Mu

张元吉　*Zhang Yuanji*

张元吉，男，1966年8月出生于青海省化隆县,为中国美术家协会会员、青海省美术家协会副主席、青海省书法家协会编辑委员会委员、现就读于中央美术学院张立辰高研班。

润笔价格：16000/平尺

Zhang Yuanji, male, born in Hualong County, Qinghai Province, in the August of 1966, is a member of China Artists Association, Vice President of Qinghai Artists Association, and committee member of Qinghai Calligraphers Association. He now attends Zhang Lichen Art Research Classes in China Central Academy of Fine Arts.

Reference price: RMB 16000 per square feet

《紫气东来》　　139cm×68cm　　*Propitious Omen*

杨燕豫 *Yang Yanyu*

杨燕豫,女,祖籍河南,生于北京,国家二级美术师,中国书法家协会会员,河南省妇女书画家协会理事,新乡市书法家协会副主席,新乡市女子书法家协会委员会主席,新乡市卫滨区第六届、第七届政协委员。

润笔价格:6000/平尺

Yang Yanyu, female, with her family from Henan Province, born in Beijing, is a National Class B artist, member of China Calligraphers Association, and council member of Henan Women Calligraphers Association. Yang is also Vice President of Xinxiang Calligraphers Association, President of Xinxiang Women Calligraphers Association, and the Sixth and Seventh CPPCC member of Weibin District of Xinxiang.

Reference price: RMB6000 per square feet

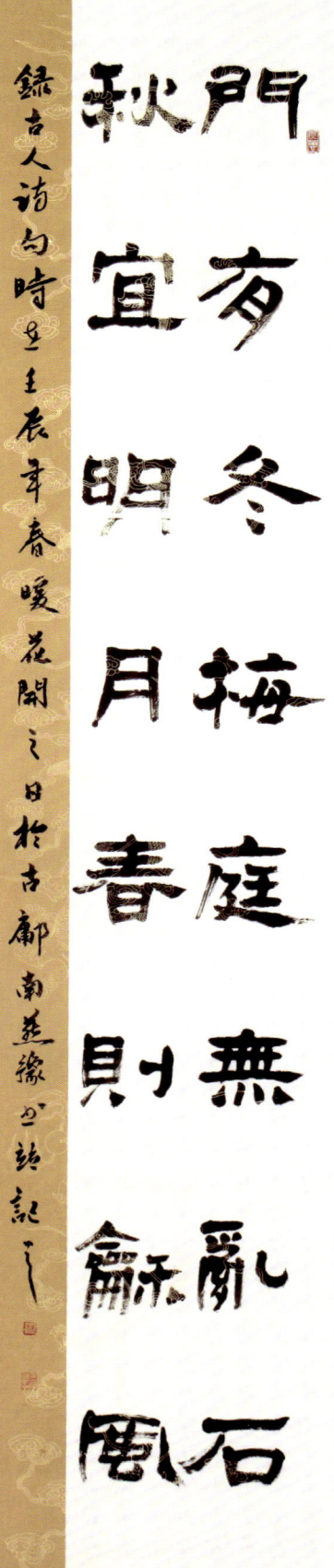

《录古人诗句》　　180cm×43cm　　*Ancient lines*

骆云　*Luo Yun*

骆云，男，字云峰，号山人，祖籍河北衡水。中国美协河北分会会员、河北山水画研究会理事、中国书画家协会理事、中国伏羲文化研究会理事、国际奥林匹克书画大赛特聘画家。

润笔价格：16000/平尺

Luo Yun, male, with Yunfeng as his courtesy name and with Shanren as his literary name, was born in Hengshui, Hebei Province. Luo is a member of Hebei Artists Association, council member of Landscape Painting Research Society of Hebei, and of China Calligrapher and Painter Association. He is also a member of China Fuxi Culture Research Institute, and especially employed painter with International Olympic Calligraphy and Painting Contest.

Reference price: RMB 16000 per square feet

《云泉涌太行》　69cm×180cm　*Bubbling Springs in Taihang Mountains*

宋传中　*Song Chuanzhong*

宋传中，男，1962年生，现为河南省书法家协会会员，作品被国内外人士收藏。
润笔价格：7000/平尺

Song Chuanzhong, male, born in 1962, is a member of Henan Calligraphers Association, whose works have been widely collected by people in and out of China.
Reference price: RMB 7000 per square feet

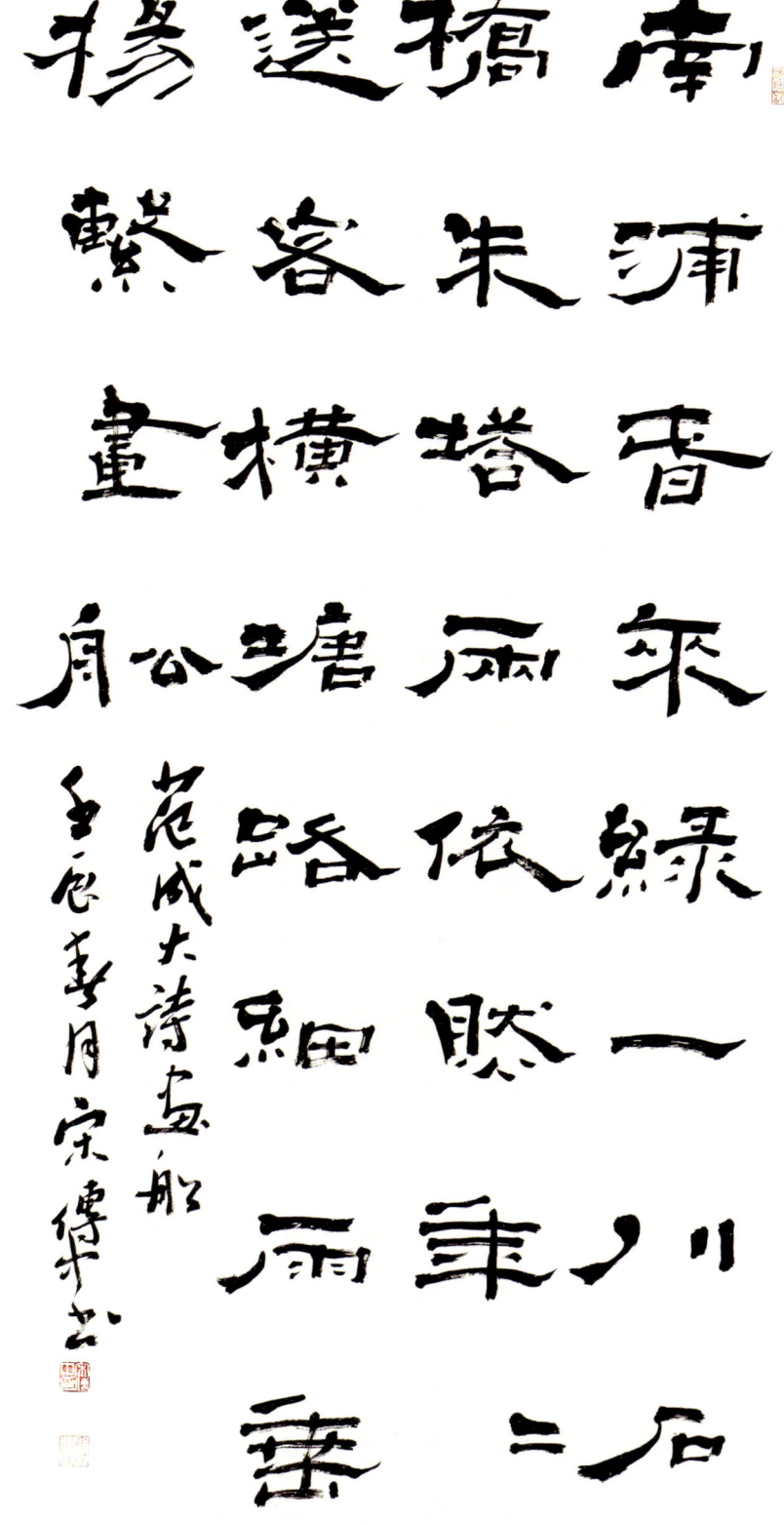

《范成大诗一首》　　138cm×69cm　　*A Poem by Fan Chengda*

寒山转苍翠 秋水日潺湲 倚杖柴门外 临风听暮蝉 渡头馀落日 墟里上孤烟 复值接舆醉 狂歌五柳前

王维诗一首 壬辰季宋传乐书

《王维诗一首》 179cm×48cm A Poem by Wang Wei

胡向麟 *Hu Xianglin*

胡向麟，男，1943年生于江苏丰县，自幼酷爱绘画，1971年正式拜京都名家许麟庐为师。1986年至1988年入西安美术学院中国画系研修，现为江苏省美术家协会会员，高级画师，南京画院特邀画师。

润笔价格：12000/平尺

Hu Xianglin, male, born in Feng County, Jiangsu Province, in 1943, has been an ardent lover of painting since his childhood, formally became a disciple of his mentor Mr. Xu Linlu in 1971, and later studied at Department of Traditional Chinese Painting at Xi'an Academy of Fine Arts from 1986 to 1988. He now is a senior painter, and member of Jiangsu Artists Association, and especially employed painter with Nanjing Painting Art Gallery.

Reference price: RMB 12000 per square feet

《兰花》 92cm×47cm *Orchids*

《白莲花开佛情见》　　139cm×69cm　　*Lotus*

王永峰　*Wang Yongfeng*

王永峰，男，字湘泰，号泳棠。1957年8月生，河南新乡人。中国书法家协会会员，河南省书法家协会篆刻创作委员会委员，河南书画院特聘书法家，东方艺术研究院终身名誉院长，新乡市书法家协会常务理事，新乡市书法家协会篆刻艺术委员会副主任兼秘书长，新乡市山水画艺委会副主任兼秘书长，新乡县书法家协会主席。

润笔价格：5000/平尺

Wang Yongfeng, male, with Xiangtai as his courtesy name and Yongtang as his literary name, was born in Xinxiang, Henan Province, in the August of 1957. He is a member of China Calligraphers Association, of Seal Cutting Committee of Henan Calligraphers Association, and an especially employed calligrapher with Henan Calligraphy and Painting Academy. Wang is lifelong Honorary President of Oriental Art Research Institute, Deputy Director and Secretary General of Seal Cutting Committee and standing council member of Xinxiang Calligraphers Association. He also bears the position of Deputy Director and Secretary General of Xinxiang Landscape Art Committee, and President of Xinxiang Calligraphers Association.

Reference price: RMB 5000 per square feet

《梅花诗—苏轼》　　179cm×48cm　　*Plum Flowers by Su Shi*

郝志国　*Hao Zhiguo*

郝志国，男，1944年生，中国美术家协会会员，中国版画家协会理事，大同大学美术教授，中国优秀版画家鲁迅奖获得者。

润笔价格：20000/平尺

Hao Zhiguo, male, born in 1944, is a member of China Artists Association, council member of China Printmakers Association, professor of Fine Arts with Datong University, and winner of Lu Xun Prize for Excellent Printmakers in China.
Reference price: RMB 20000 per square feet

《仕女图》　69cm×69cm　　*Court Ladies*

张寿石 *Zhang Shoushi*

张寿石，男，法号印池、潢泰山人，字为君、乃芝、永旭，斋号珍石山房、镂云书屋，河北安国人。现任中国书法家协会会员，中国文联书画艺术交流中心理事，世界艺术家协会副会长，中国王羲之艺术研究会研究员，中国齐白石艺术研究会副会长，中国荣宝斋推荐书画家，中国炎黄印社社长，当代肖行印社副社长，中国国际经典书画院荣誉院长，中华湖社画会常务理事艺委会主任，中国国家画院特聘书法篆刻家。

润笔价格：4000/平尺

Zhang Shoushi, male, with Yinchi and Huangtai Shanren as his monastic name, with Weijun, Naizhi and Yongxu as his courtesy name, and Zhenshi Shanfang and Louyun Study as his study's name, was born in Anguo, Hebei Province. He is a member of China Calligraphers Association, council member of Art Exchange Center of China Federation of Literary and Art Circles, Vice President of Worldwide Calligraphers Association, researcher with Wang Xizhi Art Research Institute of China, and Vice President of Qi Baishi Research Institute. Zhang is also a recommended painter by China Rongbaozhai, President of China Yanhuang Society of Seal Arts, Vice President of Contemporary Xiaohang Society of Seal Arts, Honorary President of China International Classical Calligraphy and Painting Gallery, and standing council member and Director of Arts Committee of China Hushe Painting Society as well. He is an especially employed seal calligrapher with China National Academy of Painting.

Reference Price: RMB4000 per square feet

《仁寿》　53cm×83cm　*Benevolent Longevity*

《福寿》　　136cm×68cm　　Blessing Longevity

刘振洲 *Liu Zhenzhou*

刘振洲，男，字元石，号青山居士，河北省雄县张庄村人，著名画家娄师白弟子。河北省书协、美协会员，中国楹联学会会员，雄县书协、美协会员，白洋淀诗书画院会员，中华诗词协会会员，中国书法艺术研究院理事，中国画家协会理事。

润笔价格：8000/平尺

Liu Zhenzhou, male, with Yuanshi as his courtesy name, and with Qingshan Jushi (Buddhist in Green Hills) as his literary name, was born in Zhangzhuang, Xiong County, Hebei Province. Liu learned painting with famed painter Mr. Lou Shibai, and now is a member of Hebei Calligraphers Association, of Hebei Artists Association, of Yinglian Society of China, and of Xiong County Calligraphers Association. He is also a member of Xiong County Artists Association, of Baiyangdian Gallery of China, of Chinese Poetry Association, council member of Chinese Calligraphy Art Research Institute, and of China Calligrapher and Painter Association.

Reference price: RMB 8000 per square feet

《竹报平安》　78cm×180cm　　*Bamboos that Reports Safety and Peace*

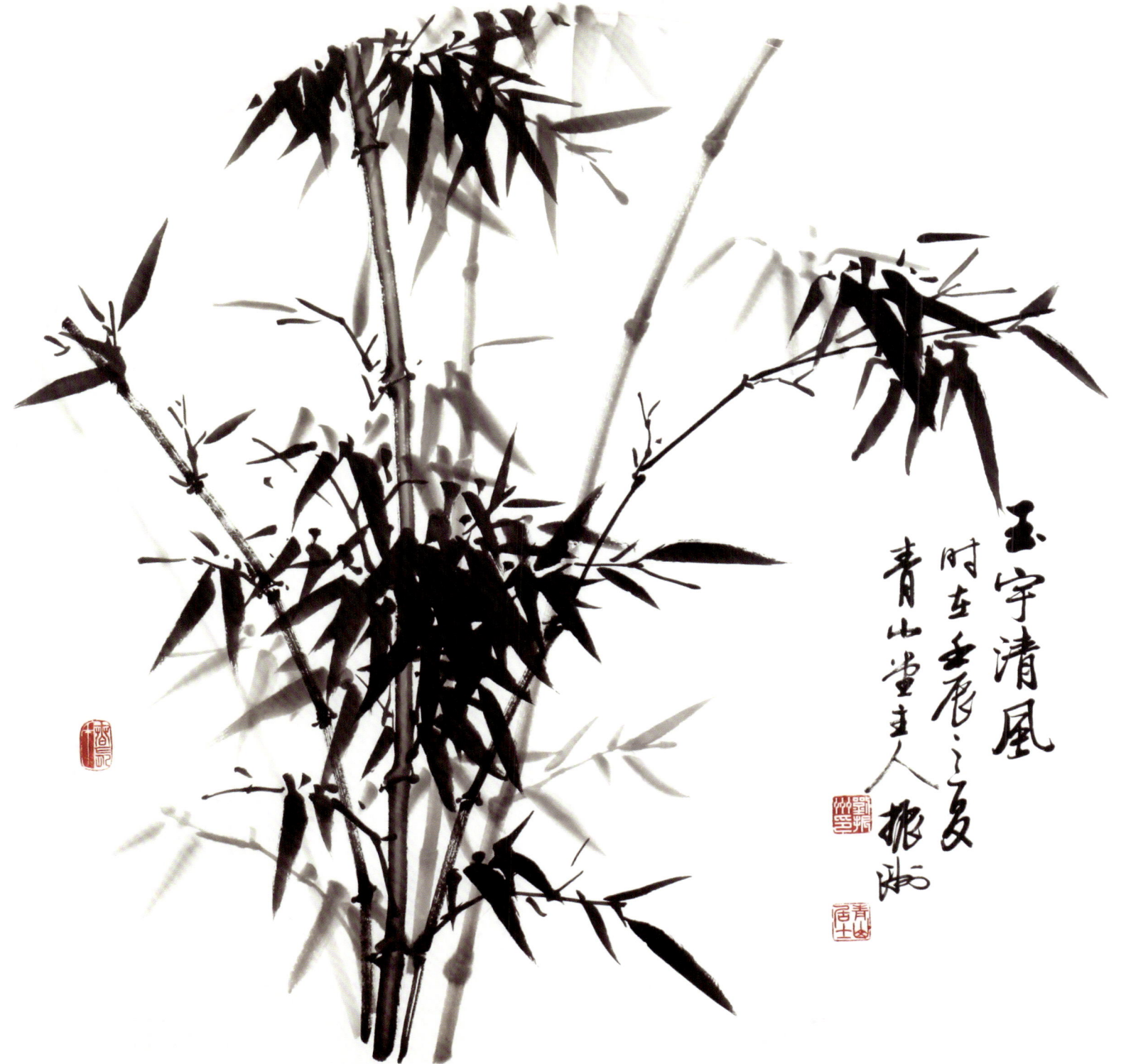

《玉宇清风》　68cm×68cm　　*Breeze through the Palace*

古凤林　*Gu Fenglin*

古凤林，男，现为国务院国（宾）礼特供艺术家；大同市书法家协会常务副秘书长、大同市诗书画印协会副会长；大同市云冈书画院学术委员。被中国名人文化研究会聘为学术委员，二级书画师。

润笔价格：6000/平尺

Gu Fenglin, male, is a Special National-Gifted Artist of State council of China, standing Vice President of Datong Calligraphers Association, and of Datong Association for Poetry, Calligraphy, Painting and Seal. He is also a member of Academic Committee of Yungang Calligraphy and Painting Institute of Datong and of Chinese Celebrity Culture Research. Gu is a Class B calligrapher and painter.

Reference price: RMB 6000 per square feet

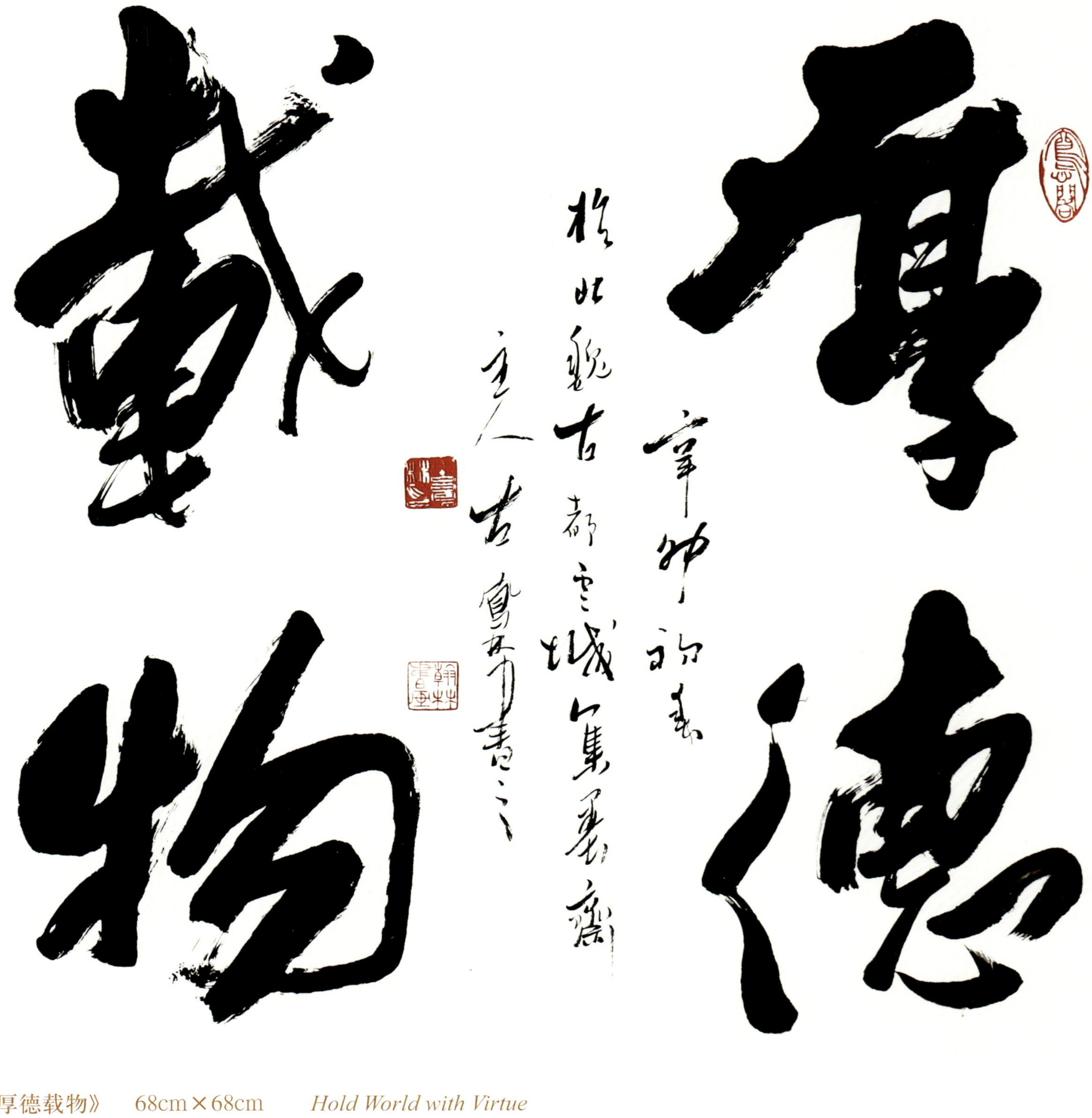

《厚德载物》　68cm×68cm　　*Hold World with Virtue*

陈立刚　*Chen Ligang*

陈立刚，男，1953年生于山东诸城，中日韩新书画家友好联盟理事、中山书画院院士、青岛市美术家协会会员、中国江都书画院特聘画师。

润笔价格：14000/平尺

Chen Ligang, male, born in Zhucheng, Shandong Province, in 1953, is a council member of Artists Alliance of China, Japan, Korea and Singapore, painter with Zhongshan Calligraphy and Painting Gallery, member of Qingdao Artists Association, and especially employed painter with Jiangdu Calligraphy and Painting Gallery of China.

Reference price: RMB 14000 per square feet

《听泉》　68cm×68cm　　*Hark the Spring*

《观瀑》　68cm×68cm　*Viewing the Waterfall*

刘远景 *Liu Yuanjing*

刘远景，男，1958年12月生，山东阳谷人，中华教育艺术家协会会员，山东硬笔书法家协会副主席，山东棵树协会常务理事，中国美协山东分会会员，中国书协山东分会会员。

润笔价格：4000/平尺

Liu Yuanjing, male, born in Yanggu, Shandong Province, in the December of 1958, is a member of China Education Artists Association, Vice President of Shandong Association of Pen Calligraphers, and standing committee member of Shandong Tree Association. Liu is also a member of Shandong Artists Association, and of Shandong Calligraphers Association.

Reference price: RMB 4000 per square feet

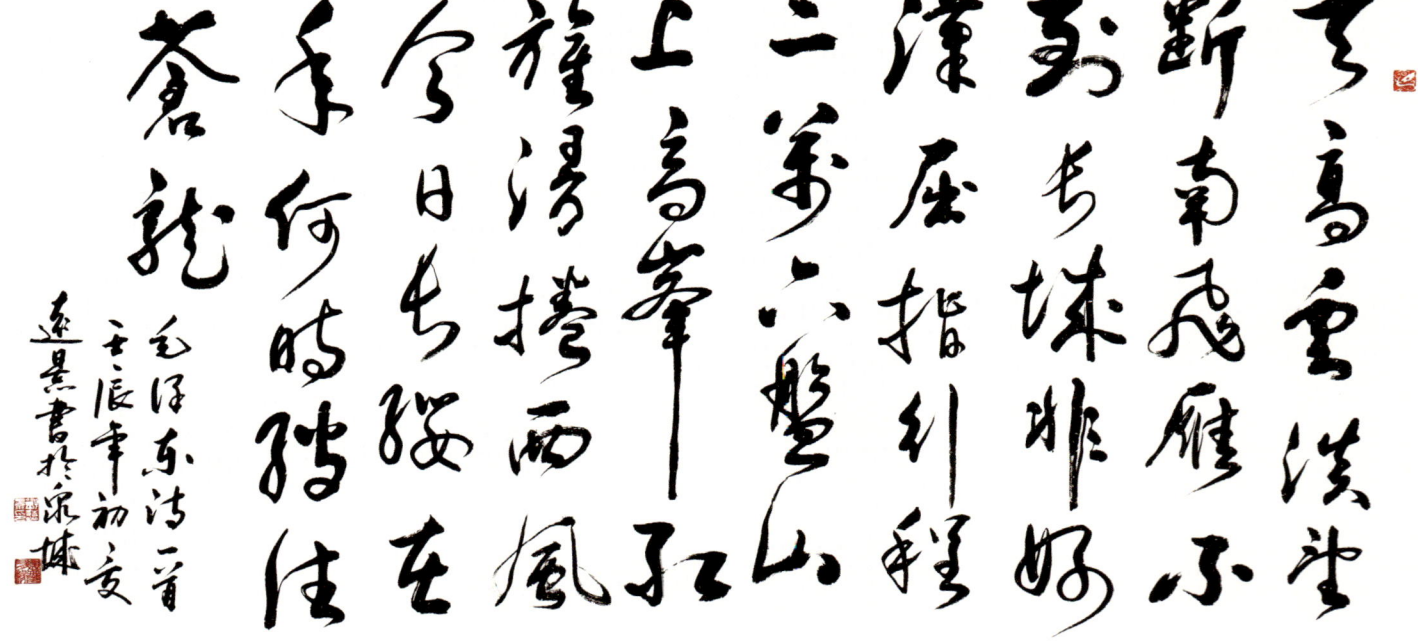

《毛泽东诗一首》　　96cm×179cm　　*A Poem by Mao Zedong*

刘岳林 *Liu Yuelin*

刘岳林，男，生于1950年，原籍河北省雄县，现居北京。中国当代画坛名家，专攻画哈密瓜，成就卓越，形成了独特的画风，被公认为画哈密瓜国手，成为名副其实的全国画哈密瓜之最的典范名家，现为中国书画家协会副主席、中国艺术品价值评审委员会副主任、新疆警官高等司法警官学院客座教授、中国人民对外友好协会艺术创作院专业画家、一级美术师。

润笔价格：25000—28000/平尺

Liu Yuelin, male, born in Xiong County, Hebei Province, in 1950, is a renowned contemporary painter, and specializes in Melon Art. With his unique painting style in Melon Art, Liu has been reverenced as the Nation Hand and master in melon painting. He is a Class A artist, Vice President of China Calligrapher and Painter Association, and Vice Director of Chinese Art Ware Appraisal Committee. Liu is also a visiting professor with Xinjiang Advanced Institute for Correctional Police, and professional painter with Art Gallery of Chinese People's Association for Friendship with Foreign Countries.

Reference price: RMB 25000-28000 per square feet

《一生钟爱》　　69cm×137cm　　Lifelong Passion

张天文 *Zhang Tianwen*

张天文，男，字瀚清，号熹微堂主人，1953年生。祖籍河南新安县，现居住北京。现任中国书画家协会常务理事、中国书法学会理事。北京长城书画院副院长，北京国防大学耕砚堂书画院艺术顾问。

润笔价格：8000/平尺

Zhang Tianwen, male, with Hanqing as his courtesy name and Xiweitang Zhuren (Host of Twilight Star Hall) as his literary name, was born in Xin'an County, Henan Province, in 1953. He is a standing council member of China Calligrapher and Painter Association, and council member of China Calligraphers Association. Zhang is also Vice President of Beijing Great Wall Calligraphy and Painting Gallery, and art consultant of Gengyantang Calligraphy and Painting Gallery of National Defense University in Beijing. He now lives in Beijing.

Reference price: RMB 8000 per square feet

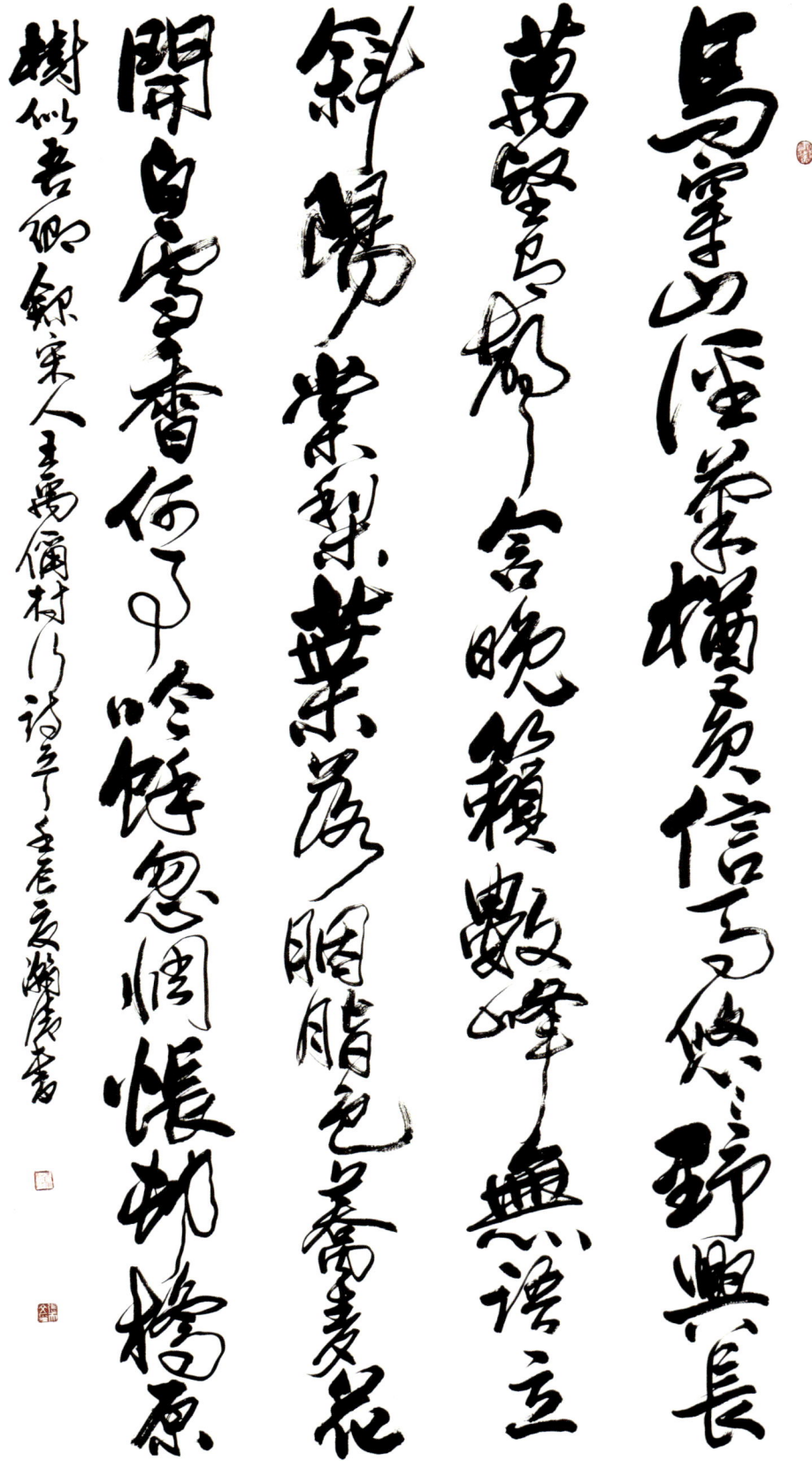

《录宋人王禹诗一首》　180×97　*A Poem by Wang Yu*

《行草条幅》　198cm×49cm　*A Scroll of Semi-cursive Script*

夏方明 *Xia Fangming*

夏方明，男，号容膝斋主，1969年生于山东安岳，现居北京。中国竹文化研究会理事，北京清晖书画院副院长，雪塘画社副社长。

润笔价格：12000/平尺

Xia Fangming, male, born in Anyue, Shandong Province, in 1969, and with Rongxi Zhaizhu (Host of Rongxi Study) as his literary name, is a council member of Chinese Bamboo Culture Research Institute, Vice President of Beijing Qinghui Calligraphy and Painting Gallery, and Vice Director of Xuetang Painting Art Gallery. He now lives in Beijing.

Reference price: RMB 12000 per square feet

《高风图》　115cm×61cm　　*Loftiness*

严海砚 Yan Haiyan

严海砚（又名海燕），男，号智空山人，1963年出生于福清市江阴半岛。严海砚现为福建省书法家协会会员，福建省逸仙艺术苑名誉理事、书法研究会会员，福建闽都画院副秘书长，福建中日书芸院秘书长。

润笔价格：3000/平尺

Yan Haiyan, male, born in Jiangyin Peninsular of Fuqing City in 1963, and with Zhikong Shanren (Wise Hermit) as his literary name, is a member of Fujian Calligraphers Association, honorary council member of Fujian Yet-Sun Art Center, and member of Calligraphy Research Institute. He is also Deputy Secretary General of Fujian Mindu Painting Art Gallery, and Secretary General of Fujian Sino-Japan Calligraphy Art Institute.

Reference price: RMB 3000 per square feet

《道》   68cm×134cm   *Dao*

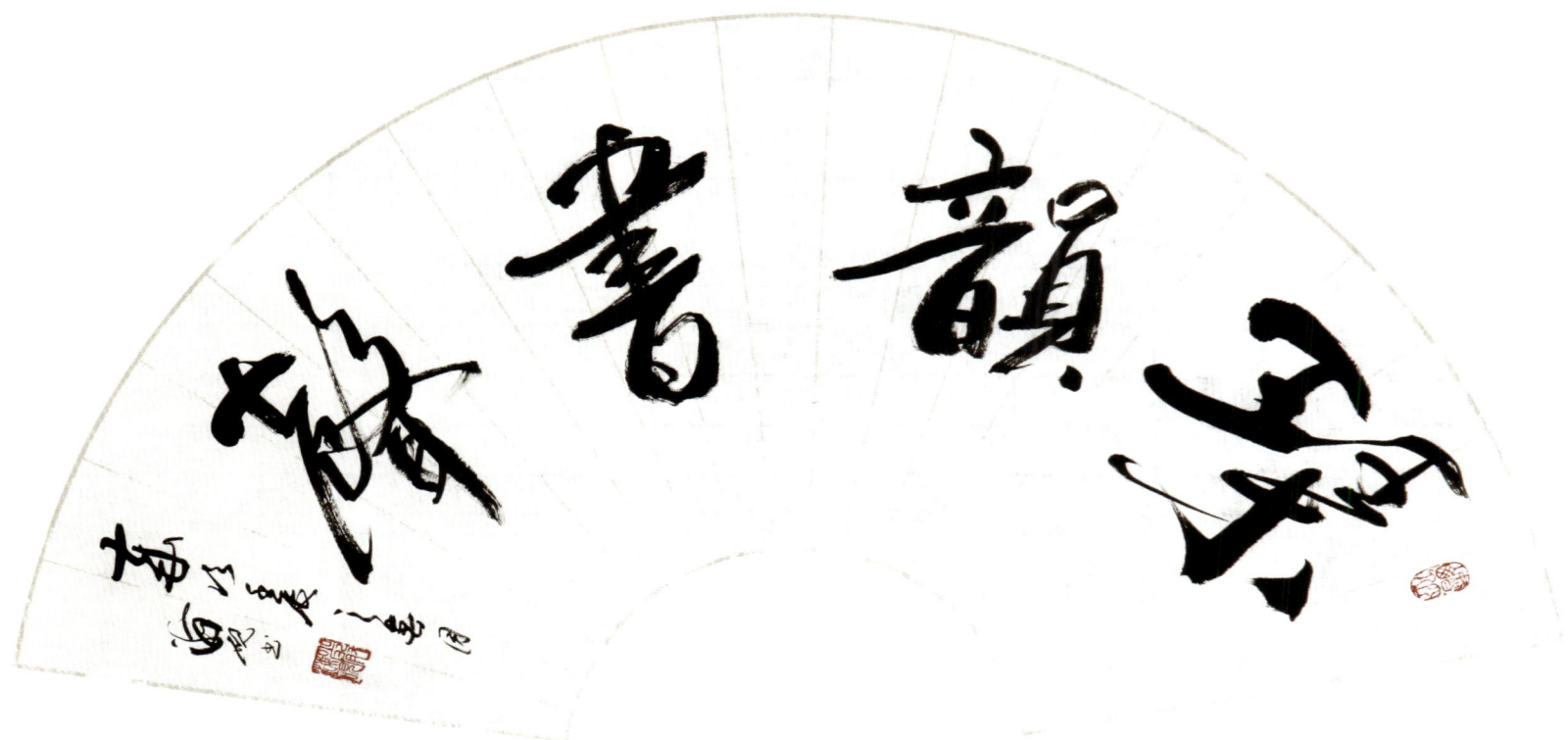

《扇面琴韵书声》　　34cm×70cm　　*Lyre and Book*

刘德君 *Liu Dejun*

刘德君，男，1953年生于河北省霸州市，字方州，号燕京堂。河北美术家协会会员，中国书画家联谊会理事，中国书画艺术研究会会员，中国国画家协会理事，霸州市美术家协会副主席，霸州市工笔画院院长，河北日报北方书画院高级画师，霸州市政协委员，中国书画院联谊会河北分会副会长。

润笔价格：14000/平尺

Liu Dejun, male, born in Bazhou, Hebei Province, in 1953, also with Fangzhou as his courtesy name and with Yanjing Hall as his literary name, is a member of Hebei Artists Association, of Chinese Calligraphy and Painting Research Institute, council member of Chinese Calligrapher and Painter Federation, and of China Association of Traditional Chinese Painting. Liu is also Vice President of Bazhou Artists Association, President of Bazhou Hue Art Society, senior painter with North China Calligraphy and Painting Gallery of Hebei Daily, and Vice Director of Hebei Branch of Chinese Calligrapher and Painter Federation. He is a CPPCC member of Bazhou City.

Reference Price: RMB 14000 per square feet

《猫》　70cm×46cm　　*Cat*

《猫》　90cm×49cm　　*Cat*

汤禄仕 *Tang Lushi*

汤禄仕，男，1966年6月生于江苏扬州宝应，国家级职业书法家。现为中国书法家协会会员、中国"扬州八怪"遗风继承与创新者、扬州市宝应县书法家协会副主席，作品《毛泽东词沁园春·雪》被人民大会堂收藏。

润笔价格：6000/平尺

Tang Lushi, male, born in Baoying of Yangzhou, Jiangsu Province, in the June of 1966, is a State-level professional calligrapher. He is a member of China Calligraphers Association, and inheritor and innovator of Eight Eccentrics of Yangzhou. Tang is also Vice President of Baoying Calligraphers Association, and his work Qinyuanchun•Snow by Mao Zedong has been collected in Great Hall of the People.

Reference price: RMB 6000 per square feet

《沁园春 雪》　68cm×34cm×4

李智民 *Li Zhimin*

李智民，男，1952年生，河北曲周县人。现为中国书画家协会会员、河北省美术家协会会员、河北省书法家协会会员。

润笔价格：8000/平尺

Li Zhimin, male, born in Quzhou County, Hebei Province, in 1952, is a member of China Calligrapher and Painter Association, of Hebei Artists Association, and of China Calligraphers Association.
Reference price: RMB 8000 per square feet

《雄视》 136cm×68cm *Overwhelming View*

丁卓辉 *Ding Zhuohui*

丁卓辉，男，1941年8月生于广东潮安县。现为中国当代艺术家协会理事，中国书画研究院艺术委员，广东省老年书画家协会会员，广东潮州市书法家协会会员。

润笔价格：7000/平尺

Ding Zhuohui, male, born in Chao'an, Guangdong Province, in the August of 1941, is a council member of China Contemporary Artists Association, member of Arts Committee of China Calligraphy and Painting Research Institute, of Guangdong Senior Calligrapher and Painter Association, and of Chaozhou Calligraphers Association.

Reference price: RMB 7000 per square feet

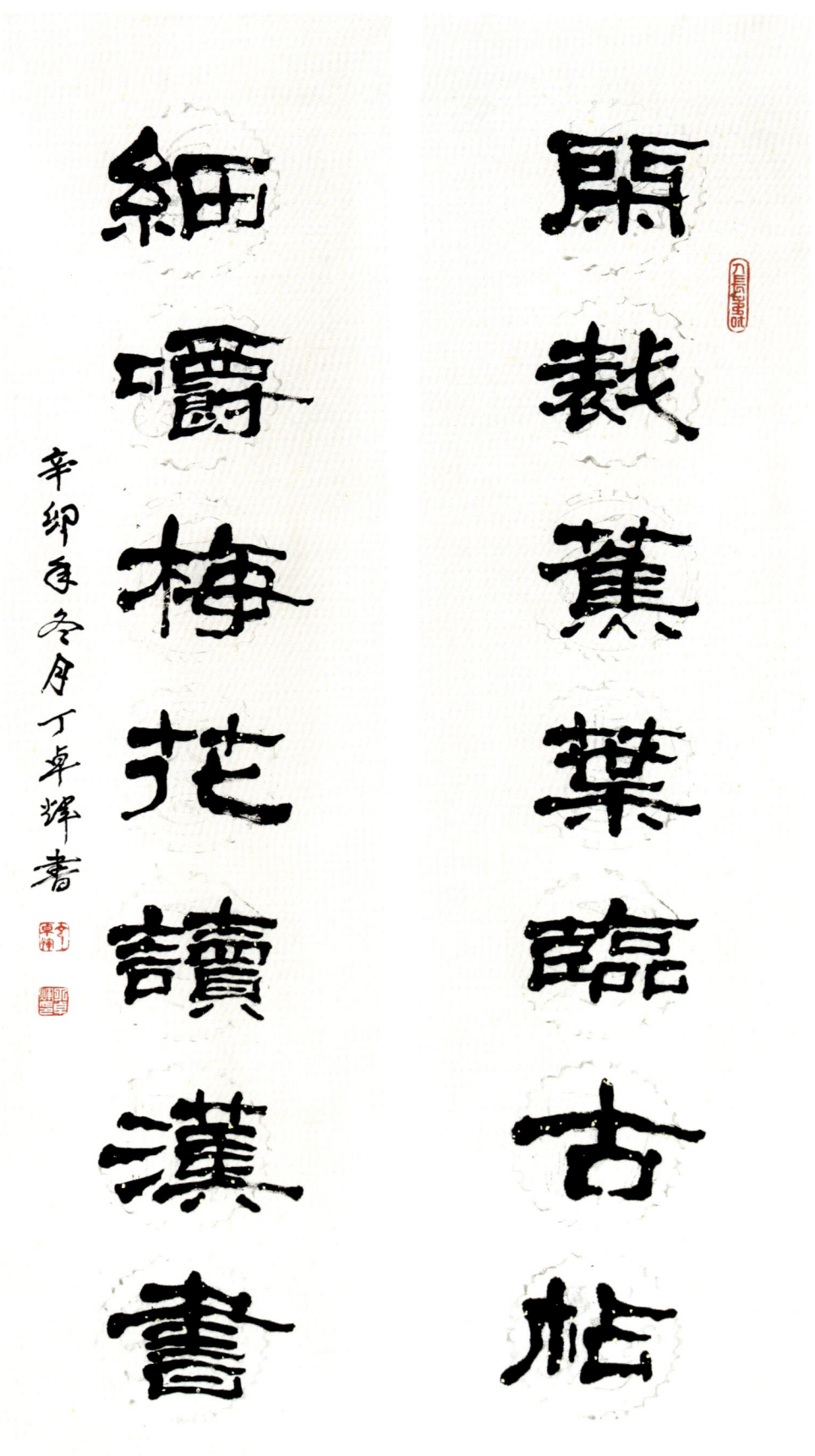

《对联一副》　136cm×32cm×2　*A Couplet*

沈忠信 *Shen Zhongxin*

沈忠信，男，号思米山翁，1950年生，河北省迁安市人，现为中国书画艺术促进会常务理事，中国书画研究会、翰墨书画院理事、顾问、高级书画师。

润笔价格：8000/平尺

Shen Zhongxin, male, born in Qian'an, Hebei Province, in 1950, and with Simi Shanweng as his literary name, is a standing committee member of China Calligraphy and Painting Art Promotion Society, consultant, council member and senior calligrapher and painter of China Calligraphy and Painting Research Institute, and of Hanmo Calligraphy and Painting Gallery.
Reference price: RMB 8000 per square feet

《母子情深》　　69cm×46cm　　*Mother and Son*

耿协生　*Geng Xiesheng*

耿协生，男，1949年生于安徽临泉，宿州中院退休副院长，安徽省美术家协会会员，中国国画家协会会员，中国美协培训中心特聘画师，中国书法研究院艺术委员会会员，宿州市美协会员、书协常务理事。

润笔价格：7000/平尺

Geng Xiesheng, male, born in Linquan, Anhui Province, in 1949, is a retired Vice President of Suzhou Intermediate People's Court, member of Anhui Artists Association, and of China Association of Traditional Chinese Painting. He is also an especially employed painter with Training Center of China Artists Association, member of Arts Committee of China Calligraphy Art Research Institute, of Suzhou Artists Association, and council member of Suzhou Calligraphers Association.

Reference price: RMB 7000 per square feet

《毛泽东诗词一首》　　69cm×35cm　　*A Poem by Mao Zedong*

张天文　*Zhang Tianwen*

张天文，男，字瀚清，号熹微堂主人，1953年生。祖籍河南新安县，现居住北京。现任中国书画家协会常务理事、中国书法学会理事。北京长城书画院副院长，北京国防大学耕砚堂书画院艺术顾问。

润笔价格：15000/平尺

Zhang Tianwen, male, with Hanqing as his courtesy name and Xiweitang Zhuren (Host of Twilight Star Hall) as his literary name, was born in Xin'an County, Henan Province, in 1953. He is a standing council member of China Calligrapher and Painter Association, and council member of China Calligraphers Association. Zhang is also Vice President of Beijing Great Wall Calligraphy and Painting Gallery, and art consultant of Gengyantang Calligraphy and Painting Gallery of National Defense University in Beijing. He now lives in Beijing.

Reference price: RMB 15000 per square feet

《花鸟》　180cm×97cm　*Birds and Flowers*

冯步明 *Feng Buming*

冯步明，男，1947年7月生于河南汤阴，现为河南省书法家协会会员。

润笔价格：6000/平尺

Feng Buming, male, born in Tangyin, Henan Province, in the July of 1947, is a member of Henan Calligraphers Association.

Reference price: RMB 6000 per square feet

《隶书杜甫诗一首》　138cm×69cm　*A Poem by Du Fu in Clerical Script*

谢天成　*Xie Tiancheng*

谢天成，男，1950年11月生，广东省茂名市信宜县人，现任刘海粟艺术研究院院长、北京大学资源学院客座教授、美国世界美术家联盟会副会长、世界华人协会艺术总监、世界收藏家联合会艺术总监、美国中美文化艺术交流促进理事、美国新奥尔良美术学院名誉教授、美国国际文化艺术交流学会副会长兼艺术总监。

润笔价格：14000/平尺

Xie Tiancheng, male, born in Xinyi County, Maoming City, Guangdong Province, in the November of 1950, is President of Liu Haisu Art Research Institute, visiting professor with Resource College of Peking University, and Vice Director of World Artists Alliance of America. Xie is also Art Director of Worldwide Association of Chinese and of Worldwide Collectors Alliance, council member of Sino-US Culture and Art Exchange and Promotion Society, honorary professor with New Orleans Academy of Fine Arts, and Vice Director and Art Director of America International Culture and Art Exchange Society.

Reference price: RMB 14000 per square feet

《漓江万竿烟雨中》　69cm×138cm　*Lijiang River in Misty Rain*

高菲 *Gao Fei*

高菲，男，祖籍山东烟台，现居北京。师从中央美院博士生导师邱振中，毕业于中国国家画院书法高研班。现为中国文联艺术指导委员会艺术研究员、中国左笔书画家协会主席、中国扇子艺术协会理事、国际工商总会左笔书法委员会主席、在当今书法界独树一帜的高菲左书。

润笔价格：10000/平尺

Gao Fei, male, born in Yantai, Shandong Province, learned with Mr. Qiu Zhenzhong, Doctoral Supervisor of China Central Academy of Fine Arts, and graduated from Art Research Class of China National Academy of Painting. He is a researcher with Art Steering Committee of China Federation of Literary and Art Circles, President of China Association of Left-Hand Calligraphy and Painting, and council member of China Association of Fan Arts. Gao is also President of Left-Hand Calligraphy Committee of International Federation of Commerce and Industry, whose left-hand calligraphy is unique in contemporary calligraphy circles.

Reference price: RMB 10000 per square feet

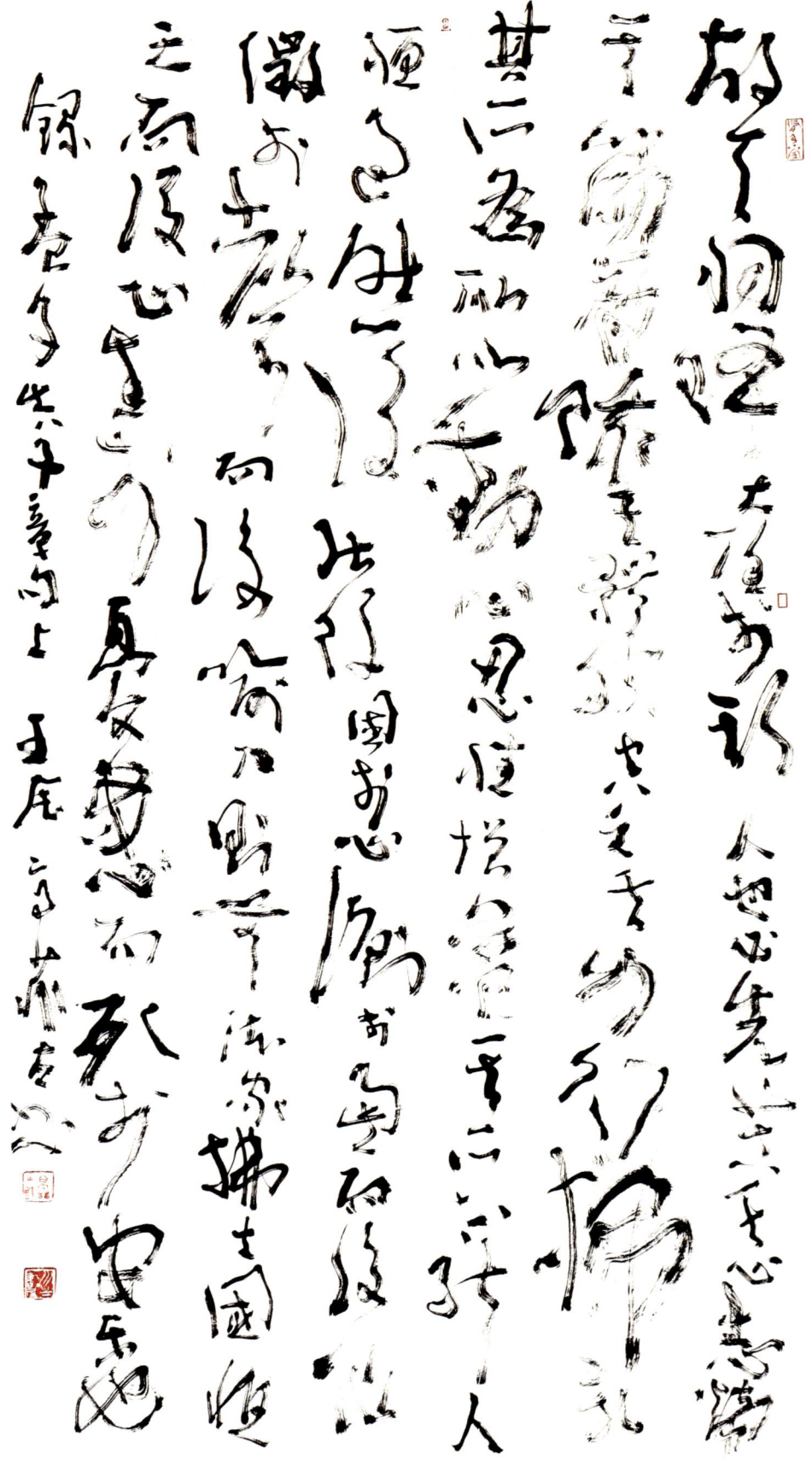

《录孟子句》　　180cm×97cm　　*Lines by Mencius*

李云光 *Li Yunguang*

李云光，男，湖南湘潭人，1965年师范毕业。湖南省美术教育研究会会员，湖南省美术家协会会员，湖南省书法家协会会员，湖南省湘潭市雨湖区美术家协会副主席。

润笔价格：10000/平尺

Li Yunguang, male, born in Xiangtang, Hunan Province, graduated in a normal university in 1965. Li is a member of Hunan Art Education Association, and of Hubei Artists Association. He is also a member of Hubei Calligraphers Association, and Vice President of Xiangtan Yuhu District Artists Association, Hunan.

Reference price: RMB 10000 per square feet

《报春图》　68cm×68cm　　*Heralding Spring*

汤锋 *Tang Feng*

汤锋、男、1979年出生，山东省邹城市人，字拂锐，别署雨润堂主、滴砚楼主人。中国书法家协会会员、山东省书法家协会会员。

润笔价格：4000/平尺

Tang Feng, male, with Furui as his courtesy name and Yurun Tangzhu (Host of Yurun Hall) and Diyanlou Zhuren (Host of Diyan Tower) as his literary name, was born in Zoucheng, Shandong Province, in 1979. He is a member of China Calligraphers Association and of Shandong Calligraphers Association.
Reference price: RMB 4000 per square feet

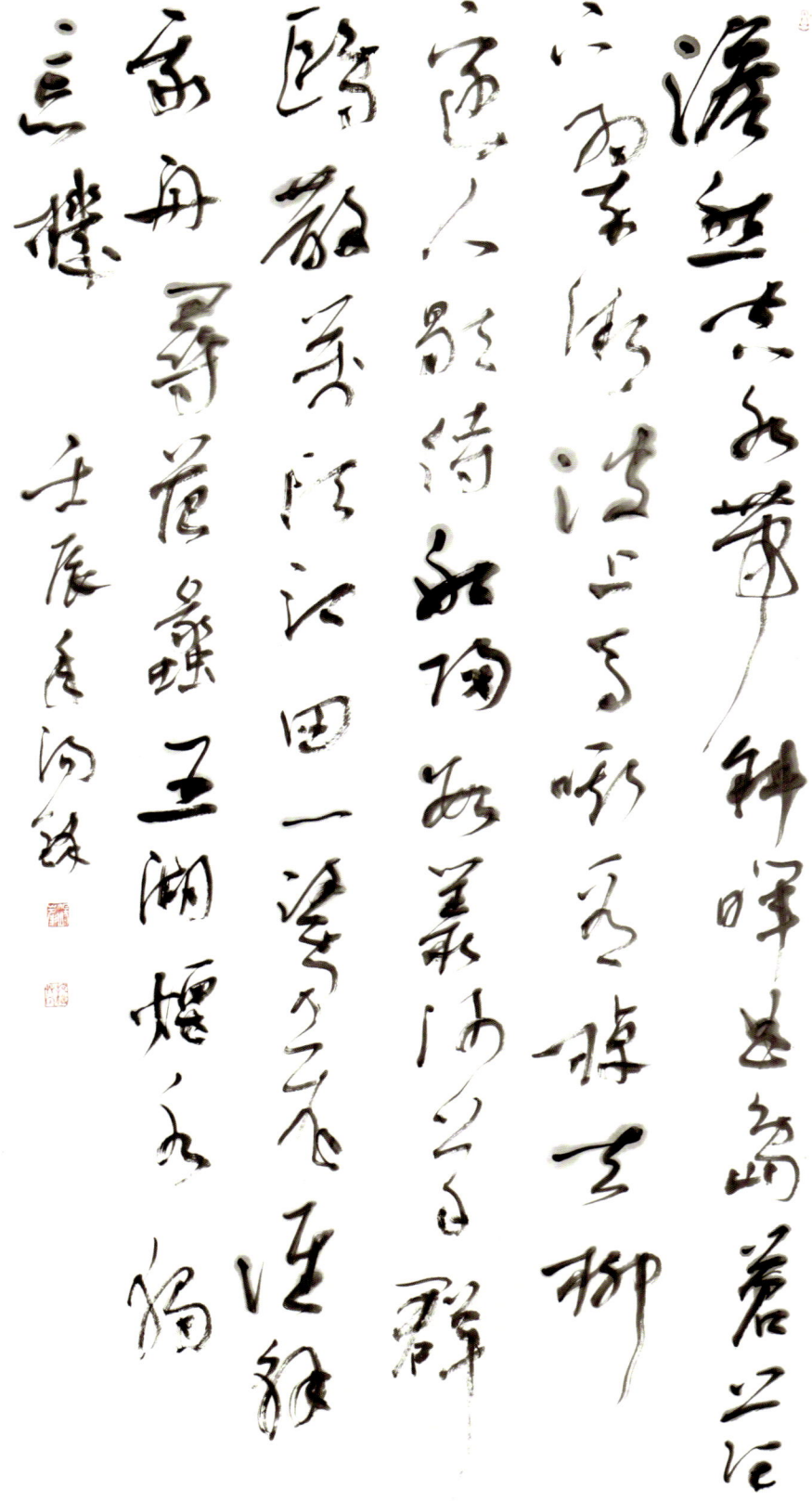

《草书一幅》　138cm×69cm　　*A Scroll of Cursive Script*

《草书一幅》　196cm×46cm　　*A Scroll of Cursive Script*

陈宏光 *Chen Hongguang*

陈宏光，男，山东东营市人。毕业于山东师范大学美术系，现任东营电视书画院院长，国家一级美术师，国家画院龙瑞工作室画家。中国电视艺术家协会会员，中国书画家协会理事，山东省美术家协会会员，东营市美术家协会常务副主席。

润笔价格：10000/平尺

Chen Hongguang, male, born in Dongying, Shandong Province, graduated in Department of Fine Arts in Shandong Normal University. Chen is a National Class A artist, President of Dongying Television Calligraphy and Painting Gallery, and painter with Longrui Studio of China National Academy of Painting. He is also a member of Chinese Television Artists Association, of Shandong Artists Association, council member of China Calligrapher and Painter Association, and Vice President of Dongying Artists Association.

Reference price: RMB 10000 per square feet

《紫藤挂云》　　69cm×68cm　　*Chinese Wisteria*

《花鸟》 68cm×68cm　*Flowers and Birds*

槐芳　*Huai Fang*

槐芳，男，1943年6月生于河北安平县。现为中国书画家联谊会会员、世界民间文艺家协会会员、中国书画家协会会员、中国文人书法家协会理事等。

润笔价格：2000/平尺

Huai Fang, male, born in Anping County, Hebei Province, in the June of 1943, is a member of Chinese Calligrapher and Painter Federation, of International Folk Artists Association, of China Calligrapher and Painter Association, and council member of China Literary Calligraphers Association. He also bears some other positions.

Reference price: RMB 2000 per square feet

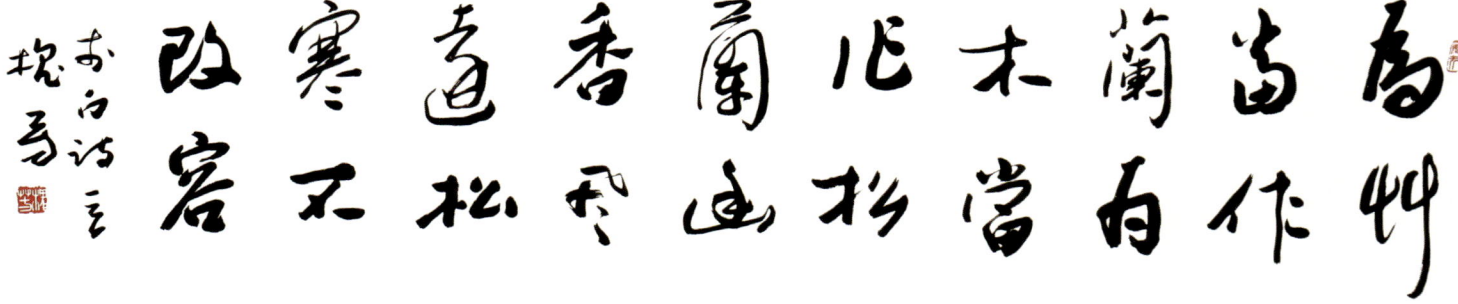

《李白诗一首》　　137cm×35cm　　*A Peom by Li Bai*

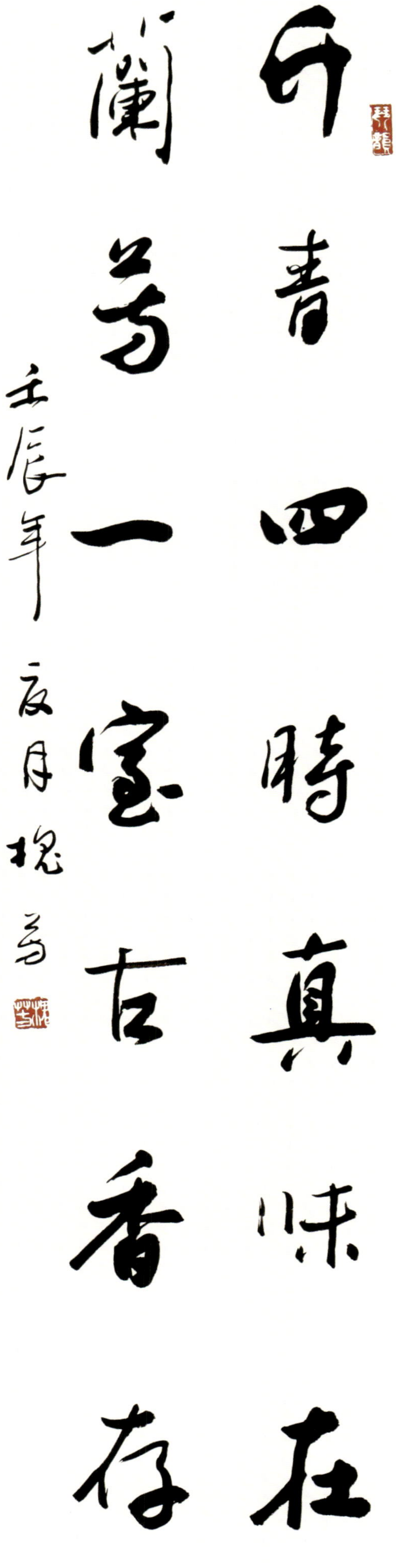

丹青四时真味在

兰芳一室古香存

壬辰年夏月槐高书

《兰芳一室古香存》　35cm×137cm　　The Antique Sweet in a Room Full of Orchid Fragrance

孔德馨 Kong Dexin

孔德馨，男，字泉石，乐砚斋主人。1963年生于山东省滕州市山东省书法家协会会员、山东省美术家协会会员、中国国画院院士。现为张立辰花鸟高研博士班学员。

润笔价格：12000/平尺

Kong Dexin, male, with Quanshi as his courtesy name, and with Master of Leyanzhai (Leyan Study) as his literary name, was born in Tengzhou, Shandong Province, in 1963. He is a member of Shandong Calligraphers Association, of Shandong Artists Association, and painter with China Traditional Chinese Painting Institute. Kong is now attending the Zhang Lichen Doctoral Art Research Classes on Bird-and-Flower Painting.

Reference price: RMB 12000 per square feet

《蕉阴赏菊》   68cm×137cm   *Beauty of Chrysanthemums*

《大吉大利》　137cm×68cm　　*Auspicious Luck*

刘心敏 *Liu Xinmin*

刘心敏，男，字宜朴，2000年退休前任本地文联主席，书协主席，现专职书画，系中国书协会员，杭州西湖书画研究院特聘书画师，宁波敏兰画院院长。

润笔价格：5000/平尺

Liu Xinmin, male, with Yipu (Being Simple) as his courtesy name, is Ex-President of local Federation of Literary and Art Circles and of local Calligraphers Association before his retirement in 2000. He now is a professional calligrapher and painter, member of China Calligraphers Association, especially employed painter with Hangzhou Xihu (West Lake) Calligraphy and Painting Research Institute, and President of Ningbo Minlan Painting Art Gallery.

Reference price: RMB 5000 per square feet

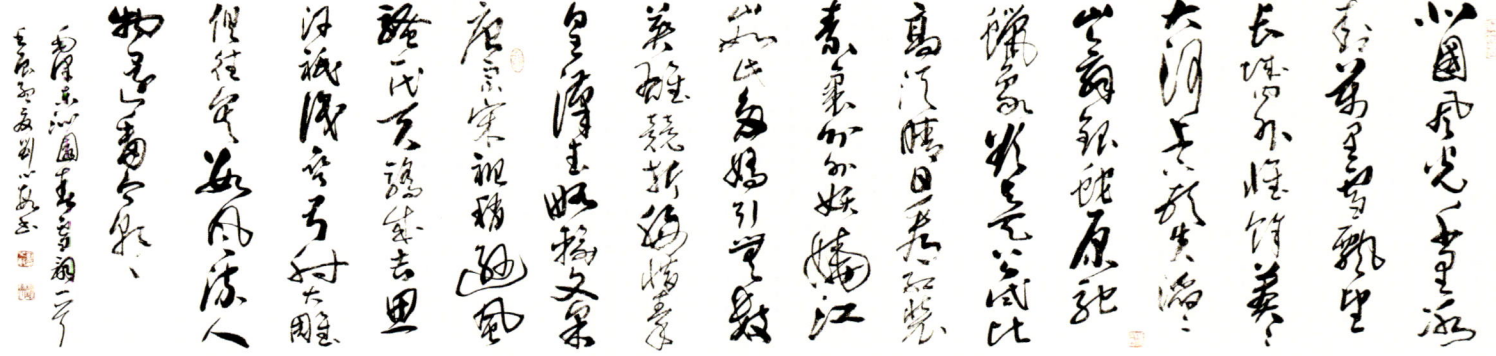

《沁园春－雪》　　180cm×49cm　　*Qinyuanchun•Snow*

《苏轼念奴娇》　　180cm×53cm　　*Meditations on the Red Cliff by Su Shi*

米占芳　*Mi Zhanfang*

米占芳（家山），男，河南郑州人，专职山水画家，作品曾参加第四届、第六届、第七届、第八届、第九届、第十届河南省中国画艺术展、河南省第十一届美术作品展并有获奖。现为河南省美术家协会会员，河南省国画家协会会员。

润笔价格：12000/平尺

Mi Zhanfang, male, also known as Jiashan, was born in Zhangzhou, Henan Province. He is a professional landscape painter, member of Henan Artists Association and of Henan Association of Traditional Chinese Painting as well, whose works won awards in the Fourth, Sixth, Seventh, Eighth, Ninth, and Tenth Henan Chinese Painting Art Exhibition, as well as in the Eleventh Henan Art Exhibition.

Reference price: RMB 12000 per square feet

《黄河奔腾》　69cm×136cm　*The Galloping Yellow River*

《大河惊涛》　69cm×136cm　*Raging Waves*

张文贵　Zhang Wengui

张文贵，男，1958年8月生，陕西志丹县人。现为陕西毛泽东书法研究会会员，中国书法研修院教育委员会会员，北京日月腾飞文化艺术交流中心签约书画理事，中国文人书法家协会会员，华夏京都书画艺术研究院书画师，吴道子艺术馆理事，东方书法研修院院士，中国书画家协会会员，中国收藏家协会会员，世界华人艺术家协会理事，中国国际文艺家协会高级书画师等。

润笔价格：3000/平尺

Zhang Wengui, male, born in Zhidan County, Shanxi Province, in the August of 1958, is a member of Mao Zedong Calligraphy Art Research Institute of Shanxi, of Education Committee of China Calligraphy Research Institute, of China Literary Calligraphers Association, of China Calligrapher and Painter Association, and of China Association of Collectors. He is a contracted council member of Beijing Riyue Tengfei Exchanges Center of Chinese Culture and Art, painter with China Calligraphy and Painting Art Research Institute of Beijing, and with Oriental Calligraphy Research Institute. Zhang is also a council member of Wu Daozi Art Museum, of WCNAA, and senior calligrapher and painter with CIALA.

Reference price: RMB 3000 per square feet

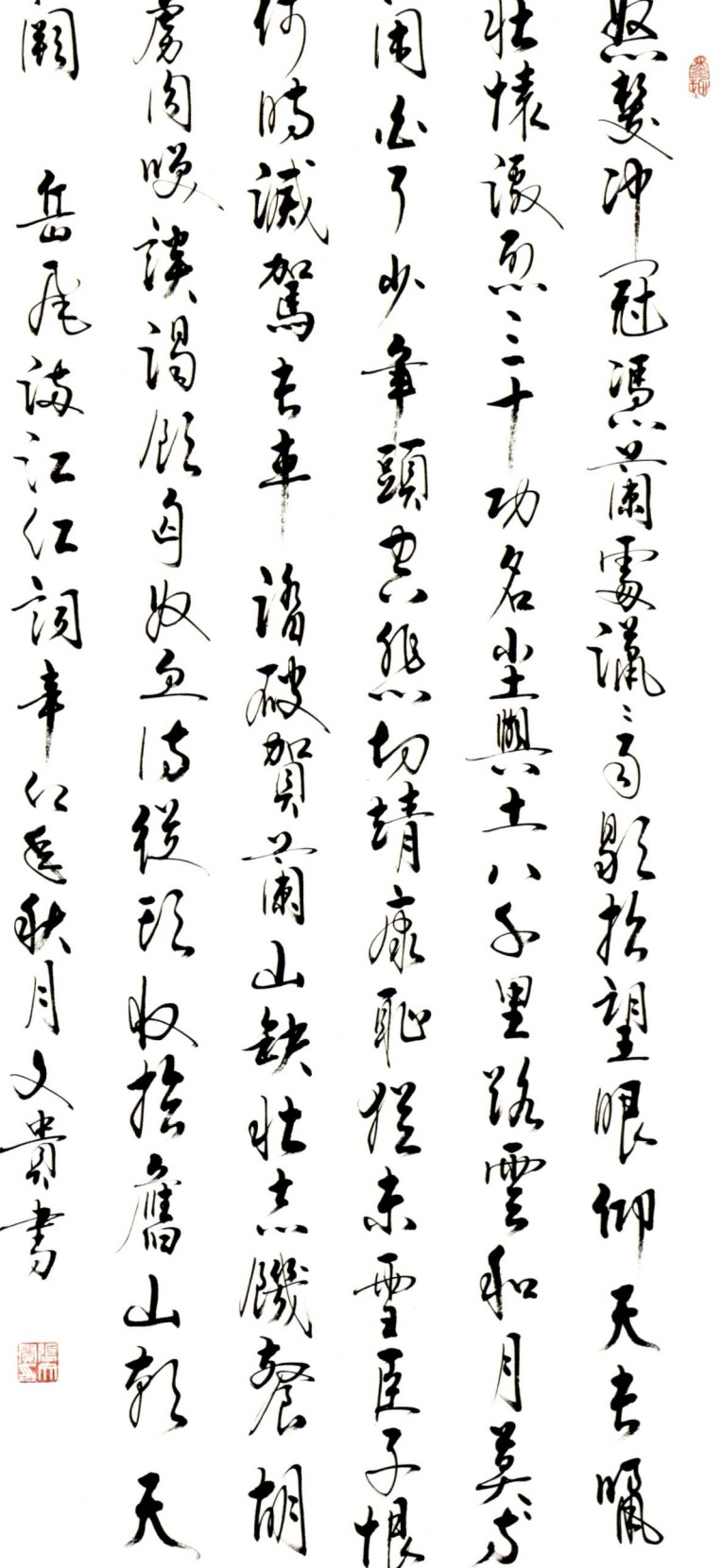

岳飞 《满江红》　138cm×69cm　*Man Jiang Hong by Yue Fei*

北国风光，千里冰封，万里雪飘。望长城内外，惟余莽莽；大河上下，顿失滔滔。山舞银蛇，原驰蜡象，欲与天公试比高。须晴日，看红装素裹，分外妖娆。江山如此多娇，引无数英雄竞折腰。惜秦皇汉武，略输文采；唐宗宋祖，稍逊风骚。一代天骄，成吉思汗，只识弯弓射大雕。俱往矣，数风流人物，还看今朝。 辛卯岁书

《沁园春 雪》　138cm×69cm　Qinyuanchun·Snow

王铁中 *Wang Tiezhong*

王铁中，男，1950年生，国家高级美术师，洛阳国画研究院院长，世界世家协会高级会员。
润笔价格：18000/平尺

Wang Tiezhong, male, born in 1950, is a national senior artist. He is also President of Luoyang Traditional Chinese Painting Art Research Institute, and senior member of International Family Association.
Reference price: RMB 18000 per square feet

《积翠空》　138cm×69cm　　*Multiplied Greenness*

《深谷隐秀》　138cm×69cm　*Indistinct Beauty in Ravine*

常福清 *Chang Fuqing*

常福清，男，笔名醉墨，号静觉山人，1943年生，唐山市丰润区沙流河镇安家坨村人。现为中国书法家协会会员、唐山市书法家协会会员、唐山市硬笔书法家协会理事、中国文化艺术城特聘高级书画师、世界教科文卫组织专家成员、中国海峡两岸书画家协会会员。

润笔价格：4000/平尺

Chang Fuqing, male, with Zuimo as his pseudonym, and with Jingjue Shanren (Quiet Sensation Hermit) as his literary name, was born in Anjiatuo of Shaliuhe Town, Fengrun District of Tangshan City, in 1943. He is a member of China Calligraphers Association, of Tangshan Calligraphers Association, and council member of Tangshan Association of Pen Calligraphers. Chang is also an especially employed senior calligrapher and painter with Chinese Culture and Art City, expert with WESCHO, and member of China Cross-Strait Research Institute of Calligraphy and Painting.

Reference price: RMB 4000 per square feet

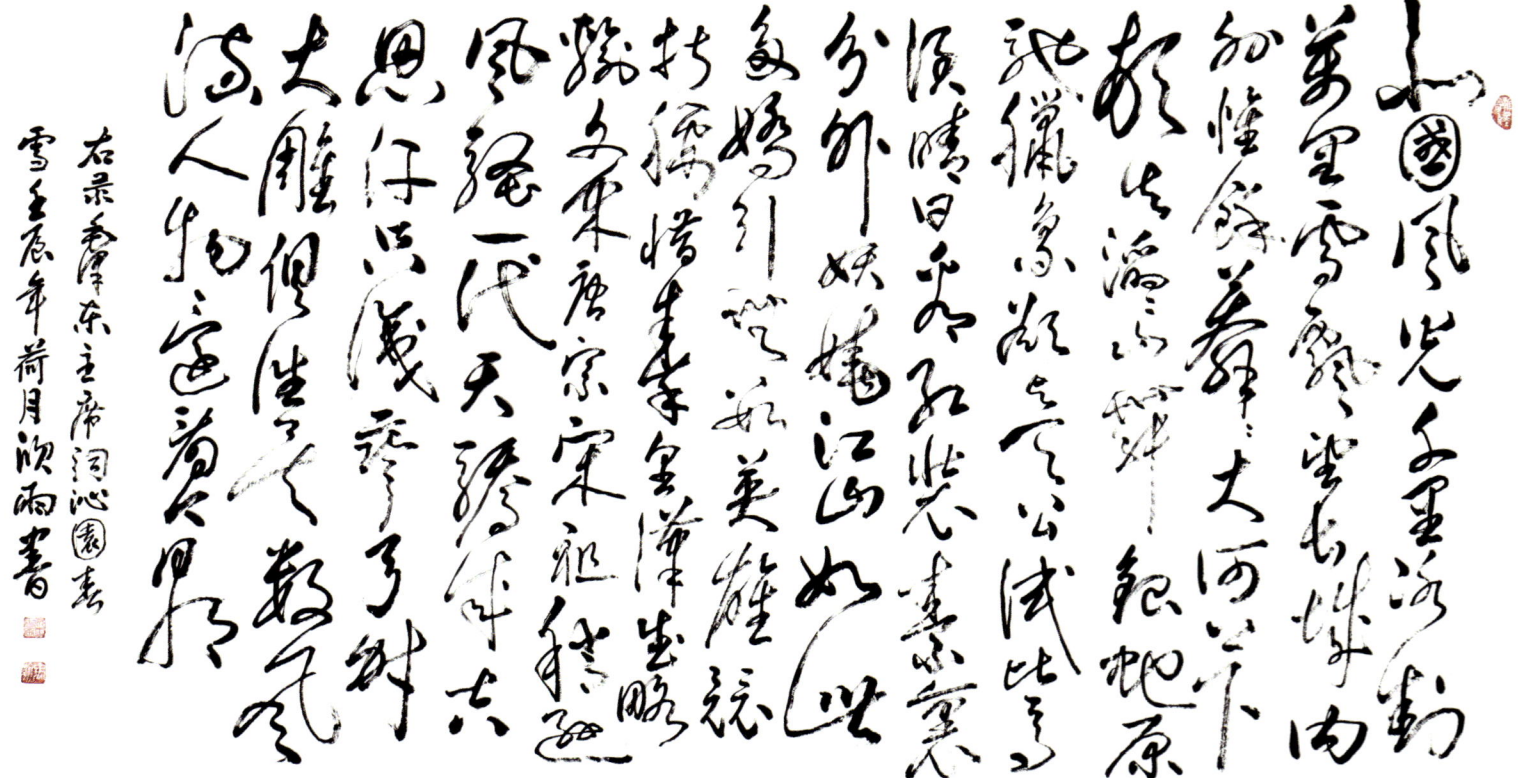

《沁园春 雪》　　97cm×180cm　　*Qinyuanchun Snow*

王斌　*Wang Bin*

王斌，男，字子夏，1960年生于江苏太仓。现为江苏省美术家协会会员、太仓市美术家协会副主席、太仓市书画院院务委员、宋文治艺术馆特聘画师。

润笔价格：12000/平尺

Wang Bin, male, with Zixia as his courtesy name, was born in Taicang, Jiangsu Province, in 1960. He is a member of Jiangsu Artists Association, Vice President of Taicang Artists Association, committee member of Taicang Calligraphy and Painting Gallery, and especially employed painter with Song Wenzhi Art Museum.

Reference price: RMB 12000 per square feet

《云山秋韵》　97cm×179cm　*Autumn Charm of Yun Mount*

李欣雨　*Li Xinyu*

李欣雨（字禹翰），男，汉族，研究生学历。1959年9月出生于齐鲁大地山东省平原县。菲律宾《世界日报》，《香港日报》专刊特约书法家，北京翰墨流芳书画文化有限公司顾问，中国少数民族文化交流书画研究院院长，世界华人艺术家联合会执行主席，和谐中国十大书法家，中国民族书画家协会副秘书长、中国海峡两岸书画家协会会员。

润笔价格：4000/平尺

Li Xinyu, male, with Yuhan as his courtesy name, was born in Pingyuan County, Shandong Province, in September, 1959, and is a post-graduate. He is an especially employed calligrapher with World Journal of Philippines and Hong Kong Daily, consultant with Beijing Hanmo Liufang Calligraphy and Painting Culture company, Ltd., and President of Calligraphy and Painting Research Institute for China Ethnic Minority Culture Exchange. Li is also one of the Top Ten Calligraphers of Harmonious China, Executive President of WCNAA, Deputy Secretary General of China National Calligraphers and Painters Association, and member of China Cross-Strait Research Institute of Calligraphy and Painting.

Reference price: 4000 per square feet

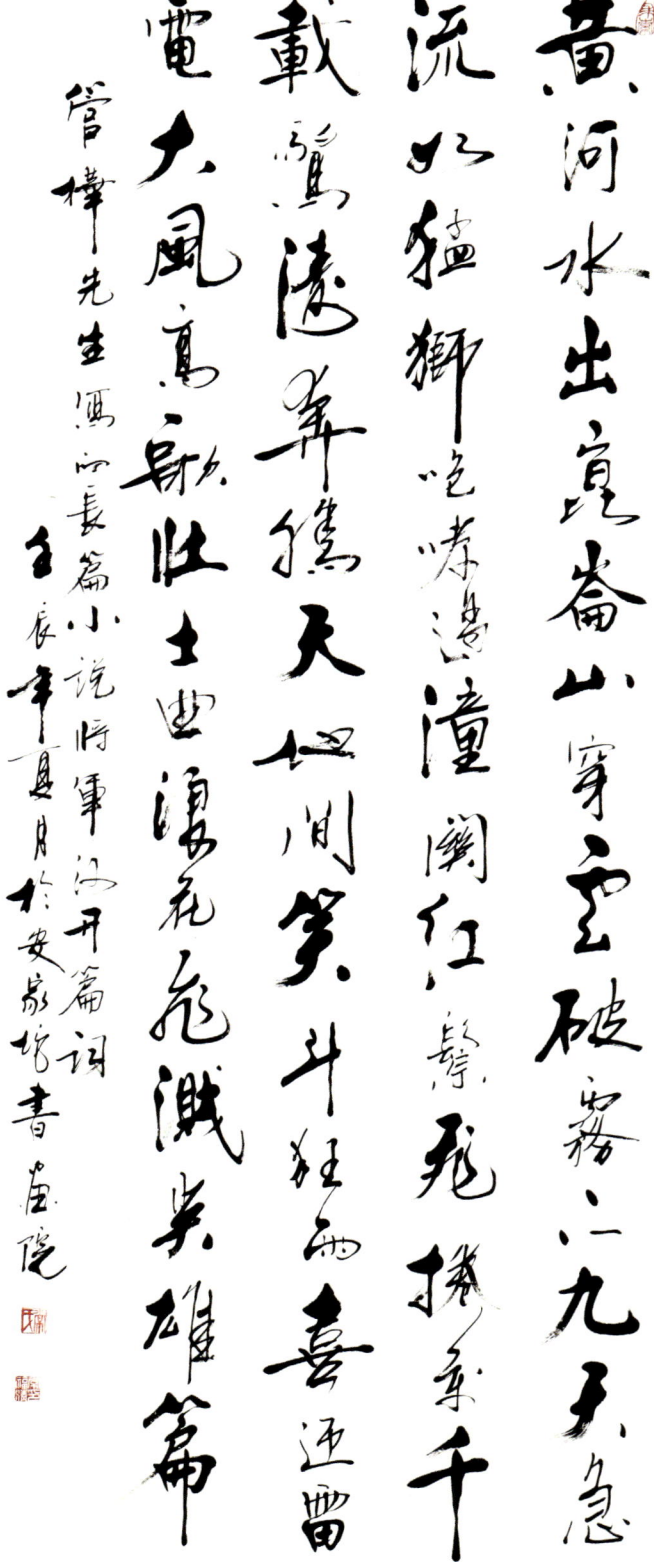

《小说开篇词》　　180cm×90cm　　The Opening Poem of a Novel

辛晋瑛 *Xin Jingying*

辛晋瑛，男，1932年6月生，河北辛集人。国家一级美术师，中国美术家协会会员，石家庄市美术家协会名誉主席，市老年书画研究会顾问，石家庄市老年大学顾问，石家庄书画院院长、名誉院长。

润笔价格：10000/平尺

Xin Jingying, male, born in Xinji, Hebei Province, in the June of 1932, is a National Class A artist, member of China Artists Association, and honorary President of Shijiazhuang Artists Association. He is also a consultant of Shijiazhuang Calligraphy and Painting Research Institute for Seniors, of Shijiazhuang University for the Aged, and President and honorary president of Shijiazhuang Calligraphy and Painting Gallery.

Reference price: RMB 10000 per square feet

《壶口瀑布》　94cm×280cm　　*Hukou Waterfall*

唐栓怀 *Tang Shuanhuai*

唐栓怀，男，字仁德，1959年生，陕西省岐山县人。现任宁夏军区转业干部办公室副师职主任，大校军衔，中国书法家协会会员，中国书画家协会理事，中国收藏家协会会员，宁夏青年书院副院长等。

润笔价格:4000/平尺

Tang Shuanhuai, male, born in Qishan, Shaanxi Province, in 1959, and with Rende (Virtue of Kindness) as his courtesy name, is Deputy Director of Office for Transferred Military Officers of Ningxia Military Region and a Senior Colonel bearer. He is a member of China Calligraphers Association, council member of China Calligrapher and Painter Association, member of China Association of Collectors, and Vice President of Ningxia Calligraphy Art Gallery for Youth.

Reference price: RMB 4000 per square feet

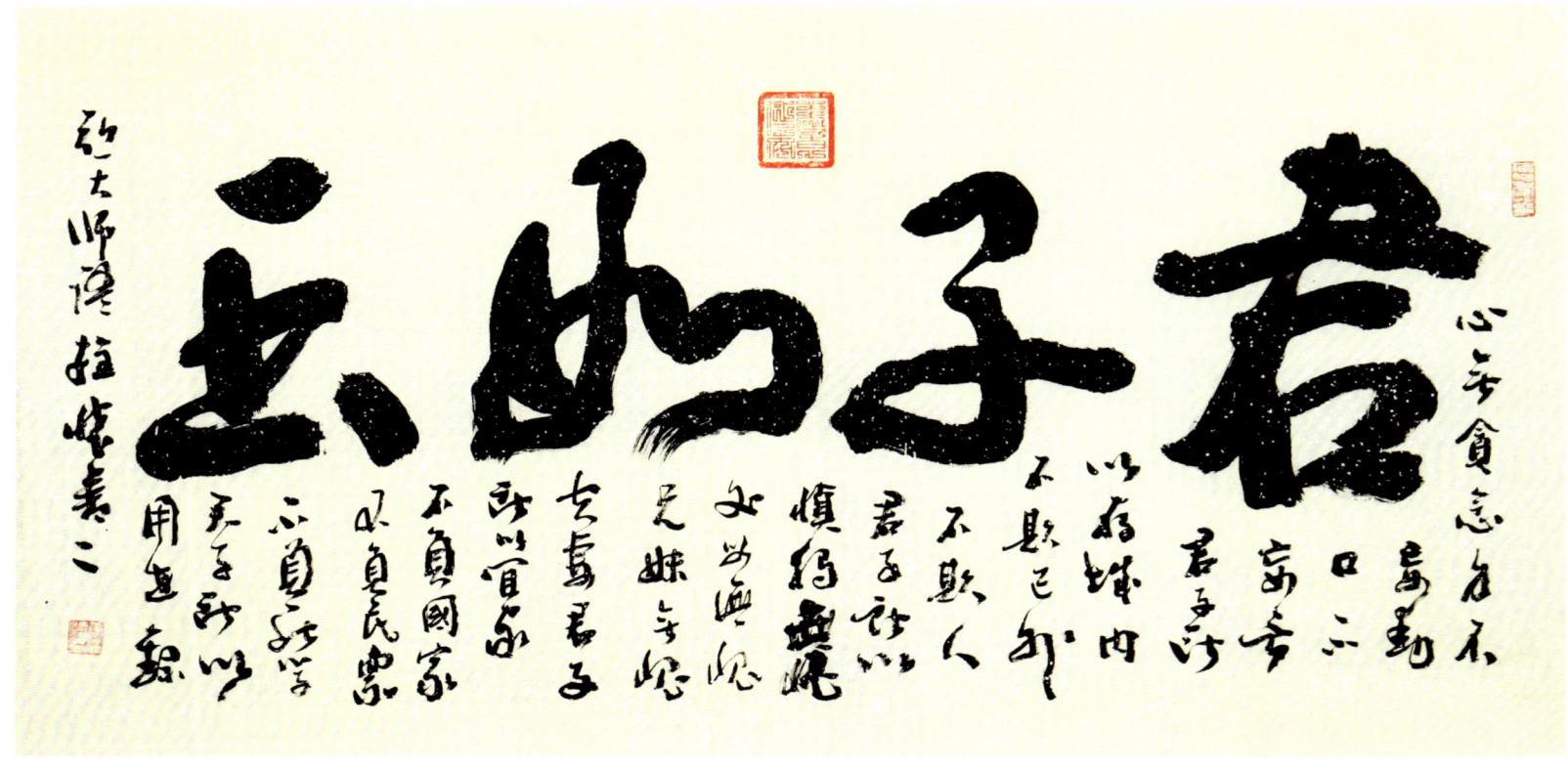

《君子如玉》　138cm×69cm　*Jade-like Gentleman*

刘峰　Liu Feng

刘峰，男，1966年3月生于湘潭，大学毕业。现任湘都书画院院长、安全生产书画院法人代表、中国国际竞争力促进会副秘书长。

润笔价格：8000/平尺

Liu Feng, male, born in Xiangtan, in the March of 1966, is a university graduate, and now is President of Xiangdu Calligraphy and Painting Gallery, Legal Representative of Work Safe Calligraphy and Painting Gallery, and Deputy Secretary General of China Association for International Competitiveness.

0Reference price: RMB 8000 per square feet

《龙腾》　48cm×180cm　Soaring Dragons

高丽华　*Gao Lihua*

高丽华，女，现为世界华人华侨联合会会员，中国海峡两岸书画协会会员，炎黄书画院院士，黑龙江省老年书画研究会创作员。

润笔价格：4000/平尺

Gao Lihua, female, is a member of World Overseas Chinese Federation, of China Cross-Strait Research Institute of Calligraphy and Painting, painter with Yanhuang Calligraphy and Painting Gallery, and creative artist with Heilongjiang Calligraphy and Painting Art Research Institute for Seniors.

Reference price: RMB 4000 per square feet

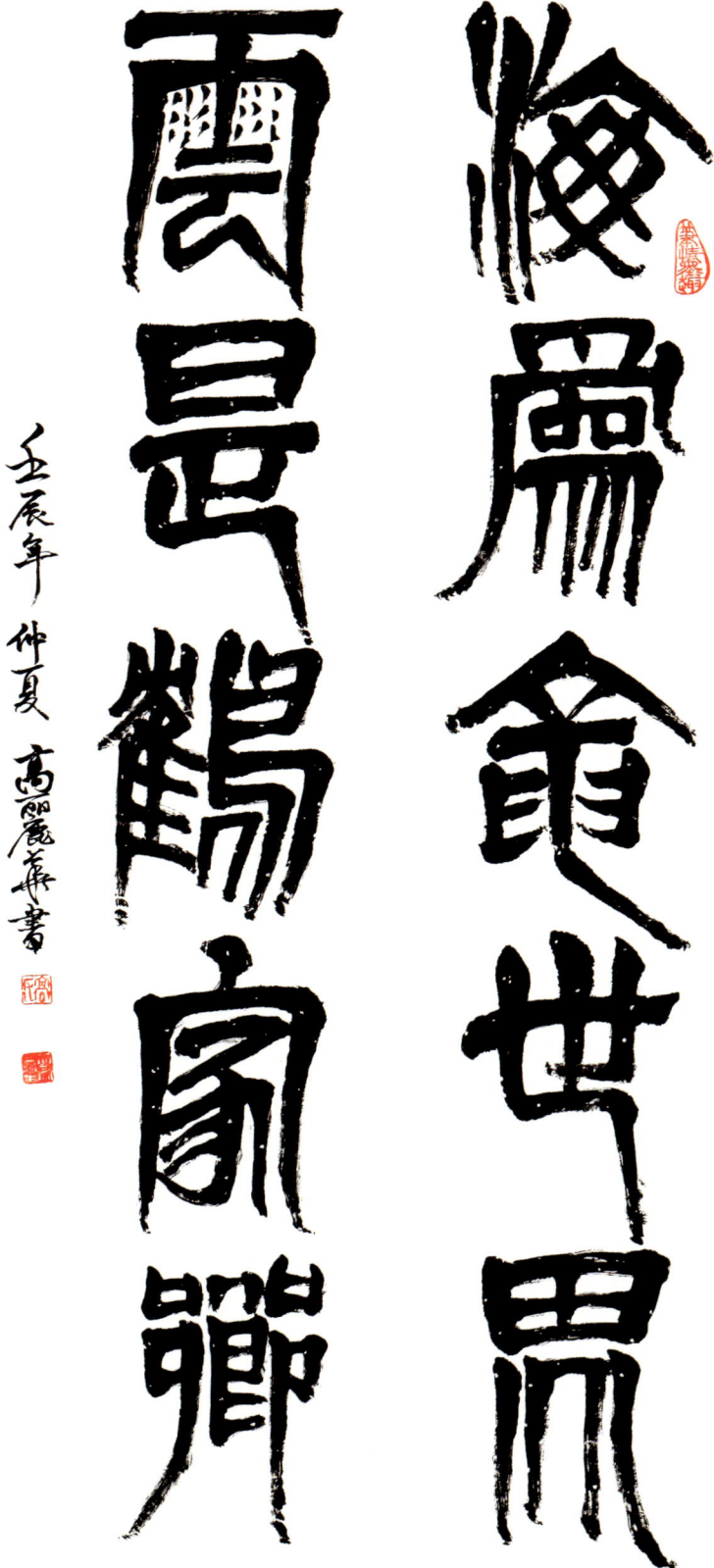

《海为龙世界》　132cm×65cm　　*Sea as the World of Dragons*

刘远景 *Liu Yuanjing*

刘远景，男，1958年12月生，山东阳谷人，中华教育艺术家协会会员，山东硬笔书法家协会副主席，山东棵树协会常务理事，中国美协山东分会会员，中国书协山东分会会员。

润笔价格：12000/平尺

Liu Yuanjing, male, born in Yanggu, Shandong Province, in the December of 1958, is a member of China Education Artists Association, Vice President of Shandong Association of Pen Calligraphers, and standing committee member of Shandong Tree Association. He is also a member of Shandong Artists Association, and of Shandong Calligraphers Association.

Reference price: RMB 12000 per square feet

《贡嘎神韵》　　180cm×97cm　　*Charm of Mount Gongga*

张春生 *Zhang Chunsheng*

张春生，男，号墨齐，1957年生于福建厦门，中国书协会员，世界张氏书画家协会会员。
润笔价格：1000/平尺

Zhang Chunsheng, male, born in Xiamen, Fujian Province, in 1957, and with Moqi as his literary name, is a member of China Calligraphers Association, and of Worldwide Society for Calligrapher and Painter Zhangs.
Reference price: RMB 1000 per square feet

《清人诗一首》　　139cm×69cm　　*A Poem*

侯延峰 *Hou Yanfeng*

侯延峰，男，1965年生于陕北，现居北京。2002年师从王明明，现为中国国画家协会理事，北京文采书画院秘书长，陕西国际书画交流协会副会长，陕西省书协、美协会员。

润笔价格：12000/平尺

Hou Yanfeng, male, born in the north of Shaanxi, in 1965, learned with Mr. Wang Mingming from 2002. Hou is a council member of China Association of Traditional Chinese Painting, Secretary General of Beijing Wencai Calligrapher and Painting Gallery, and Vice President of International Calligraphy and Painting Exchange Society of Shaanxi. He is also a member of Shaanxi Calligraphers Association and of Shaanxi Artists Association. He now lives in Beijing.

Reference price: RMB 12000 per square feet

《牡丹》　97cm×52cm　　*Peonies*

邢顺华 *Xing Shunhua*

邢顺华，男，1935年生于河北正定，现为中国书画家协会会员、中国书画艺术研究会理事、南京市长江书画家协会名誉主席、中国书法家协会理事。

润笔价格：5000/平尺

Xing Shunhua, male, born in Zhengding, Hebei Province, in 1935, is a member of China Calligrapher and Painter Association, and council member of Chinese Calligraphy and Painting Research Institute. He is also Honorary President of Changjiang (Yangtze River) Calligrapher and Painter Association of Nanjing, and council member of China Calligraphers Association.

Reference price: RMB 5000 per square feet

《三国演义开篇词》　　178cm×48cm　　*A Scroll of Oracle-bone Script*

刘金锡 *Liu Jinxi*

刘金锡，男，汉族，1957年生于山东青岛。系北京湖社画会理事、北京湖社画会青岛创作基地主任、山东省美术家协会会员、山东省收藏家协会会员、青岛市收藏与鉴赏研究会常务理事，青岛市市南区政协书画联谊会会员。现任青岛市市南区人民法院工会主席，司法警察一级警督。

润笔价格：8000/平尺

Liu Jinxi, male, born in Qingdao, Shandong Province, in 1957, is a council member of Beijing Hushe Painting Society, Director of Creation Base of Beijing Hushe Painting Society, member of Shandong Artists Association, and of Shandong Association of Collectors. Liu is a standing committee member of Qingdao Collection and Appraisal Institute, and member of Calligraphers and Painters Society of South District CPPCC of Qingdao as well. He is also the Chairman of the Union of the People's Court of South District, Qingdao, and judicial policeman of First Class Police Inspector.

Reference price: RMB 8000 per square feet

《墨竹》　180cm×97cm　　*Dark Bamboos*

刘景堂 *Liu Jingtang*

刘景堂，男，1949年1月生，毕业于西安书法学院，现为山东省书协会员、菏泽市书协会员、定陶县书协会员。

润笔价格：4000/平尺

Liu Jingtang, male, born in the January of 1949, graduated at Xi'an Calligraphy College. He is a member of Shandong Calligraphers Association, of Heze Calligraphers Association, and Dingtao Calligraphers Association.

Reference price: RMB 4000 per square feet

《古诗文一首》　　136cm×68cm　　*An Ancient Poem*

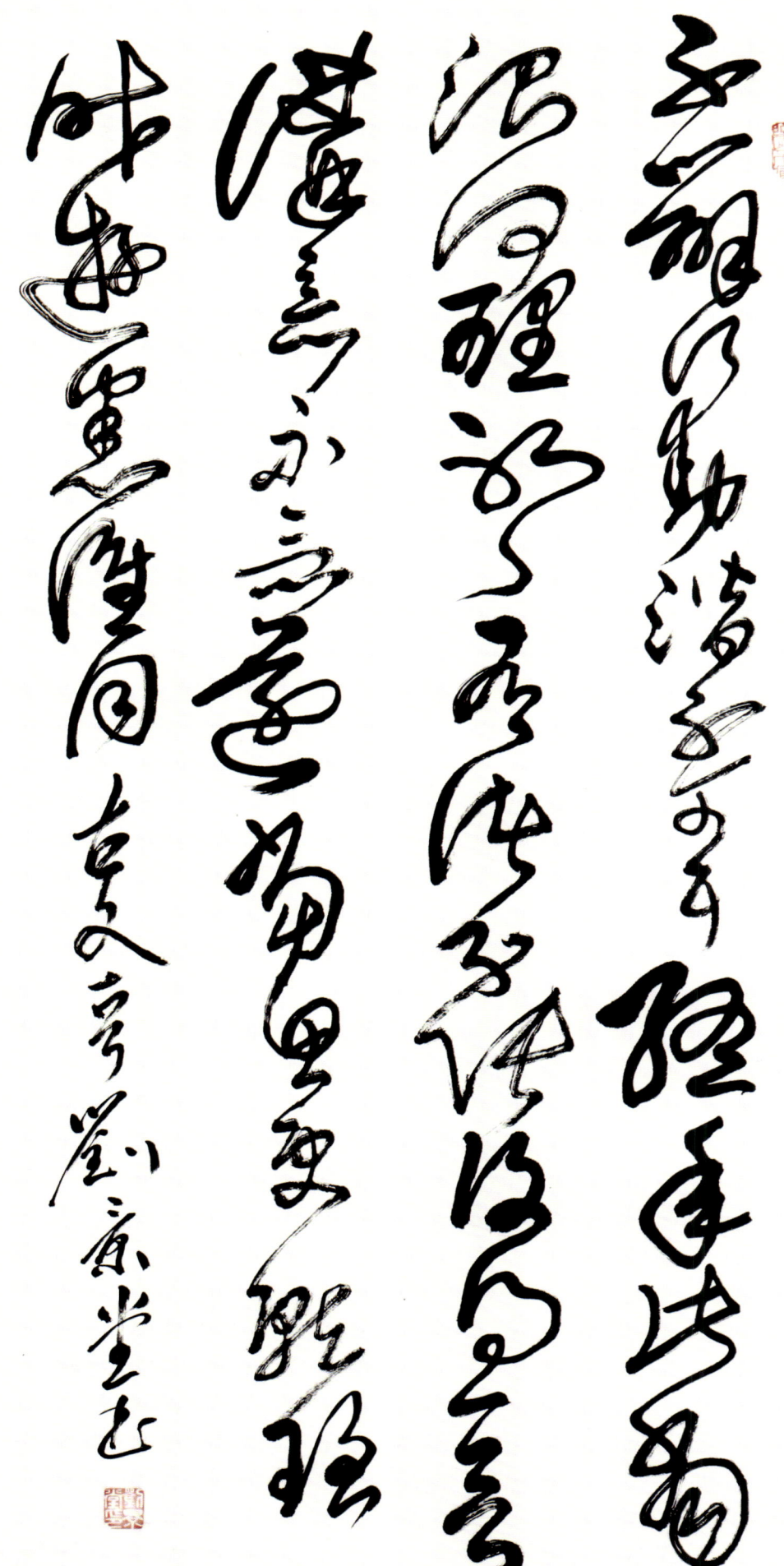

《古文一首》　136cm×68cm　　*An Ancient Prose*

潘电风 *Pan Dianfeng*

潘电风，男，又名殿风，闲墨斋主，1940年生于辽宁台安，中国书画家协会会员、盘锦市美术家协会会员、老年大学专职书画家。

润笔价格：14000/平尺

Pan Dianfeng, male, also by the name of Dianfeng and with Xianmo Zhaizhu (Host of Ease Study) as his literary name, was born in Tai'an, Liaoning Province, in 1940. Pan is a member of China Calligrapher and Painter Association, of Panjing Artists Association, and professional calligrapher and painter with the Universities for the Aged.

Reference Price: RMB 14000 per square feet

《秋晴》 67cm×67cm *Sunshiny Autumn*

《雨过清香发》　67cm×136cm　*Fresh Scent after Rain*

蒋光前 *Jiang Guangqian*

蒋光前，男，1941年生，西安人，陕西省书协会员、中国煤矿文联书协会员、中国书画艺术研究会研究员、东坡书画艺术研究院艺术顾问、长城魂当代诗书画家协会名誉主席、九州枫林国际书画艺术院院士、北京墨都书画院常务高级理事、洛阳市颜真卿研究会名誉会长。

润笔价格：3000/平尺

Jiang Guangqian, male, born in Xi'an in 1941, is a member of Shanxi Calligraphers Association, of Calligraphers Association of China Coal Mine Federation of Literary and Art Circles, and researcher with Chinese Calligraphy and Painting Research Institute. He is also an art consultant with Dongpo Calligraphy and Painting Art Research Institute, Honorary President of Great Wall Soul Contemporary Poet, Calligrapher and Painter Association, and of Yan Zhenqing Research Institute of Luoyang. Jiang is also a painter with International Jiuzhou Fenglin Calligraphy and Painting Gallery, and senior council member of Beijing Modu Calligraphy and Painting Gallery.

Reference price: RMB 3000 per square feet

李清照 《月满西楼》　180cm×72cm　　*Moonlight Full in the West Building by Li Qingzhao*

夫天地者萬物之逆旅也光陰者百代之過客也而浮生若夢為歡幾何古人秉燭夜遊良有以也況陽春召我以煙景大塊假我以文章會桃李之芳園序天倫之樂事群季俊秀皆為惠連吾人詠歌獨慚康樂幽賞未已高談轉清開瓊筵以坐花飛羽觴而醉月不有佳作何伸雅懷如詩不成罰依金谷酒數

李白春夜宴詞桃李園序
浮山主人高光亮書

李白 《桃李園序》　180cm×60cm　　Prelude to Peach and Plum Garden by Li Bai

沈勤邦 *Shen Qinbang*

沈勤邦,男,1948年生,广西德保县人,广西美术家协会会员、国家特级书画师、北京尔康书画院客座教授。

润笔价格:10000/平尺

Shen Qinbang, male, born in Debao County, Guangxi Zhuang Autonomous Region, in 1948, is a member of Guangxi Artists Association, distinguished State-Level calligrapher and painter, and visiting professor with Beijing Erkang Calligraphy and Painting Gallery.

Reference price: RMB 10000 per square feet

《红色万福山》　97cm×180cm　　*Red Wanfu Mountain*

《旭日东升》　97cm×180cm　*The Rising Sun*

冯玉霞 *Feng Yuxia*

冯玉霞，女，1973年生，广东省中山人，专业书画家，多次在全国性比赛获奖。

润笔价格：3000/平尺

Feng Yuxia, female, born in Zhongshan, Guangdong Province, in 1973, is a professional calligrapher and painter, whose works won many awards in national competitions.

Reference price: RMB 3000 per square feet

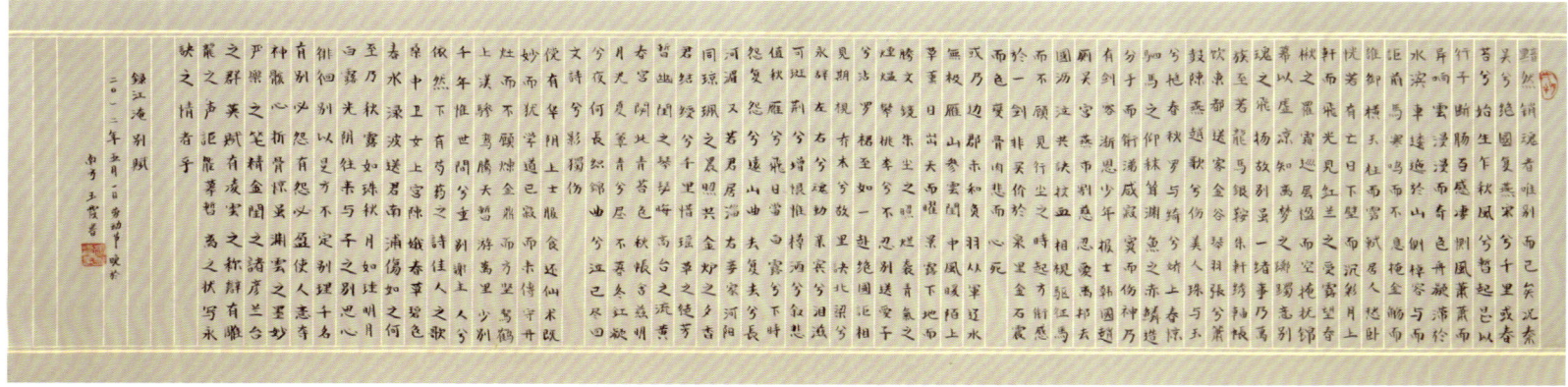

《录江淹别赋》　　34cm×130cm　　*Departure Fu by Jiang Yan*

马双彦 *Ma Shuangyan*

马双彦，男，1967年生，中国人文美术家协会会员，画家。
润笔价格：10000/平尺

Ma Shuangyan, male, born in 1967, is a painter, and member of China Literary Artists Association.
Reference price: RMB 10000 per square feet

《金色江南》　　138cm×68cm　　*Golden South China*

贺祖荣 *He Zurong*

贺祖荣，男，1938年出生，祖籍重庆市奉节县，专业军人，退休干部，中国书画家协会会员，中国书画研究院艺术委员会会员，世界华人艺术家联合会会员，山东省枣庄市书法家协会会员，山东省书法家协会会员，作品曾多次在国内外大赛中获奖，并入编作品集。

润笔价格：5000/平尺

He Zurong, male, born in Fengjie County, Chongqing, in 1938, is a retired veteran and cadre. He is a member of China Calligrapher and Painter Association, of Art Committee of China Calligraphy and Painting Research Institute, and Zaozhuang Calligraphers Association. He is also a member of WCNAA, and of Shandong Calligraphers Association, whose works won many awards in domestic and international exhibitions, and have been complied into collections.

Reference price: RMB 5000 per square feet

《对联一幅》　206cm×36cm×2　*A Couplet*

《镜心诗三首》　170cm×69cm　Three Poems

李政贤 *Li Zhengxian*

李政贤，男，号藏海道人，1975年生于云南武定，现为中国美术家协会会员，作品多次荣获国内外大奖。

润笔价格：12000/平尺

Li Zhengxian, male, born in Wuding, Yunnan Province, in 1975, and with Zanghai Taoist as his literary name, is a member of China Artists Association, whose works won numerous domestic and international awards.
Reference price: RMB 12000 per square feet

《人物一幅》　138cm×69cm　　*A Figure*

《花鸟一幅》　　138cm×69cm　　*Flowers and Birds*

吕能华 *Lü Nenghus*

吕能华，男，字略震、号竹溪居士，1955年生于安徽徽州，作品被海内外收藏家重视，大获好评。
润笔价格：4000/平尺

Lü Nenghus, male, with Luezhen as his courtesy name and Zhuxi Jushi (Householder by Zhuxi) as his literary name, was born in Huizhou, Anhui Province, in 1955. His works have been highly praised by collectors in and out of China.
Reference price: RMB 4000 per square feet

《岁通盛世》　35cm×133cm　　*Prosperous Age*

龙吟盛世神州添福寿
笔谱宏图华夏贺康宁

《楹联一幅》 134cm×34cm×2　A Couplet

邵建刚 *Shao Jiangang*

邵建刚，男，字墨妄言，生于1958年，现居北京。现为中国美术学会会员、中国书画研究院委员、中国书画创作院院士、中国当代艺术家协会理事、东方艺术家协会委员、特聘中国当代艺术家协会培训中心教授。

润笔价格：14000/平尺

Shao Jiangang, male, born in 1958, and with Mowangyan as his courtesy name, is a member of China Artists Association, committee member of Chinese Calligraphy and Painting Research Institute, and painter with China Calligraphy and Painting Art Creation Institute. Shao is also a council member of China Contemporary Artists Association, committee member of Oriental Artists Association, and especially employed professor with Training Center of China Association of Contemporary Artists. He now lives in Beijing.

Reference price: RMB 14000 per square feet

《寒林瑞雪图》　69cm×139cm　*Winter Forest with Auspicious Snow*

《静心图》　97cm×180cm　*Ataraxia*

郝英辉 *Hao Yinghui*

郝英辉，又名郝应辉，男，1976年2月生于山东省宁阳县，现为山东省书协会员、东营市书法家协会会员。

润笔价格：3000/平尺

Hao Yinghui, male, born in Ningyang County, Shandong Province, in the February of 1976, is a member of Shandong Calligraphers Association, and of Dongying Calligraphers Association.

Reference price: RMB 3000 per square feet

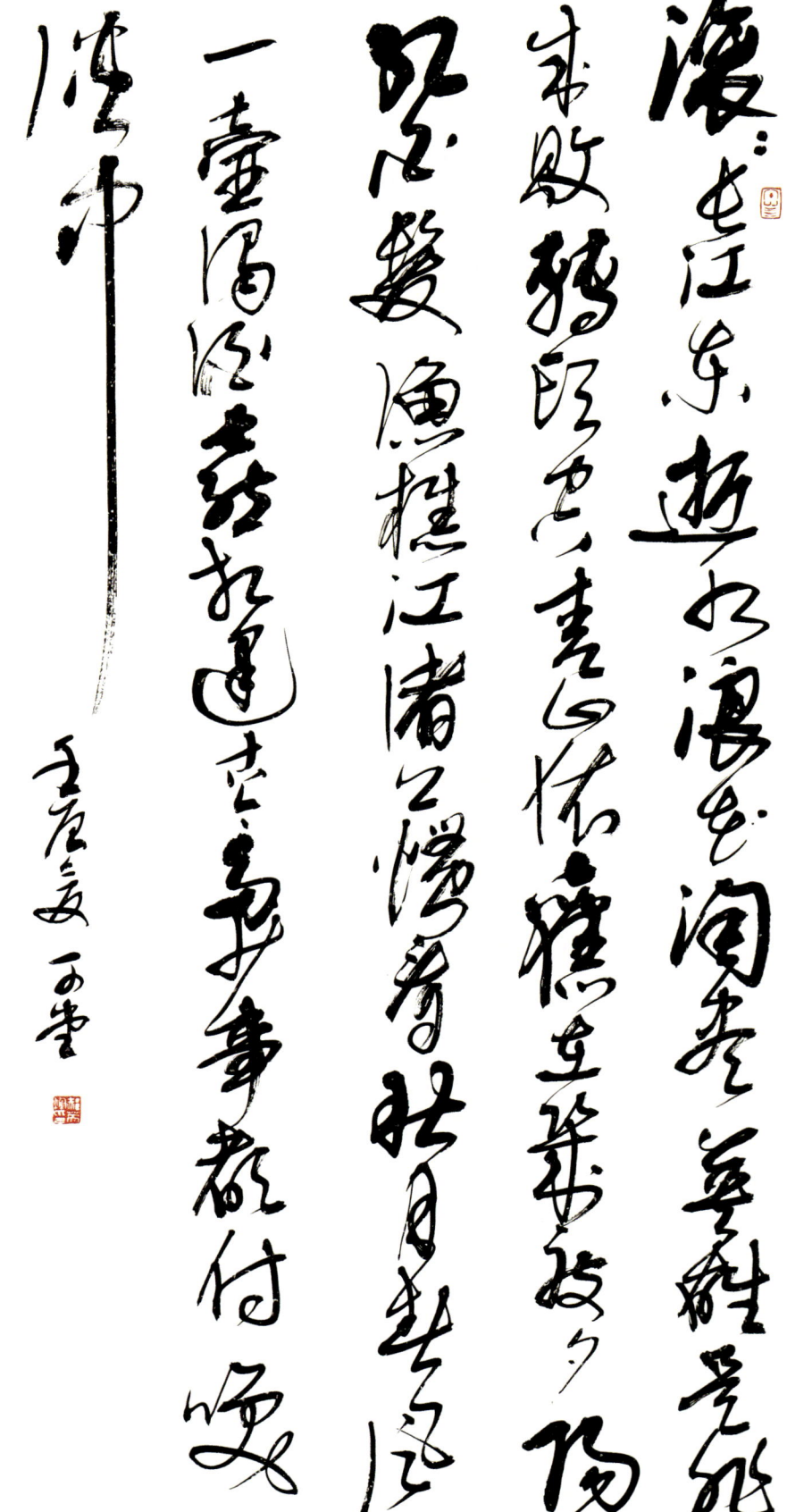

《三国演义开篇词》　　138cm×69cm　　*The Opening Poem in The Romance of Three Kingdoms*

张弓强 *Zhang Gongqiang*

张弓强、男，笔名弓强，斋名碧玉阁，1939年4月出生，河南省新安县人，高级工艺美术师。现为中国美术家协会会员，中国书画家协会理事，中国书画研究院理事，中国工艺美术学会会员，洛阳金谷印社理事。

润笔价格：8000/平尺

Zhang Gongqiang, male, also known as Gongqiang and with his study as Jasper Hall, was born in Xin'an County, Henan Province, in the April of 1939. He is a senior crafts artist, member of China Artists Association, and council member of China Calligrapher and Painter Association. Zhang is also a council member of China Calligraphy and Painting Research Institute, member of China Arts and Crafts Association, and council member of Luoyang Jingu Society of Seal Arts.

Reference price: RMB 8000 per square feet

《国花神韵》　68cm×138cm　*Charm of National Flowers*

李光泉　*Li Guangquan*

李光泉，男，1955出生于湘潭。中国书协会员、中国书法名城联谊会常务理事、中国书画家协会常务理事、湖南省书协理事、湘潭市文联副主席、湘潭市书协主席。现任湘潭市政协副主席。

润笔价格：5000/平尺

Li Guangquan, male, born in Xiangtan in 1955, is a member of China Calligraphers Association, standing council member of Federation of Chinese Calligraphers in Big Cities, and of China Calligrapher and Painter Association. He is also a council member of Hunan Calligraphers Association, Vice President of Xiangtan Federation of Literary and Art Circles, and President of Xiangtan Calligraphers Association. Li is Vice President of Xiangtan CPPCC.

Reference price: RMB 5000 per square feet

《天道酬勤》　53cm×115cm　*Fortune Favors the Diligent*

张传森　*Zhang Chuansen*

张传森，男，号金溪渔翁，1944年5月生，山东费县人，现为国家一级美术师、中国国画院院士、中国艺术研究院创作委员、中华人民共和国人事部艺术家学部委员会一级国画艺术委员、北京东方欣正书画院执行院长、中艺名北京书画院院长、中国国画院花鸟画艺术创作委员会副主席、日本东京中国书画院特聘院士、国务国（宾）礼特供艺术家。

润笔价格：6000/平尺

Zhang Chuansen, male, born in Fei County, Shandong Province, in the May of 1944, and with Jinxi Fisher as his literary name, is a National Class A artist, painter with China Traditional Chinese Painting Institute, and member of School of Fine Arts of Chinese National Academy of Arts. Zhang is also Class A member of Traditional Chinese Painting of Arts Committee of Ministry of Human Resources and Social Security, standing President of Beijing Oriental Xinzheng Calligraphy and Painting Gallery, President of Beijing Zhongyiming Calligraphy and Painting Gallery, and Vice President of Bird-and-Flower Painting Art Committee of China Traditional Chinese Painting Institute. He is an especially employed painter with Tokyo Institute of Traditional Chinese Painting, and receiver of State allowance.

Reference price: RMB 6000 per square feet

《前程似锦》　68cm×138cm　　*Prosperous Expectation*

贺书元　*He Shuyuan*

贺书元，男，1942年生，系湖南省湘潭市房产局退休干部、湖南省书法家协会会员、湖南帛书研究会会员、湘潭市书法家协会艺术顾问、潭州书画院艺术总监。

润笔价格：3000/平尺

He Shuyuan, male, born in 1942, is a retired cadre of Xiangtan Real Estate Bureau of Hunan Province, who is a member of Hunan Calligraphers Association, and of Hunan Silk Texts Research Institute. He is also an art consultant of Xiangtan Calligraphers Association, and art director of Xiangtan Calligraphy and Painting Gallery.

Reference price: RMB 3000 per square feet

《孔子名句》　58cm×137cm　　*Famous Quotations of Confucius*

闫道辉 *Yan Daohui*

闫道辉，男，名留迷，字浑人，1957年生于河南，现为外交部书画协会副书长。曾先后在意大利举办个展。

润笔价格：6000/平尺

Yan Daohui, male, also by the name of Liumi, and with Hunren (an undisciplined person) as his courtesy name, was born in Henan Province in 1957. He is Vice Director of Calligraphy and Painting under Ministry of Foreign Affairs, whose works have been exhibited on his one-man show in Italy.

Reference price: RMB 6000 per square feet

《神龙》　98cm×178cm　　*Dragon*

白银禄　*Bai Yinlu*

白银禄，男，又名白云禄，又名云露，1939年生于河北省石家庄市，历任中国长城书画院画家、中国榜书艺术研究会会员，中国美术家协会河北分会会员。

润笔价格：2000/平尺

Bai Yinlu, male, also by the name of Bai Yunlu, was born in Shijiazhuang, Hubei Province, in 1939. He is a painter with China Changcheng (Great Wall) Calligraphy and Painting Gallery, member of China Bangshu Art Research Society, and of Hebei Branch of China Artists Association.

Reference price: RMB 2000 per square feet

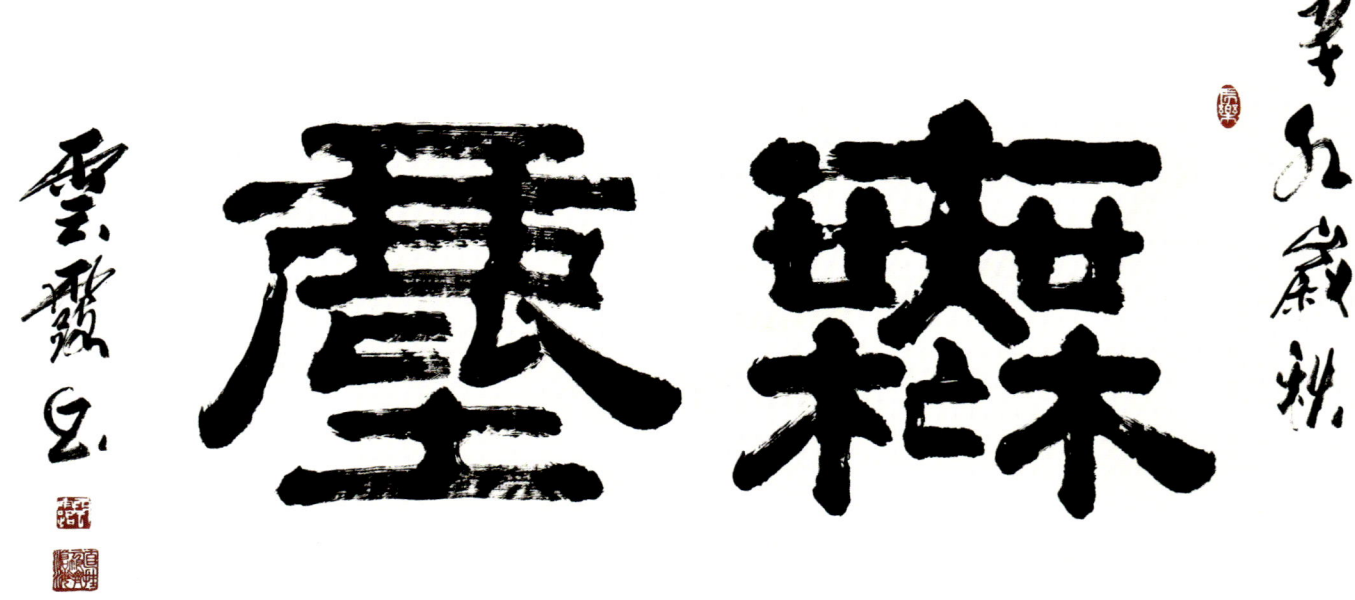

《无尘》　138cm×69cm　　*Free from Dirt*

黄国建 *Huang Jianguo*

黄国建，男，1962年生，湖北襄阳人。北京美术家协会区县委员会委员，文化部侨联文华阁书画院艺术委员，中华书画协会常务副主席，北京慈善艺术院副院长，中国世界民族文化交流促进会理事、北京书法家协会会员、中国收藏家协会会员。

润笔价格：12000/平尺

Huang Jianguo, male, born in Xiangyang, Hubei Province, in 1962, is a committee member of District and County Artists Association of Beijing, member of Art Committee of Wenhua Hall Calligraphy and Painting for Returned Oversea Chinese under Ministry of Culture, and standing President of Calligraphy and Painting Association of China. Huang is also Vice President of Beijing Charity Arts Institute, council member of Worldwide National Culture Promotion Society of China, member of Beijing Calligraphers Association, and of Beijing Association of Collectors.

Reference price: RMB 12000 per square feet

《渐远峡江映雾谙》　　98cm×178cm　　*Foggy Xiajiang*

陈明逊 Chen Mingxun

陈明逊，男，1933年12月出生，四川安县人。系成都市美协会员，中国书协会员，中国书画家协会理事。

润笔价格：4000/平尺

Chen Mingxun, male, born in An County, Sichuan Province, in the December of 1933, is a member of Chengdu Artists Association, of China Calligraphers Association, and council member of China Calligrapher and Painter Association.

Reference price: RMB 4000 per square feet

《明杨慎诗一首》　138cm×69cm　　*A Poem by Yang Shen*

邓承敏 *Deng Chengmin*

邓承敏，男，1964年生于广西玉林市，国家一级书画师，现为当代书画家协会会员，东坡书画院常务理事，北京尔康书画院院士。

润笔价格：4000/平尺

Deng Chengmin, male, born in Yulin, Guangxi Zhuang Autonomous Region, in 1964, is a National Class A artist, and member of Contemporary Calligrapher and Painter Association. He is also a standing committee member of Dongpo Calligraphy and Painting Academy, and painter with Beijing Erkang Calligraphy and Painting Gallery.

Reference price: RMB 4000 per square feet

《乾坤清气》　138cm×69cm　*Fresh Air*

李鸿超 *Li Hongchao*

李鸿超，男，号竹园居士，1950年生于河南扶沟，现为职业书画师、中国国画家协会理事、中国书法家协会会员、中国老年美协理事、中国书画研究院研究员、扶沟书画研究会会长。

润笔价格：4000/平尺

Li Hongchao, male, born in Fugou, Henan Province, in 1950, and with Zhuyuan Jushi (Householder of Bamboo Garden), is a professional calligrapher and painter, council member of China Association of Traditional Chinese Painting, and of China Senior Artists Association. He is also a member of China Calligrapher Association, researcher with China Calligraphy and Painting Research Institute, and President of Fugou Calligraphy and Painting Research Institute.

Reference price: RMB 4000 per square feet

《隶书一幅》　　139cm×68cm　　*A Scroll of Clerical Script*

李兴建　*Li Xingjian*

李兴建，男，1938年生于山东临沂，现为中国书画家协会会员，东方艺术研究院名誉院长，文化部侨联文华阁书画院书画师等。

润笔价格：4000/平尺

Li Xingjian, male, born in Linyi, Shandong Province, in 1938, is a member of China Calligrapher and Painter Association, Honorary President of Oriental Art Research Institute, and calligrapher and painter with Wenhua Hall Calligraphy and Painting for Returned Oversea Chinese under Ministry of Culture. He also bears other positions.

Reference price: RMB 4000 per square feet

《山水一副》　66cm×44cm　　*A Picture of Landscape*

陈维国 *Chen Weiguo*

陈维国，男，字怡博，1952年生于山东。现为中国书画艺术研究院高级研究员、副秘书长。

润笔价格：4000/平尺

Chen Weiguo, male, born in Shandong in 1952, and with Yibo as his courtesy name, is a senior researcher and Deputy Secretary General of Chinese Calligraphy and Painting Research Institute.

Reference price: RMB 4000 per square feet

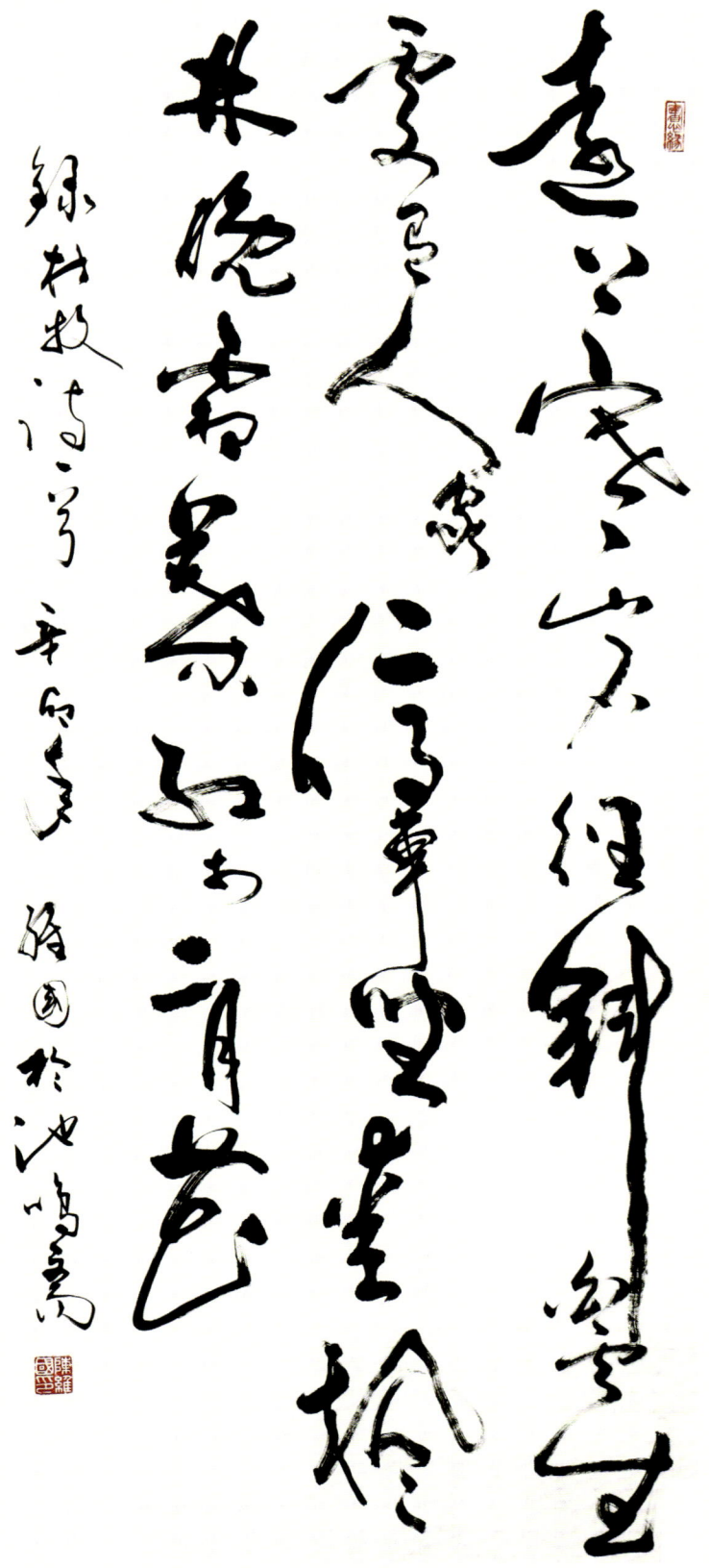

《录杜牧诗一首》　　138cm×69cm　　*A Poem by Du Mu*

姜立法 *Jiang Lifa*

姜立法，男，山东省聊城市东昌府区人，现任联合国美术家协会副主席、中国书画协会副主席、中国国画家协会理事、山东省聊城市政协委员、聊城市书画研究会会长(主席)。

润笔价格：4000/平尺

Jiang Lifa, male, born in Dongchangfu District of Liaocheng City, Shandong Province, is Vice President of United Nations Artists Association, of China Calligrapher and Painter Association, and council member of China Association of Traditional Chinese Painting. Jiang is also a CPPCC member of Liaocheng City, and President of Liaocheng Calligraphy and Painting Research Institute.

Reference price: RMB 4000 per square feet

《群龙图》   138cm×69cm   *Dragons*

党正 *Dang Zheng*

党正，男，77岁，陕西富平县人。现任富平县书法协会会长，薛镇乡书协会长。

润笔价格：3000/平尺

Dang Zheng, male, 77-year-old, was born in Fuping County, Shanxi Province. He is President of Fuping Calligraphers Association, and of Xuezhen Calligraphers Association.

Reference price: RMB 3000 per square feet

《陋室铭》　　137cm×70cm　　Ode to My Humble Room

张传文　*Zhang Chuanwen*

张传文，男，号无极，1974年生于山东省荷泽市单县。师从米南阳，先后在国内外发表作品近千件。

润笔价格：10000/平尺

Zhang Chuanwen, male, born in Shan County of Heze City, Shandong Province, in 1974, and with Wuji as his literary name, learned with Mr. Mi Nanyang about painting. He has published thousands of works in and out of China.
Reference price: RMB 10000 per square feet

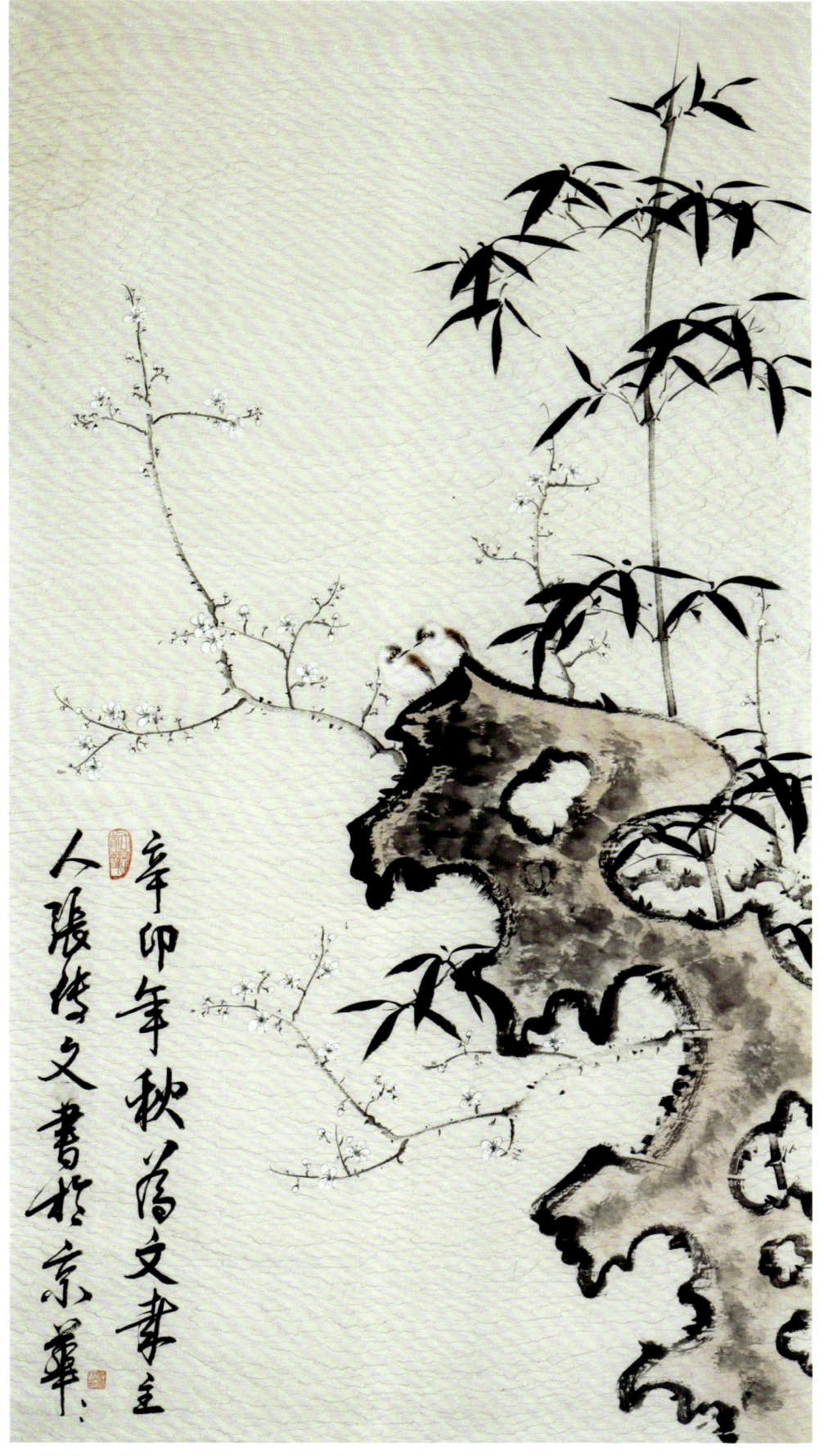

《花鸟一幅》　180cm×98cm　　*A picture of Flowers and Birds*

苟中元　*Gou Zhongyuan*

苟中元，男，四川广元昭化人，系中国书画家协会理事，中国青年书法家协会会员等。

润笔价格：6000/平尺

Gou Zhongyuan, male, born in Zhaohua of Guangyuan, Sichuan Province, is a council member of China Calligrapher and Painter Association, and China Young Calligraphers Association, etc.

Reference price: RMB 6000 per square feet

《岳阳楼记》　131cm×66cm　　*Account of Yueyang Building*

王丽荣　*Wang Lirong*

王丽荣，女，澄心堂主人，1970年生，天津美院霍春阳研究生在读，现为中国画家协会副主席,中国美术家协会宁夏分会理事。

润笔价格：14000/平尺

Wang Lirong, female, born in 1970, and with Host of Chengxin Hall as her literary name, is a graduate student at Huo Chunyang Art Classes at Tianjin Academy of Fine Arts. She is also Vice President of China Painters Association, and council member of Ningxia Artists Association.

Reference price: RMB 14000 per square feet

《前程似锦》　68cm×68cm　*Promising Future*

郭瑞 *Guo Rui*

郭瑞，男，于1999年拜大同市书法家协会副主席古凤林先生为师。现为大同市书法家协会主席团委员，大同市青年书法家协会副主席。

润笔价格：3000/平尺

Guo Rui, male, learned with Mr. Gu Fenglin, Vice President of Datong Calligraphers Association, in 1999. He is a now member of Presidential Committee of Datong Calligraphers Association, and Vice President of Datong Young Calligraphers Association.

Reference price: RMB 3000 per square feet

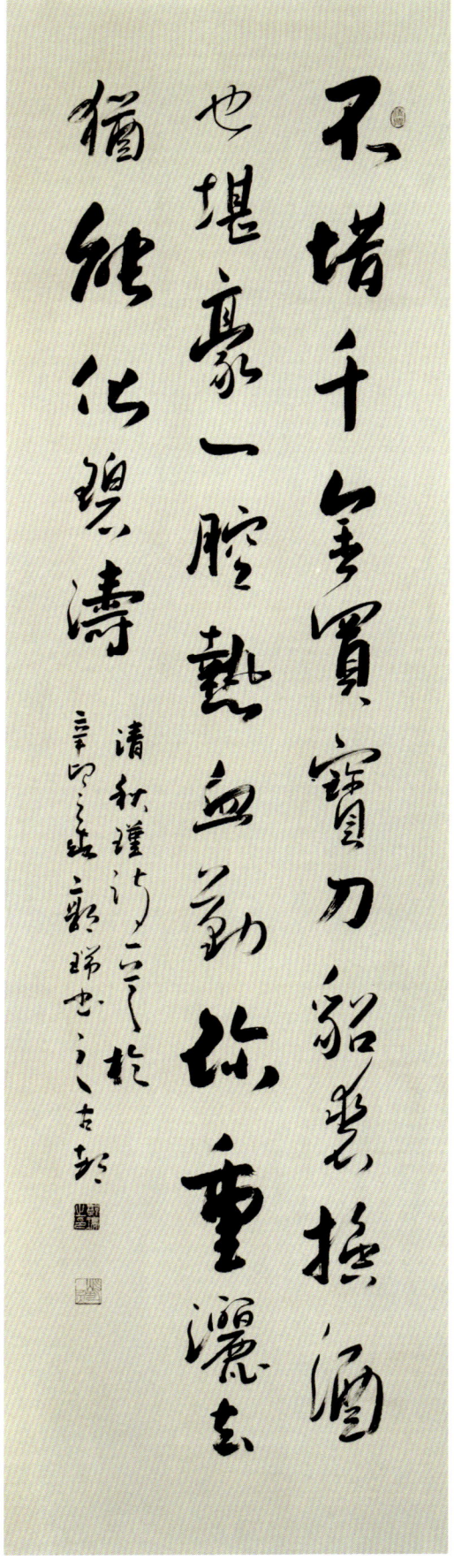

《清秋瑾诗一首》　　180cm×50cm　　*A Poem by Qiu Jin*

童威尧 *Tong Weiyao*

童威尧，男，字夏歌，1964年生，浙江江山人。中国美术艺术家协会会员，中国艺术家协会理事，中国名家书画研究院院士，中国画院会员、中国书画院院士、中国书画家联谊会会员、东城美术家协会会员，中国诗酒文化协会诗书画院一级画师，和谐中国书画院会员。

润笔价格：6000/平尺

Tong Weiyao, male, born in Jiangshan, Zhejiang Province, in 1964, and with Xiage as his courtesy name, is a member of China Artists Association, council member of China Artists Association, painter with Chinese Master Calligraphy and Painting Research Institute, member of China Art Academy, and painter with China Calligraphy and Painting Research Institute as well. Tong is also a member of Chinese Calligrapher and Painter Federation, of Dongcheng Artists Association, Class A Painter with Poetry, Calligraphy and Painting Gallery of China Cultural Association of Poetry and Wine, and member of Harmonious Research Institute of Calligraphy and Painting.

Reference price: RMB 6000 per square feet

《天香一品》 138cm×69cm *Heaven Fragrance*

霍炬 *Huo Ju*

霍炬,男,1969年生于黑龙江省宝清县。现为双鸭市书法家协会会员,北大荒书法家协会会员。
润笔价格:2000/平尺

Huo Ju, male, born in Baoqing County, Helongjiang Province, in 1969, is a member of Shuangya Calligraphers Association, and of Beidahuang Calligraphers Association.
Reference price: RMB 2000 per square feet

《腾龙》　180cm×97cm　　*Soaring Dragon*

《雄风》　180cm×97cm　　*Invincible Might*

刘武宏 Liu Hongwu

刘武宏，男，1946年生于西安，毕业于西安美院。现任中国美术家协会会员、陕西省美术家协会会员、延安市美术家协会理事、陕西英才组织委员会专业画家、西部文化交流联谊会会长等职，被业内同行推崇为"延安窑洞画派"创始人。

润笔价格：10000/平尺

Liu Hongwu, male, born in Xi'an, in 1946, graduated from Xi'an Academy of Fine Arts. He now is a member of China Artists Association, of Shaanxi Artists Association, council member of Yan'an Artists Association, and painter with Organization Committee of Shaanxi Excellence Society. Liu is also Director of West China Cultural Exchange Federation, who has been reverend as the Founder of Yan'an Cave Painting. He also bears some other positions.

Reference price: RMB 10000 per square feet

《陕北高原处处春》　83cm×149cm　*Spring in Northern Shaanxi Plateau*

柯明　*Ke Ming*

柯明，男，汉族，1963年出生，湖北大冶市人。现任中国艺术研究院文化艺术市场研究中心创作员、中国书画家协会理事、世界书画家协会会员、中华书法研究会会员，黄河书画院特邀书画师，中国黄石同舟行书画院书画师。

润笔价格：3000/平尺

Ke Ming, male, born in Daye, Hubei Province, in 1963, is a calligrapher and painter. He is a creator with Research Center of Culture and Arts Market of Chinese National Academy of Arts, council member of China Calligrapher and Painter Association, and member of International Calligraphers and Painters Association. Ke is also a member of China Calligraphy Research Society, especially employed painter with Huanghe (Yellow River) Calligraphy and Painting Gallery, and calligrapher and painter with Huangshi Tongzhouxing Calligraphy and Painting Gallery of China.

Reference price: RMB 3000 per square feet

《霹雳手段》　107cm×49cm　*Thunderbolt*

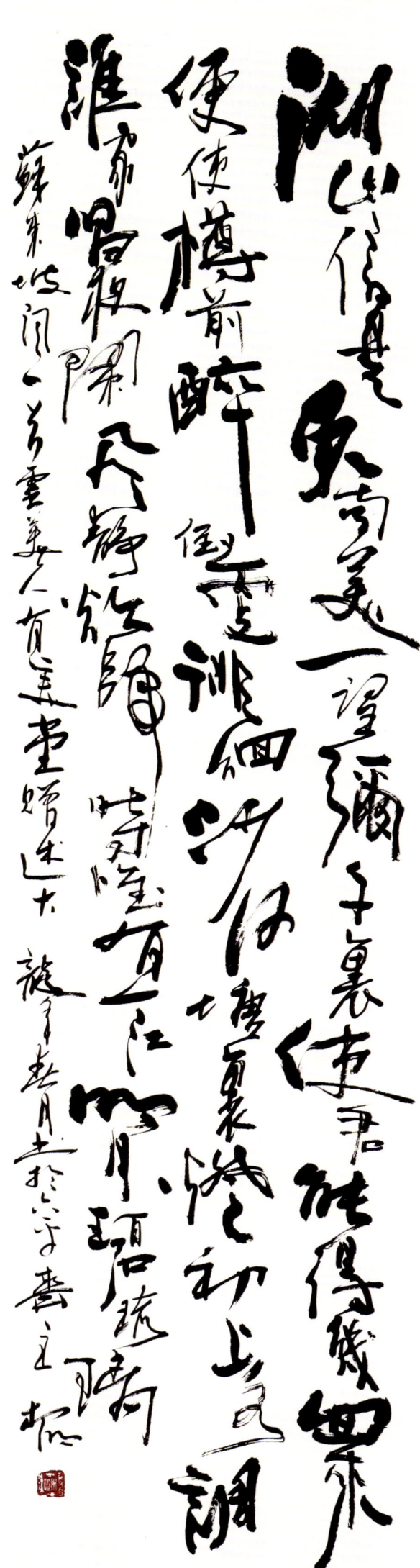

《苏东坡词》　180cm×49cm　　A Poem by Su Dongpo

陈福圣 *Chen Fusheng*

陈福圣，男，字苍秋，号苦独山人，1957年3月生于重庆，九州枫林国际书画艺术院院士，擅长山水、人物、花鸟等，作品参加国内外的各种展览，入编各种大型画册名家辞典并获奖，部分作品被海内外人士收藏。

润笔价格：10000/平尺

Chen Fusheng, male, with Cangqiu (Vigorous Autumn) as his courtesy name and with Kudu Shanren as his literary name, was born in Chongqing, in the March of 1957. Chen is now a painter with Jiuzhou Fenglin International Calligraphy and Painting Gallery, adept at painting landscape, figures, flowers and birds, etc., whose works have been exhibited in many domestic and international exhibitions, and been compiled into various dictionaries of large painting albums and awarded. Some of his works have also been collected by people in and out of China.

Reference price: RMB 10000 per square feet

《荷塘清香》　　136cm×67cm　　*Scent around the Pond of Lotus*

《菊花》　136cm×67cm　　Chrysanthemums

况路生　Kuang Lusheng

况路生，男，1963年5月生，江西省吉安市人，中国书画家协会理事，一级美术师，中国书画印研究会理事，中国书画院院士，长江书画院名誉院长。

润笔价格：6000/平尺

Kuang Lusheng, male, born in ji'an, Jiangxi Province, in the May of 1963, is a Class A artist, council member of China Calligrapher and Painter Association, and of Calligraphy, Painting and Seal Research Institute of China. He is also a painter with China Painting and Calligraphy Academy, and Honorary President of Changjiang (Yangtze River) Calligraphy and Painting Gallery.

Reference price: RMB 6000 per square feet

扇面　《物华天宝》　35cm×20cm　　Fan Calligraphy: Abundant Resources

《辛稼轩词三首》 178cm×17cm×3 Three Poems by Xin Jiaxuan

《春意盎然》　68cm×68cm　　Blooming Spring

刘从善 *Liu Congshan*

刘从善，男，1934年7月生，安徽省太和县人，现为安徽省界首市美协会员、界首市老年书画研究会副秘书长、阜阳地区老年书画研究会会员。

润笔价格：8000/平尺

Liu Congshan, male, born in Taihe County, Anhui Province, in the July of 1934, is a member of Jieshou Artists Association, Deputy Secretary General of Jieshou Calligraphy and Painting Research Institute for Seniors, and member of Fuyang Calligraphy and Painting Research Institute for Seniors.

Reference price: RMB 8000 per square feet

《雄风》　68cm×68cm　　*Vigor*

《反哺》　68cm×68cm　　Feeding

梁涛 *Liang Tao*

梁涛，男，1984年生于山东淄博，供职于淄博艺术学校，中国书画艺术研究院研究员，淄博市书法家协会会员。

润笔价格：6000/平尺

Liang Tao, male, was born in Zibo, Shandong Province, in 1984, and now works at Zibo Arts College. He is a researcher with Chinese Calligraphy and Painting Research Institute, and member of Zibo Calligraphers Association.
Reference price: RMB 6000 per square feet

山不在高有仙则名水不在深
有龙则灵斯是陋室惟吾德馨
苔痕上阶绿草色入帘青谈笑
有鸿儒往来无白丁可以调素
琴阅金经无丝竹之乱耳无案
牍之劳形南阳诸葛庐西蜀子
云亭孔子云何陋之有

《陋室铭》　138cm×68cm　*Ode to My Humble Room*

梅国庆 *Mei Guoqing*

梅国庆，男，字笑寒。湖北洪湖人。中国书画家协会会员，湖北美术家协会会员，世界名家书画院常务理事，伟人风采书画院副院长，紫龙赛虹（北京）国际书画院特聘画家。

润笔价格：6000/平尺

Mei Guoqing, male, with Xiaohan as his courtesy name, was born in Honghu, Hubei Province. He is a member of China Calligrapher and Painter Association, of Hubei Artists Association, and council member of International Master Calligraphy and Painting Institute. Mei is also Vice President of Weiren Fengcai (Elegance of the Greats) Calligraphy and Painting Gallery, and especially employed painter with Zilong Saihong International Calligraphy and Painting Gallery, Beijing.

Reference price: RMB 6000 per square feet

《山水一幅》　138cm×69cm　*A Picture of Landscape*

李鹏飞 *Li Pengfei*

李鹏飞，男，字渊石，现为中国书法家协会会员，中国硬笔书法协会会员，轩辕书画院副院长。

润笔价格：7000/平尺

Li Pengfei, male, with Yuanshi (Stone Deep in a Pool) as his courtesy name, is a member of China Calligraphers Association, of China Association of Pen Calligraphers, and Vice President of Xuanyuan Calligraphy and Painting Gallery.

Reference price: RMB 7000 per square feet

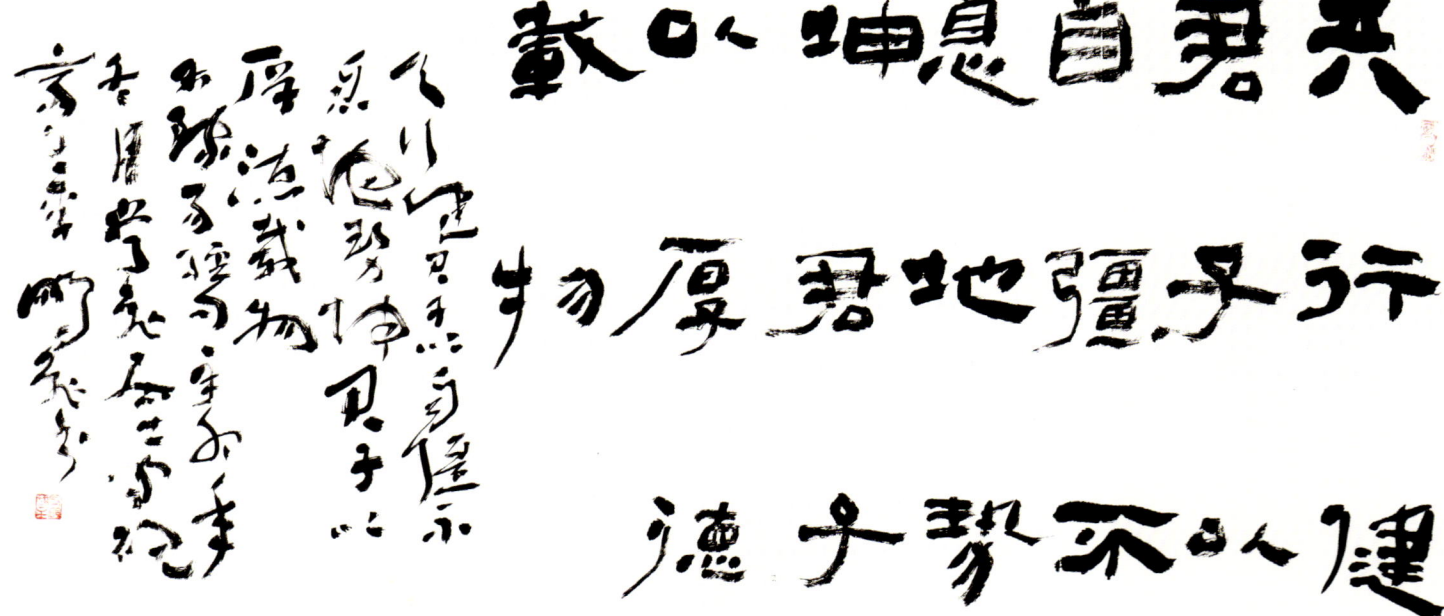

《隶书一幅》 138cm×69cm *A Scroll of Clerical Script*

《古诗九首》　180cm×97cm　Nine Poems

杨长喜 *Yang Changxi*

杨长喜，男，现为中国美术家协会会员、山东省美术家协会理事、东营市文联副主席、东营美术家协会名誉主席，中国笔墨研究院执行院长，天津师范大学课座教授。

润笔价格：8000/平尺

Yang Changxi, male, is a member of China Artists Association, council member of Shandong Artists Association, Vice President of Dongying Federation of Literary, and Honorary President of Dongying Artists Association. Yang is also Executive President of Chinese Ink Art Research Institute, and visiting professor with Tianjing Normal University.
Reference price: RMB 8000 per square feet

《紫气东来》　70cm×68cm　　*Propitious Omen*

《长寿图》　137cm×68cm　　Longevity

李新斌　*Li Xinbin*

李新斌，男，1973年生，系中国硬笔书法协会会员，浙江省书协会员，江南书画家联谊会常务副会长。

润笔价格：4000/平尺

Li Xinbin, male, born in 1973, is a member of China Association of Pen Calligraphers, of Zhejiang Calligraphers Association, and standing Vice President of Jiangnan (Regions south of Yangtze River) Federation of Calligraphers and Painters.
Reference price: RMB 4000 per square feet

《春华秋实》　135cm×35cm　*Blossoming in Spring and Fructifying in Autumn*

《海纳百川》　135cm×35cm　　*All Rivers Run into Sea*

宋学亮 *Song Xueliang*

宋学亮，男，1954年生，现为一级美术师、山东美术家协会会员、青岛老年大学教授、青岛老年书画协会副秘书长，青岛书画研究院理事。

润笔价格：10000/平尺

Song Xueliang, male, born in 1954, is a Class A artist, and member of Shandong Artists Association. He is a professor at Qingdao University for the Aged, Deputy Secretary General of Qingdao Calligraphy and Painting Association for the Seniors, and council member of Qingdao Calligraphy and Painting Research Institute.

Reference price: RMB 10000 per square feet

《黄山一线天》　68cm×69cm　　*A Thread of Sky in Mount Huang*

《山水有清音》　68cm×69cm　　*Babbling River in Mountains*

李赞集 *Li Zanji*

李赞集，男，广东人，大学毕业，中共党员，中国书画印研究院院长、中国剑光书画院院长、中国书画名家网主席、国际美术网理事长、世界书画家协会顾问、台北故宫书画院名誉院长、国家一级美术师、广东省陆河美协主席、中国书协、硬协会员等。

润笔价格：3000/平尺

Li Zanji, male, born is Guangdong Province, is a Party member and university graduate. He is a National Class A artist, President of Calligraphy, Painting and Seal Research Institute of China, of China Jianguang Calligraphy and Painting Gallery, and of Chinese Celebrated Calligrapher and Painter Net. Li is also a council member of International Arts Net, consultant of International Calligraphers and Painters Association, and Honorary President of Taibei Imperial Palace Calligraphy and Painting Institute. He also bears the positions like President of Luhe Artists Association, member of China Calligraphers Association and of China Association of Pen Calligraphers, etc.

Reference price: RMB 3000 per square feet

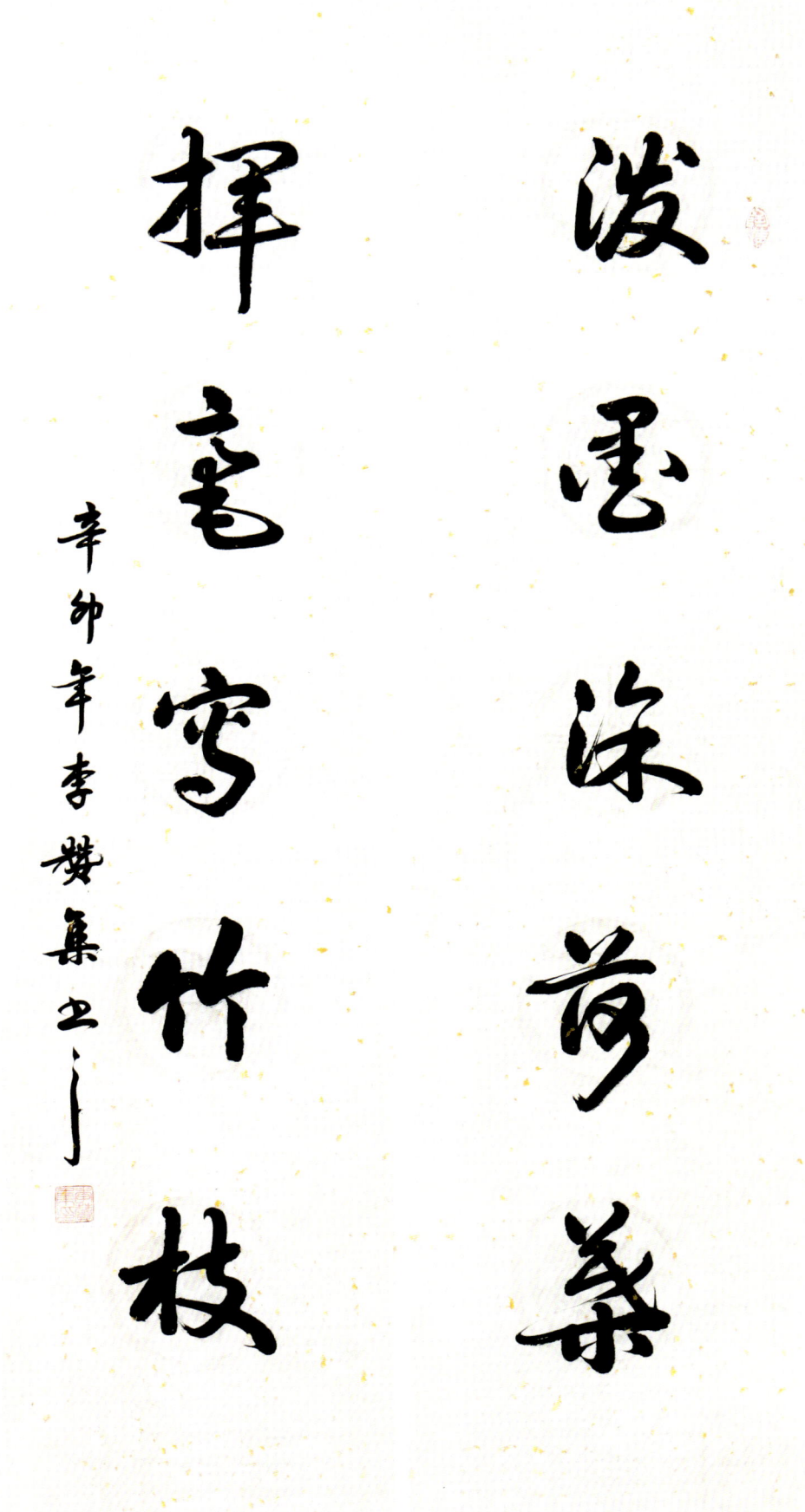

《对联一幅》　　130cm×33cm×2　　*A Couplet*

《诗一首》　138cm×68cm　　*A Poem*

王春林　*Wang Chunlin*

王春林，男，国际美术家联合会理事，美国指画艺术协会理事，国家一级美术师，中国美术家协会山东分会会员。

润笔价格：10000/平尺

Wang Chunlin, male, is a National Class A artist, council member of International Artists Alliance, and of American Finger Painting Society. He is also a member of Shandong Branch of China Artists Association.

Reference price: RMB 10000 per square feet

《觅》　68cm×68cm　　*Seeking*

《双鹰图》 68cm×68cm　　*Two Eagles*

刘军 *Liu Jun*

刘军，男，1984年生，现为福建文笔轩传播公司签约书法家。作品多次在去全国报刊、杂志发表。
润笔价格：5000/平尺

Liu Jun, male, born in 1984, is a contracted calligrapher with Fujian Wenbixuan Mass-Communication Company, whose works have been published in national newspaper and magazines.
Reference price: RMB 5000 per square feet

《云白风清》　101cm×97cm　　*White Clouds and Fresh Breeze*

《书法一幅》　190cm×65cm　　*A Calligraphy Scroll*

史文青 *Shi Wengqing*

史文青，男，1947年5月生，河北省大名县人，系辽宁省美术家协会会员，中国书画研究院院士，南京颜真卿文化研究会名誉主席。

润笔价格：14000/平尺

Shi Wengqing, male, born in Daming County, Hebei Province, in the May of 1947, is a member of Liaoning Artists Association, painter with China Calligraphy and Painting Research Institute, and honorary President of Nanjing Yan Zhenqing Art Research Institute.

Reference price: RMB 14000 per square feet

《牡丹》　178cm×96cm　　*Peonies*

《清泥不染出君子》　136cm×70cm　*Pure Gentleman*

刘万杰 *Liu Wanjie*

刘万杰，男，字三郎、又字师功，教授，中共党员，曾荣立三等军功。中国书法家协会汶上书协名誉主席、国家文化部徐悲鸿画院书画家、中国手指画研究会常务理事、中国艺术研究院创作委员、中国国画家协会常务理事等。

润笔价格：2000/平尺

Liu Wanjie, male, with Sanlang and Shigong as his courtesy name, is a Party member and professor, who was granted Class C Military Exploit. He is Honorary President of Wenshang Calligraphers Association of CCA, painter with Xu Beihong Gallery of Ministry of Culture, and council member of China Finger Painting Research Society. Liu is also member of School of Fine Arts of Chinese National Academy of Arts, standing council member of China Association of Traditional Chinese Painting, etc.

Reference price: RMB 2000 per square feet

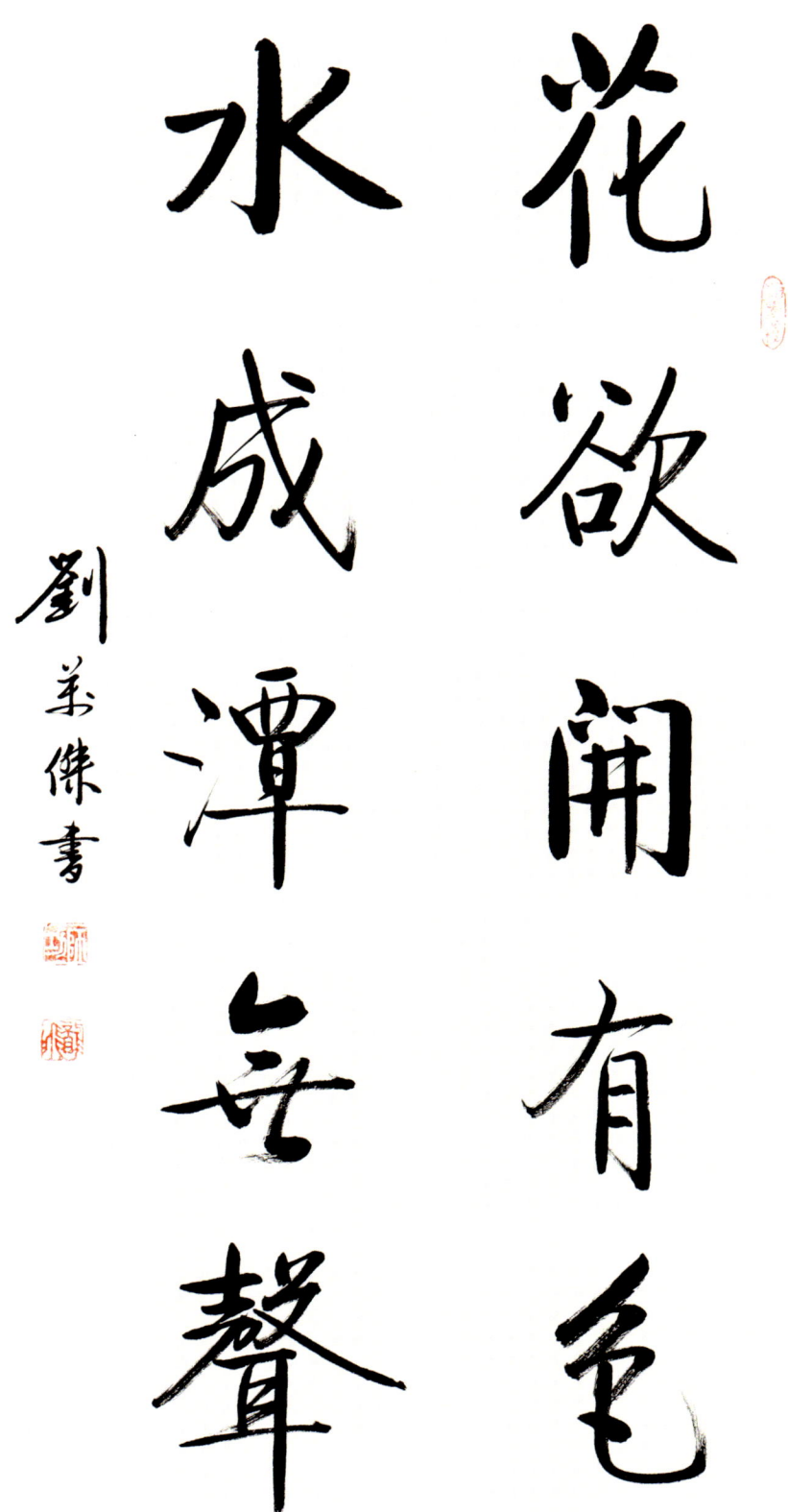

《花欲开有色》　98cm×51cm　　*Colorfully Blooming Flowers*

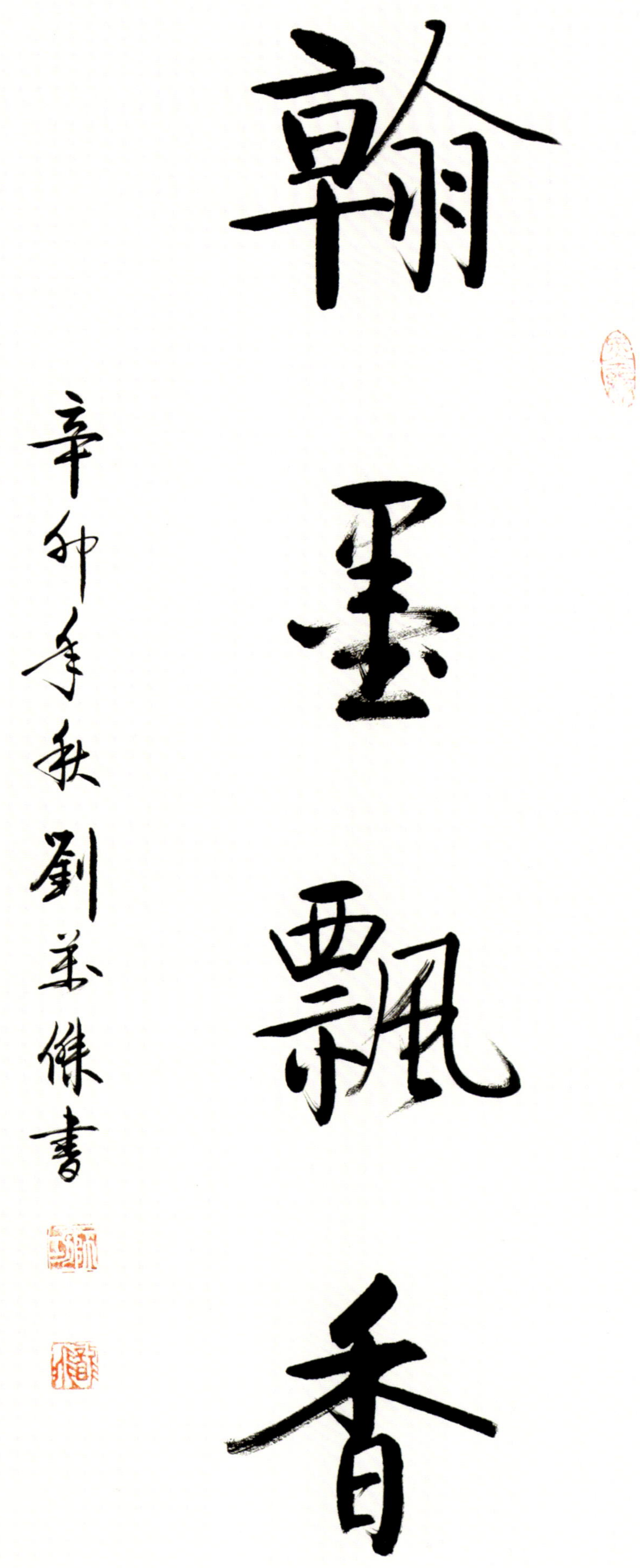

翰墨飘香

辛卯季秋 刘英杰书

《翰墨飘香》 98cm×51cm The Fragrance of Ink

唐智东 *Tang Zhidong*

唐智东、男，1952年生，四川成都人，汉族。笔名乙涧，号厚来斋主。现为中国书画家协会会员，中国书画研究院成员，成都市美术家协会会员。北京华夏国艺书画院签约书画家，颜真卿研究会会员。

润笔价格：4000/平尺

Tang Zhidong, male, also by the name of Yijian, and with Host of Houlai Study as his literary name, was born in Chengdu, Sichuan Province, in 1952. He is a member of China Calligrapher and Painter Association, of China Calligraphy and Painting Research Institute, and of Chengdu Artists Association. Tang is also a contracted painter with China Guoyi Calligraphy and Painting Gallery of Beijing, and member of Yan Zhenqing Research Institute.

Reference price: RMB 4000 per square feet

《身享鲜空气》 138cm×69cm *Fresh Air*

《使命》 138cm×69cm *Mission*

刘希舜 *Liu Xishun*

刘希舜，男，1930年生，退休前为二九0农场邮政局副局长。世界书画家协会会员，北大荒老年书画研究会会员，二九0农场美协名誉主席。

润笔价格：2000/平尺

Liu Xishun, male, born in 1930, was Deputy Director of 290 Farm Post Office before his retirement. He is member of International Calligraphers and Painters Association, of Beidahuang Calligraphy and Painting Research Institute for Seniors, and Honorary President of 290 Farm Artists Association.

Reference price: RMB 2000 per square feet

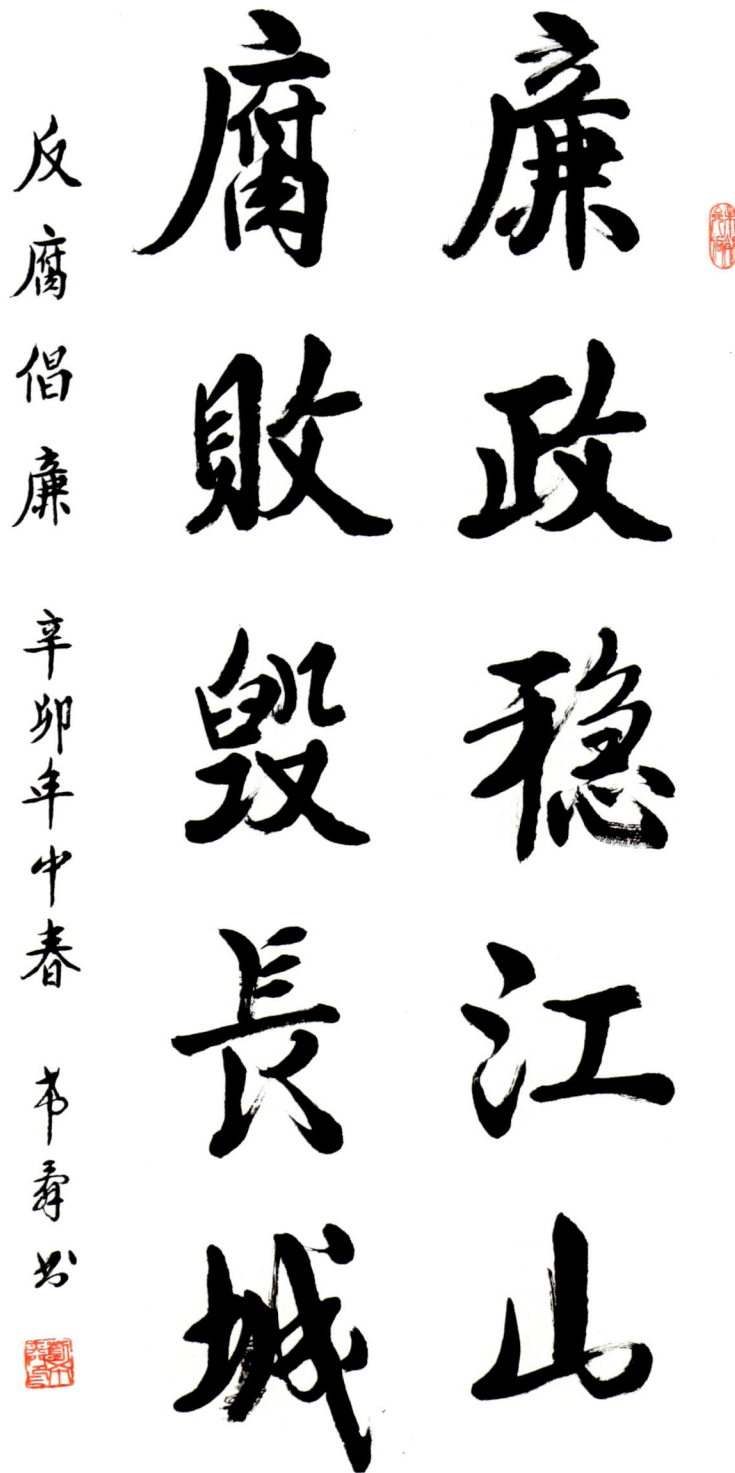

《反腐倡廉》　99cm×53cm　　*Combat Corruption and Uphold Integrity*

毛明强　*Mao Mingqiang*

毛明强，男，号明月清风、惠泉散人、梅花书屋主人，1970年生，毕业于江苏无锡书法艺术专科学校，江苏省无锡市书法家协会会员、楹联学会会员、诗词协会秘书长。

润笔价格：12000/平尺

Mao Mingqiang, male, born in 1970, and with Mingyue Qingfeng (Bright Moon and Fresh Air), Huquan Sanren and Host of Plum Blossom Study, graduated from Wuxi Academy of Calligraphy Art, Jiangsu Province. Mao is a member of Wuxi Calligraphers Association, of Yinglian Society of China, and Secretary General of Chinese Poetry Association.

Reference price: RMB 12000 per square feet

《松》　138cm×35cm　　*Pines*

刘悦波 *Liu Yuebo*

刘悦波，男，1927年生，汉族。中国艺术研究院文艺中心创作委员、中韩艺术专家委员会委员、国际金、银奖艺术家等荣誉，世界书画家协会会员。

润笔价格：2000/平尺

Liu Yuebo, male, born in 1927, is a creative member of Art Center of Chinese National Academy of Arts, member of International Calligraphers and Painters Association, and of Sino-Korean Artists Committee. He is also an international gold and silver award artist.

Reference price: RMB 2000 per square feet

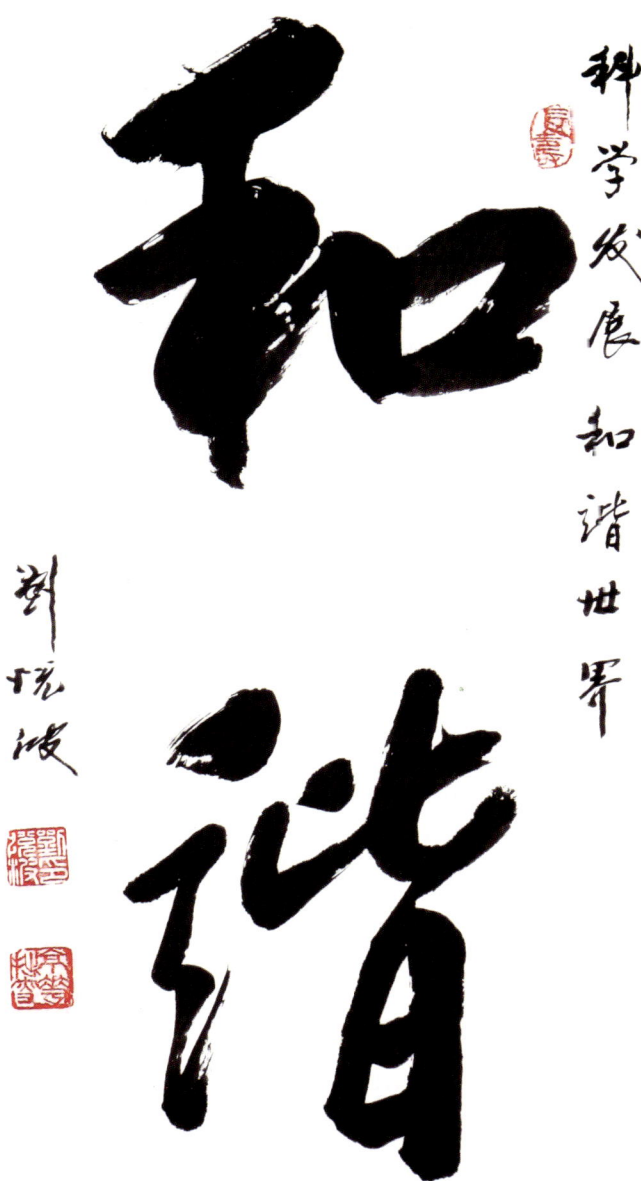

《和谐》　　100cm×50cm　　*Harmony*

《凝聚》　101cm×54cm　Condensation

何伟生　*He Weisheng*

何伟生，男，1957年生于广东揭阳，系中国工艺美术家协会会员，揭阳市美术家协会会员。

润笔价格：4000/平尺

He Weisheng, male, born in Jieyang, Guangdong Province, in 1957, is a member of China Arts and Crafts Association, and of Jieyang Artists Association.

Reference price: RMB 4000 per square feet

《春色满园》　138cm×69cm　　*Spring in Full Swing*

《长寿》　68cm×68cm　*Longevity*

潘庆五　*Pan Qingwu*

潘庆五，男，安徽南陵人，安徽省美术家协会会员，安徽省书法家协会会员，芜湖市书画研究会副会长，安徽中山画院芜湖分院副院长。

润笔价格：5000/平尺

Pan Qingwu, male, born in Nanling, Anhui Province, is a member of Anhui Artists Association, of Anhui Calligraphers Association, Vice President of Wuhu Calligraphy and Painting Research Institute, and of Wuhu Branch of Anhui Zhongshan Painting Art Gallery.

Reference price: RMB 5000 per square feet

《秋声赋》　180cm×97cm　*Ode to the Autumn*

岳陽樓記 范仲淹

慶曆四年春，滕子京謫守巴陵郡。越明年，政通人和，百廢具興，乃重修岳陽樓，增其舊制，刻唐賢今人詩賦於其上，屬予作文以記之。予觀夫巴陵勝狀，在洞庭一湖。銜遠山，吞長江，浩浩湯湯，橫無際涯；朝暉夕陰，氣象萬千，此則岳陽樓之大觀也，前人之述備矣。然則北通巫峽，南極瀟湘，遷客騷人，多會於此，覽物之情，得無異乎？

若夫霪雨霏霏，連月不開，陰風怒號，濁浪排空，日星隱耀，山岳潛形，商旅不行，檣傾楫摧，薄暮冥冥，虎嘯猿啼，登斯樓也，則有去國懷鄉，憂讒畏譏，滿目蕭然，感極而悲者矣。

至若春和景明，波瀾不驚，上下天光，一碧萬頃，沙鷗翔集，錦鱗游泳，岸芷汀蘭，郁郁青青。而或長煙一空，皓月千里，浮光躍金，靜影沉璧，漁歌互答，此樂何極！登斯樓也，則有心曠神怡，寵辱偕忘，把酒臨風，其喜洋洋者矣。

嗟夫！予嘗求古仁人之心，或異二者之為，何哉？不以物喜，不以己悲。居廟堂之高則憂其民，處江湖之遠則憂其君。是進亦憂，退亦憂；然則何時而樂耶？其必曰：先天下之憂而憂，後天下之樂而樂歟。噫！微斯人，吾誰與歸。

辛卯年盛秋，晨霧重重，浩慶台書於晚南小鎮藉山新舍記於園

《岳陽樓記》　180cm×97cm　Account of Yueyang Building

尉迟纪平　*Yuchi Jiping*

尉迟纪平，男，字君石，号无为居士。1949年生于天津。中国美术家协会天津分会会员，中国书画艺术研究会理事，天津政协书画研究会会员，天津市老年书画研究会理事，天津书画艺术鉴赏协会会员，长城画院高级书画师，津门北斗画院高级画师。

润笔价格：10000/平尺

Yuchi Jiping, male, with Junshi as his courtesy name, and with Wuwei Jushi (Inaction Buddhist) as his literary name, born in 1949 in Tianjin. He is a member of Tianjing Artists Association, of Calligraphy and Painting Research Institute of Tianjin CPPCC, and council member of Chinese Calligraphy and Painting Research Institute. Yuchi is also a coucil member of China Calligraphy and Painting Research Institute for the Seniors, member of Tianjing Calligraphy and Painting Appraisal Association, senior painter with China Great Wall Painting Art Gallery, and of Jinmen Beidou (the Big Dipper) Painting Art Gallery.

Reference price: RMB 10000 per square feet

《大展宏图》　70cm×70cm　*Promising Future*

《浩气雄风》　134cm×68cm　　*Noble Spirit*

任仲德 *Ren Zhongde*

任仲德，男，字俊德，云岗游子，1943年生，大专文化。内蒙古书法家协会会员，包头市书法家协会副主席，大汉书画院常务副院长。

润笔价格：5000/平尺

Ren Zhongde, male, born in 1943, and with Junde as his courtesy name and Yungang Youzi (Yungang Traveler) as his literary name, graduated at a college. He is a member of Inner Mongolia Calligraphers Association, Vice President of Baotou Calligraphers Association, and standing Vice President of Dahan Calligraphy and Painting Gallery.

Reference price: RMB 5000 per square feet

《自撰作品》　　200cm×53cm　　*A Self-Composed Scroll*

李贵生 *Li Guisheng*

李贵生，男，1959年生于天津，大学学历，国画家，现供职于天津美术学院。天津市美协会员，华人国际书画家协会会员。

润笔价格：6000/平尺

Li Guisheng, male, born in Tianjin, in 1959, graduated from a university and now is a Traditional Chinese Painter. He is a member of Tianjin Artists Association, and of International Calligraphers and Painters Association. He now works at Tianjin Academy of Fine Arts.

Reference price: RMB 6000 per square feet

《山水》　180cm×98cm　　*A Picture of Landscape*

沈桂林　*Shen Guilin*

沈桂林，男，1963年6月生，河南省获嘉县人。系河南省书协会员，河南省青年书法家协会会员，新乡市书画学会理事。

润笔价格：6000/平尺

Shen Guilin, male, born in Huojia County, Henan Province, in the June of 1963, is a member of Henan Calligraphers Association, of Henan Young Calligraphers Association, and council member of Xinxiang Calligraphy and Painting Research Institute.
Reference price: RMB 6000 per square feet

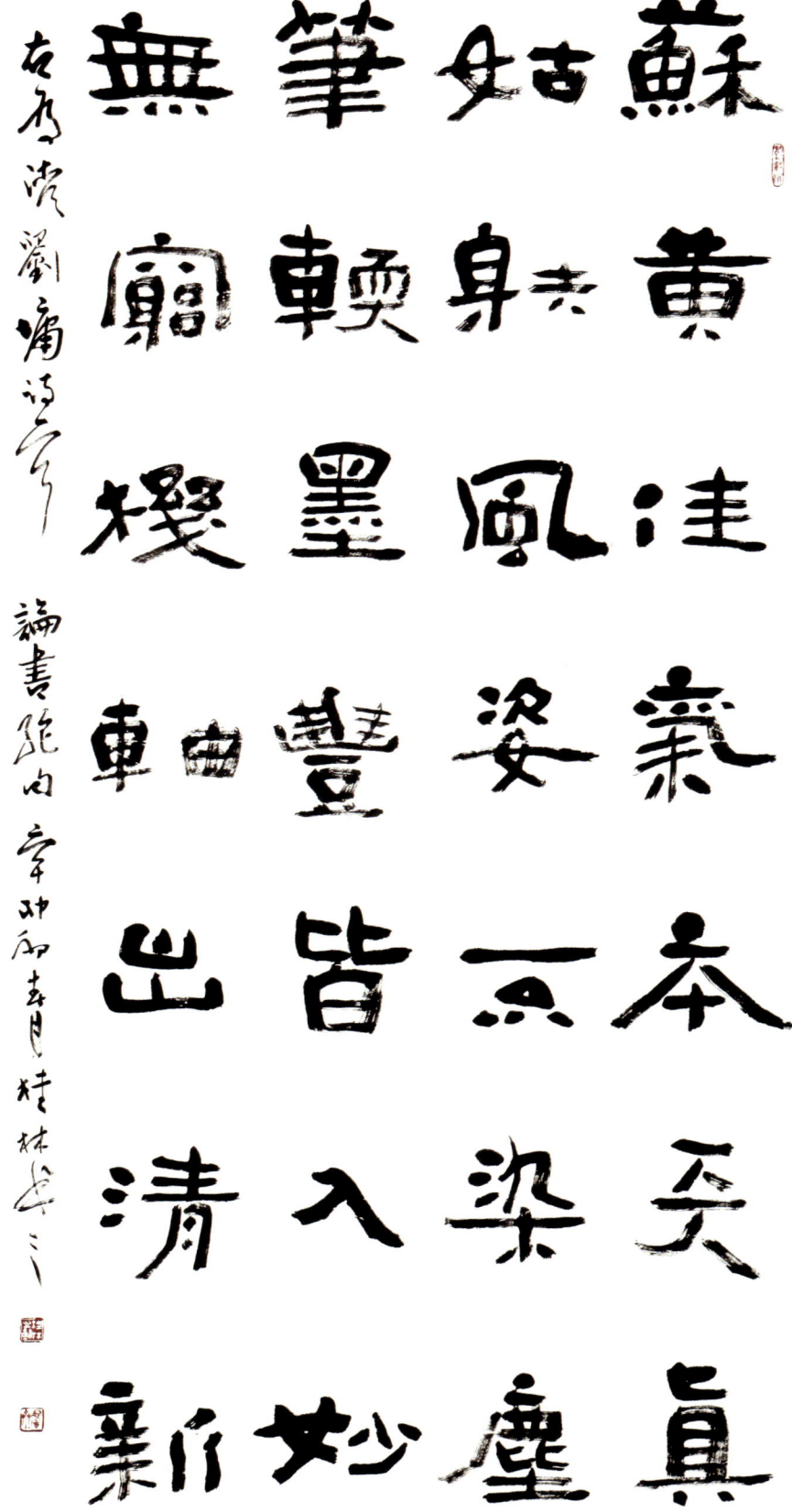

《隶属一幅》　180cm×97cm　*A Scroll of Clerical Script*

耿协生 *Geng Xiesheng*

耿协生，男，1949年生于安徽临泉，宿州中院退休副院长，安徽省美术家协会会员，中国国画家协会会员，中国美协培训中心特聘画师，中国书法研究院艺术委员会会员，宿州市美协会员、书协常务理事。

润笔价格：4000/平尺

Geng Xiesheng, male, born in Linquan, Anhui Province, in 1949, is a retired Vice President of Suzhou Intermediate People's Court. He is a member of Anhui Artists Association, and of China Association of Traditional Chinese Painting. Geng is also an especially employed painter with Training Center of China Artists Association, member of Arts Committee of China Calligraphy Art Research Institute, of Suzhou Artists Association, and council member of Suzhou Calligraphers Association.

Reference price: RMB 4000 per square feet

《早春二月》　102cm×53cm　　*Early Spring in February*

史德辉　*Shi Dehui*

史德辉，男，1954年10月生于山东淄博，就业于淄博矿务局双沟煤矿，任厂工会主席，自幼喜爱书画艺术。

润笔价格：3000/平尺

Shi Dehui, male, was born in Zibo, Shandong Province, in the October of 1954. He works at Shuanggou Mine of Zibo Mine Bureau, and is President of the Mine Labour Union. Shi has been an ardent lover of calligraphy and painting since his childhood.
Reference price: RMB 3000 per square feet

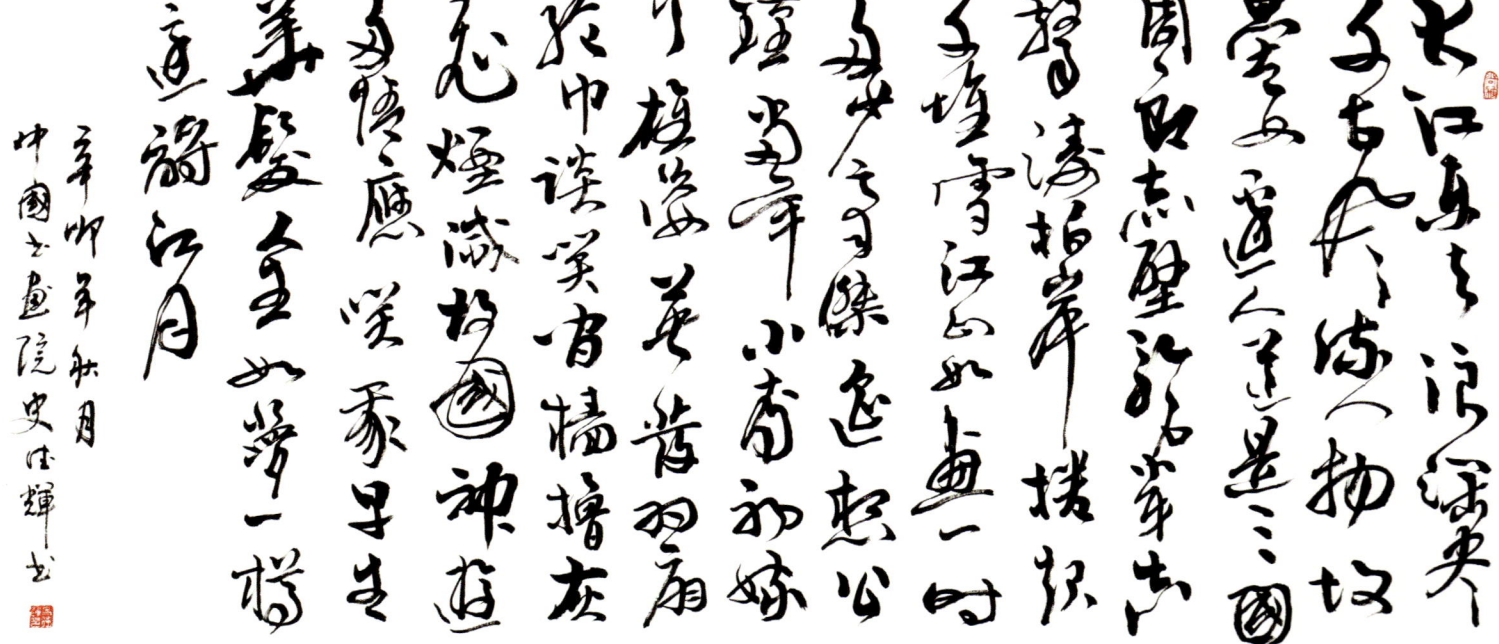

《赤壁怀古》　68cm×138cm　*Meditations on the Red Cliff*

刘谦 *Liu Qian*

刘谦，男，字谦人，1984年出生于甘肃陇南市。现为中国文人书法家协会会员。
润笔价格：4000/平尺

Liu Qian, male, with Qianren (Humble Man) as his courtesy name, born in Longnan, Gansu Province, in 1984, is a member of China Literary Calligraphers Association.
Reference price: RMB 4000 per square feet

《秋实》　48cm×48cm　　*Fruitful Autumn*

王彤富　*Wang Tongfu*

王彤富，男，1945年8月生于黑龙江省林甸县，高级书画师，现为中国书画家协会理事、中国书画家协会山东书画院常务院士、东营书法家协会会员。

润笔价格：4000/平尺

Wang Tongfu, male, born in Lindian County, Heilongjiang Province, in the August of 1945, is a senior calligrapher and painter. He is a council member of China Calligrapher and Painter Association (CCPA), painter with Shandong Calligraphy and Painting Gallery of CCPA, and member of Dongying Calligraphers Association.

Reference price: RMB 4000 per square feet

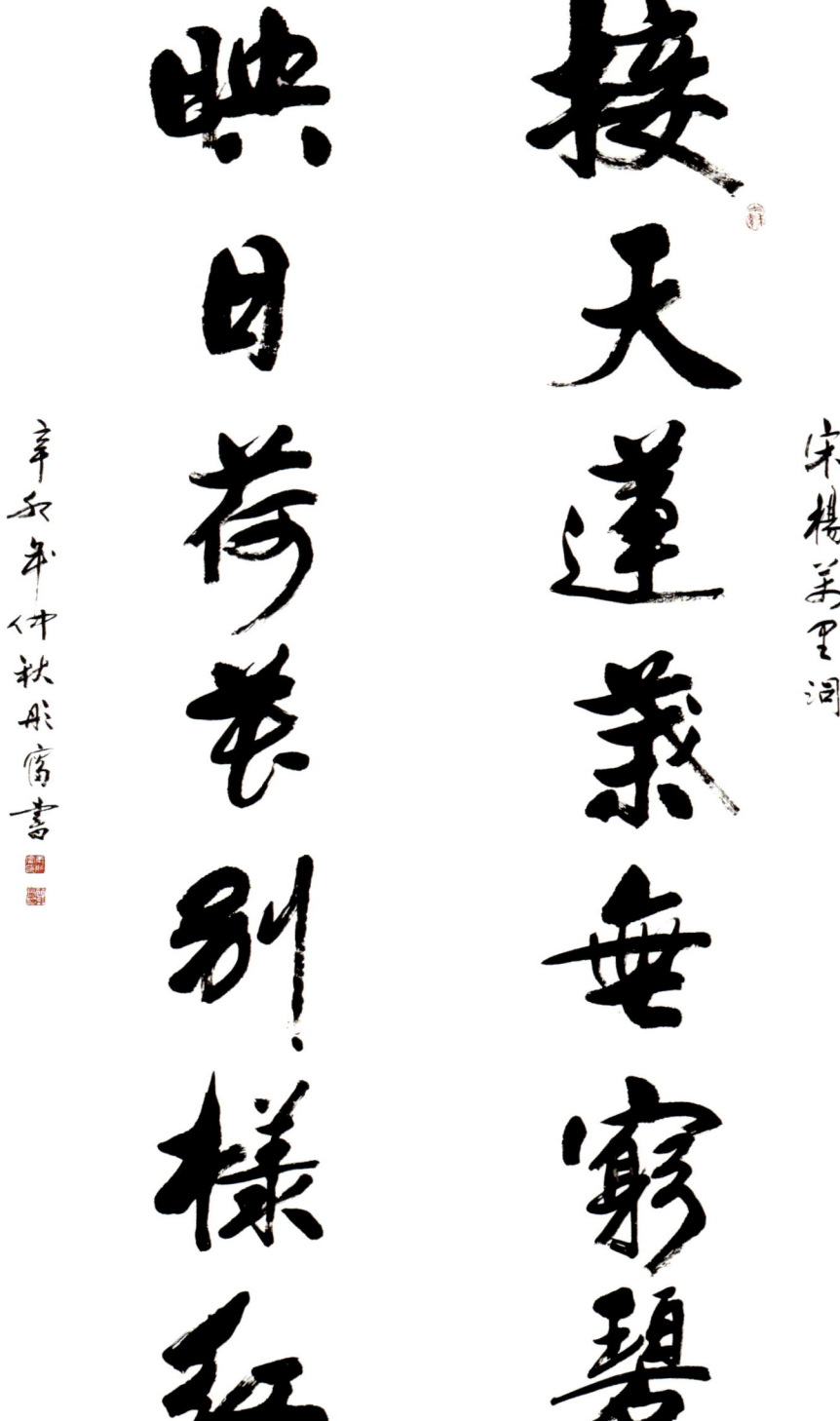

《宋杨万里诗词一首》　180cm×97cm　*A Poem by Yang Wanli*

刘占起 *Liu Zhanqi*

刘占起,男,号山野居士,1972年生于北京市房山区十渡镇,现为北京市房山区老年书画研究协会会员。

润笔价格:2000/平尺

Liu Zhanqi, male, born in Shidu of Fangshan District, Beijing, in 1972, and with Shanye Jushi (Hermit in Wild Mountain) as his literary name, is a member of Calligraphy and Painting Research Institute for Seniors of Fangshan District, Beijing.

Reference price: RMB 2000 per square feet

《山水一幅》　68cm×136cm　　*A Picture of Landscape*

苏世忠　*Su Shizhong*

苏世忠，男，55岁，内蒙古赤峰人。内蒙古自治区书法家协会会员，赤峰市书法家协会会员。工作单位为赤峰市委政研室副主任，市政协委员。

润笔价格：4000/平尺

Su Shizhong, male, 55-year-old, born in Chifeng, Inner Mongolia Autonomous Region, is a member of Inner Mongolia Calligraphers Association, and of Chifeng Calligraphers Association. He is Deputy Director of Policy Research Office of Chifeng Municipal Committee, and CPPCC member of Chifeng City.

Reference price: RMB 4000 per square feet

《长乐寿》　68cm×138cm　　*Enjoying Longevity*

《雄风》　138cm×68cm　　*Invincible Might*

崔洪良 *Cui Hongliang*

崔洪良，男，1946年生，辽宁鞍山人，中国国画家协会理事，国家友好画院特聘画师。
润笔价格：12000/平尺

Cui Hongliang, male, born in anshan, Liaoning Province, in 1946, is a council member of China Association of Traditional Chinese Painting, and especially employed painter with National Friendship Painting Art Gallery.
Reference price: 12000 per square feet

《浓春》　70cm×46cm　　*Intense Spring*

《清风》　70cm×46cm　　*Fresh Air*

孙乃恭　　*Sun Naigong*

孙乃恭，男，1932年1月生，河北涞源县山人。保定老年书画研究会会员，中国老年书画研究会会员，长城魂当代诗书画家协会会员、顾问。

润笔价格：4000/平尺

Sun Naigong, male, born in Laiyuan County, Hebei Province, in the January of 1932, is a member of Baoding Calligraphy and Painting Art Research Institute for Seniors, of China Calligraphy and Painting Art Research Institute for Seniors, and consultant and member of Changchenghun (Great Wall Soul) Contemporary Poets, Calligraphers and Painters Association.

Reference price: RMB 4000 per square feet

《曹孟德诗句》　　138cm×69cm　　*Lines by Cao Mengde*

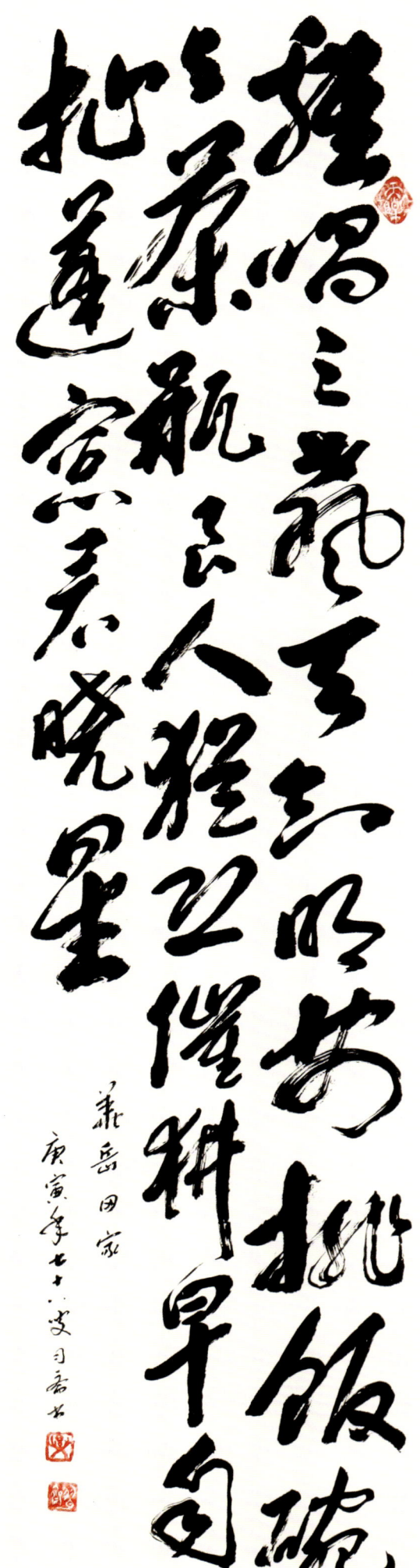

《行草一幅》　132cm×34cm　　A Scroll of Semi-cursive Script

林汉国 *Lin Hanguo*

林汉国，男，自号一粟轩主人，1954年生于广东澄海，现为中国国画家协会理事，广东省书法家协会会员。

润笔价格：8000/平尺

Lin Hanguo, male, born in Chenghai, Guangdong Province, in 1954, and with Host of Yisu Study as his literary name, is a council member of China Artists Association, and of Guangdong Calligraphers Association.
Reference price: RMB 8000 per square feet

《沐金风》　180cm×98cm　　*Breathing Golden Zephyr*

《石榴》 180cm×98cm Pomegranates

唐芳卿　Tang Fangqing

唐芳卿，男，1938年7月生于湖南。系（国际）中国书法家协会会员，世界书画协会理事，中国书画家协会理事、研究员，株洲市书法家协会会员，中原书画研究院高级研究员等。

润笔价格：5000/平尺

Tang Fangqing, male, born in Hunan Province in the July of 1938, is a member of China Calligraphers Association, council member of International Calligraphers and Painters Association, and researcher and council member of China Calligrapher and Painter Association. He is also a member of Zhuzhou Calligraphers Association, and senior researcher with Zhongyuan Calligraphy and Painting Art Academy, etc.

Reference price: RMB 5000 per square feet

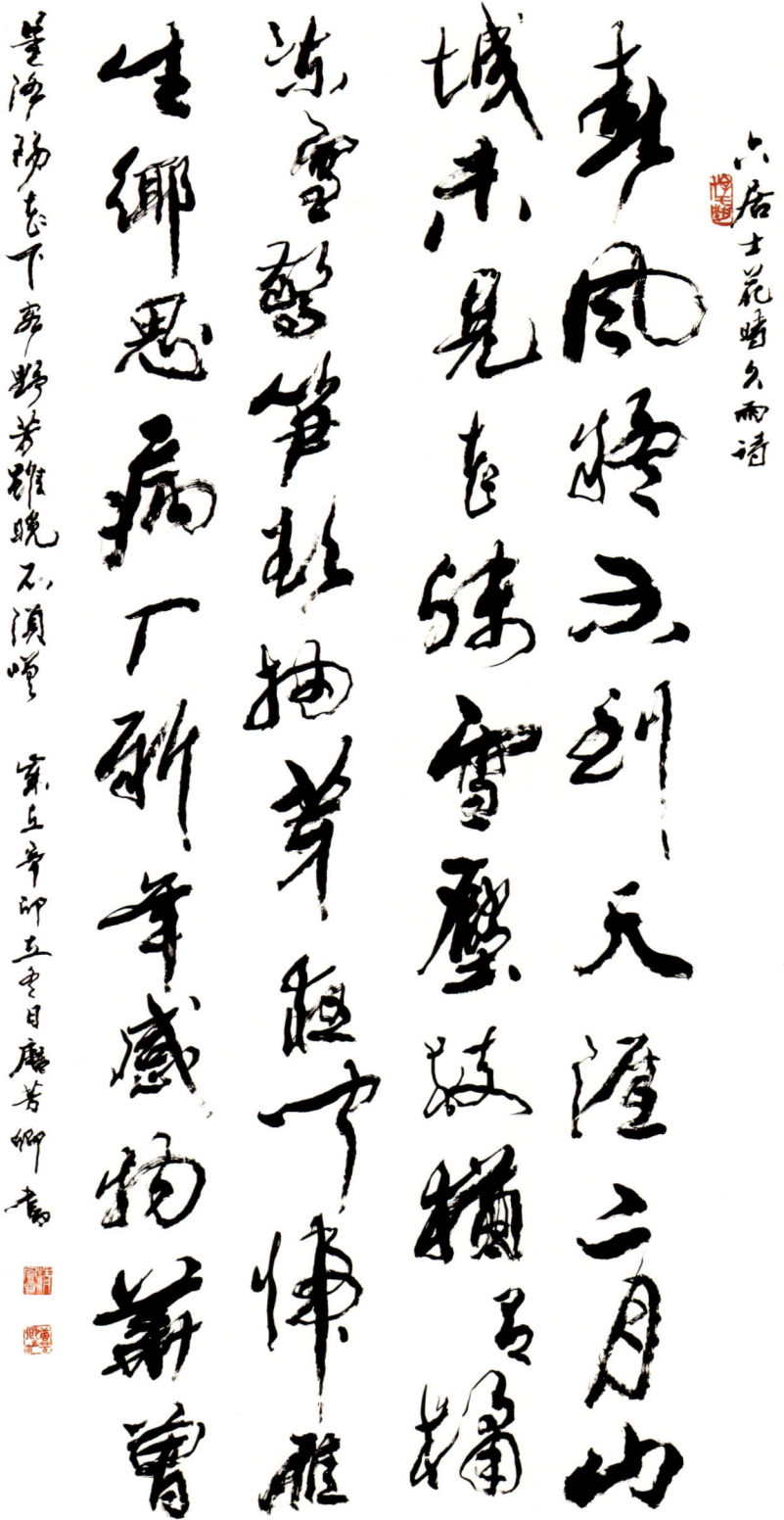

《六居士花时久雨》　　180cm×98cm　　Raining Much in Flowering Season

徐声才 *Xu Shengcai*

徐声才,男,1944年10月生,广西容县人。系中国书画促进会会员,中国乡土艺术协会会员。
润笔价格:14000/平尺

Xu Shengcai, male, born in Rong County, Guangxi Zhuang Autonomous Region, in the October of 1944, is a Chinese Calligraphy and Painting Art Promotion Society, and of Folk Arts Association of China.
Reference Price: RMB 14000 per square feet

《走在故乡的土地上》　180cm×97cm　*Walking in Hometown*

谭英群 *Tan Yingqun*

谭英群，男，1943年生，河北省栾城县人。现为石家庄市化肥厂学校教师，省少儿美术研究协会理事，上海民族画院院士，画师，理事，东方美术教育家协会理事。社会科学协会会员。

润笔价格：5000/平尺

Tan Yingqun, male, born in Luancheng, Hebei Province, in 1943, teaches at School of Shijiazhuang Fertilizer Plant. He is a council member of Hebei Children's Arts Research Institute, painter and council member with Shanghai National Calligraphy and Painting Academy, and council member of Oriental Art Educationists Association. Tan is also a member of National Social Science Association.

Reference price: RMB 5000 per square feet

《行草一幅》　　137cm×35cm　　*A Scroll of Semi-cursive Script*

空山不见人，但闻人语响。返景入深林，复照青苔上。独坐幽篁里，弹琴复长啸。深林人不知，明月来相照。中庭地白树栖鸦，冷露无声湿桂花。今夜月明人尽望，不知秋思落谁家。

庚寅冬之吉 苇庐 篆（印）

《诗三首》　137cm×35cm　Three Poems

赵贺庭 *Zhao Heting*

赵贺庭，男，1946年生，河北省卢龙县人，系中国书画家协会会员。

润笔价格：2000/平尺

Zhao Heting, male, born in Lulong County, Hebei Province, in 1946, is a member of China Calligrapher and Painter Association.

Reference price: RMB 2000 per square feet

《迎春图》　138cm×69cm　　*Welcoming Spring*

《喜看河虾又丰收》　138cm×69cm　　*Bumper Harvest of Shrimps*

童兆炉　Tong Zhaolu

童兆炉，男，字昌宾，1937年生，江西玉山人。现为中国书画艺术委员会委员，中国国画家协会理事，中国书画艺术创作中心高级书画师，怀玉山书画院院长。

润笔价格：书法3000/平尺　国画4000/平尺

Tong Zhaolu, male, born in Yushan, Jiangxi Province, in 1937, and with Changbin as his courtesy name, is a member of China Art Committee of Calligraphy and Painting, and council member of China Association of Traditional Chinese Painting. He is also a senior painter with Creative Center of Chinese Calligraphy and Painting, and President of Mount Huaiyu Calligraphy and Painting Gallery.

Reference price: Calligraphy RMB 3000 per square feet　Traditional Chinese painting RMB 4000 per square feet

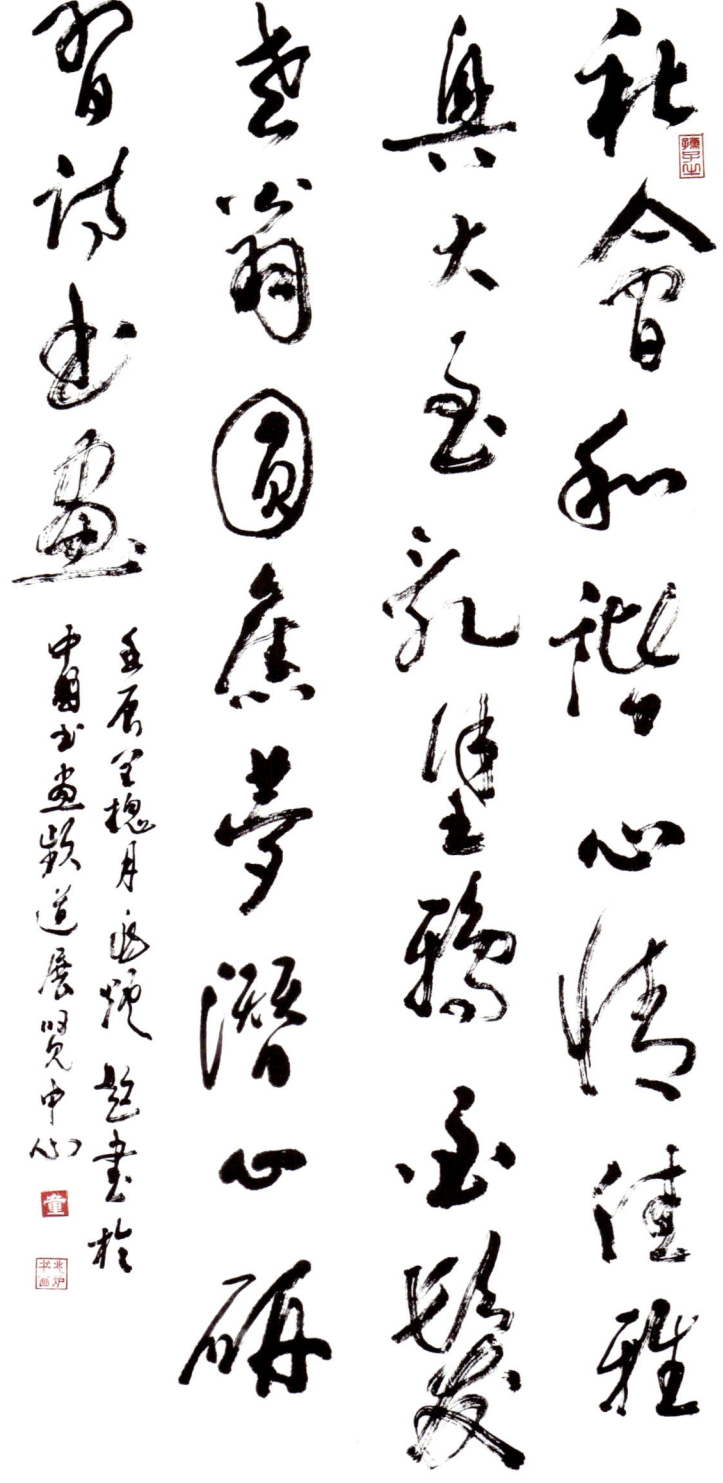

《和谐社会》　138cm×69cm　Harmonious Society

《朝阳大吉》　138cm×68cm　　Propitious Rising Sun

王宽中　*Wang Kuanzhong*

王宽中，男，字砚熙。1954年5月生，山东淄博临淄人。现为中国书画艺术院院士，中国书画艺术研究院高级研究员，中国书画院副秘书长。

润笔价格：3000/平尺

Wang Kuanzhong, male, born in Zibo, Shandong Province, in the May of 1954, is a painter with Chinese Painting and Calligraphy Art Academy, senior researcher with Chinese Calligraphy and Painting Research Institute, and Deputy Secretary General of China Painting and Calligraphy Academy.

Reference price: RMB 3000 per square feet

《杜甫诗一首》　138cm×68cm　　*A Poem by Du Fu*

陈鸿娟　*Chen Hongjuan*

陈鸿娟，女，艺名寒梅。淮安市美协会员，中国书画家协会会员，美阿艺术中心高级创作员。

润笔价格：2000/平尺

Chen Hongjuan, female, with Hanmei (Plum in Winter) as her literary name, is a member of Huai'an Artists Association, of China Calligrapher and Painter Association, and senior artist with Mei'e Art Center.

Reference price: RMB 2000 per square feet

《莲年有余》　138cm×69cm　　*Lotus that Embodies the Richness in Successive Years*

王程 *Wang Cheng*

王程，男，1968年生，四川都江堰人，现为中国硬笔书法协会会员，四川硬笔书法协会会员，中国书画家联谊会会员，阿坝州书协理事，

润笔价格：4000/平尺

Wang Cheng, male, born in Dujiangyan, Sichuan Province, in 1968, is a member of China Association of Pen Calligraphers, and of Sichuan Association of Pen Calligraphers. He is also a member of Chinese Calligrapher and Painter Federation, and council member of Aba Prefecture.

Reference price: RMB 4000 per square feet

《苏东坡诗一首》　　136cm×34cm　　*A Poem by Su Dongpo*

黄梅时节家家雨,青草池塘处处蛙。有约不来过夜半,闲敲棋子落灯花。

宋赵师秀诗一首 辛卯初冬王程书

《宋 赵师秀 诗一首》 136cm×34cm　*A Poem by Zhao Shixiu*

魏仕龙 *Wei Shilong*

魏仕龙，男，1951年生，四川成都人，现为成都市美协会员，四川张大千、徐悲鸿研究院研究员，四川西岭书画院创作研究员。

润笔价格：8000/平尺

Wei Shilong, male, born in Chengdu, Sichuan Province, in 1951, is a member of Chengdu Artists Association, researcher with Sichuan Zhang Daqian Research Institute and with Xu Beihong Research Institute as well. He is also a creative researcher of Xiling Calligraphy and Painting Gallery of Sichuan.

Reference price: RMB 8000 per square feet

《三峡夔门》　69cm×136cm　*Kuimen of the Three Gorges*

《剑山行旅》　69cm×136cm　*Jianshan Progress*

王德凯 *Wang Dekai*

王德凯，男，1965年生，中国翰林书画艺术院副院士，中国书画名家网艺委副主席，江苏唐伯虎书法院副院长。

润笔价格：2000/平尺

Wang Dekai, male, born in 1965, is an associate painter with Hanlin Calligraphy and Painting Art Academy of China, Vice President of Art Committee of China Calligraphy and Painting Celebrities Net, and of Jiangsu Tang Bohu Calligraphy Institute.
Reference price: RMB 2000 per square feet

《藏头诗》　129cm×66cm　　*An Acrostic Poem*

陈昭华 *Chen Zhaohua*

陈昭华，男，1962年生，江苏省扬州人。曾先后入天津市、上海市美协会员，中国书画名家协会会员，中国硬笔书法家协会会员，中国画虎艺术研究院特聘高级画师，上海东方画院副院长。

润笔价格：8000/平尺

Chen Zhaohua, male, born in Yangzhou, Jiangsu Province, in 1962, is a member of Tianjin Artists Association, of Shanghai Artists Association, and of Chinese Celebrated Calligrapher and Painter Association. He is also a member of China Association of Pen Calligraphers, especially employed senior painter with Chinese Tiger Painting Art Institute, and Vice President of Shanghai Oriental Painting Art Gallery.

Reference Price: RMB 8000 per square feet

《高瞻远瞩》　　128cm×69cm　　*Lofty Vision*

王高宣　*Wang Gaoxuan*

王高宣，男，笔名文如，1927年8月生。中国国学研究会研究员，中国书画艺术促进会理事，中国当代艺术协会终身名誉主席。

润笔价格：3000/平尺

Wang Gaoxuan, male, born in the August of 1927, and with Wenru as his pseudonym, is a researcher with China Guoxue Seminar, council member of China Calligraphy and Painting Art Promotion Society, and lifelong Horornary President of China Contemporary Artists Association.

Reference price: RMB 3000 per square feet

《沁园春·雪》　　100cm×52cm　　*Qinyuanchun Snow*

栾谨魁 *Luan Jinkui*

栾谨魁,男,1939年生,现为景德镇市美术家协会会员,景德镇市老年书画协会理事,中国老年书画研究会会员,中国书画家协会会员。

润笔价格:2000/平尺

Luan Jinkui, male, born in 1939, is a member of Jingdezhen Artists Association and council member of Jingdezhen Calligraphy and Painting Association for Seniors. He is also a member of China Calligraphy and Painting Research Institute for Seniors, and of China Calligraphers and Painters Association.

Reference price: RMB 2000 per square feet

《春游图》　138cm×69cm　*Spring Tour*

王更新 *Wang Gengxin*

王更新，男，1943年生，河北辛集人。现为辛集市书协会员，中国书画创作院院士。

润笔价格：3000/平尺

Wang Gengxin, male, born in Xinji, Hebei Province, in 1943, is a member of Xinji Calligraphers Association, and painter with China Calligraphy and Painting Creation Institute.

Reference price: RMB 3000 per square feet

《毛泽东词一首》　180cm×48cm　　*A Poem by Mao Zedong*

《屋莲湖水琴书润》　131cm×51cm　*Reading and Playing the Qin in a Room near a Lake*

梁骜 *Liang Ao*

梁骜，男，号寒石，1967年生于黑龙江省哈尔滨市，现任教于哈尔滨艺术与设计学院。黑龙江省美协会员，陕西美术馆特聘美术师，中国书画家协会理事，一级美术师。

润笔价格：6000/平尺

Liang Ao, male, born in Harbin, Heilongjiang Province, in 1967, and with Hanshi as his literary name, is a Class A artist, member of Heilongjiang Artists Association, and especially employed painter with Shaanxi Art Museum. He is also a council member of China Calligrapher and Painter Association. He now teaches at Art and Design College of Harbin University.

Reference price: RMB 6000 per square feet

《高瞻远瞩图》　136cm×69cm　*Lofty Vision*

《在山之阿》　136cm×69cm　　In the Mountains

王金光　*Wang Jinguang*

王金光，男，1946年生福建福州人，现任国家一级书画师，作品多次在国内外获奖。
润笔价格：3000/平尺

Wang Jinguang, male, born in Fozhou, Fujian Province, in 1964, is a National Class A calligrapher and painter, whose works won many awards in and out of China.
Reference price: RMB 3000 per square feet

《厚德载物》　138cm×72cm　　*Hold World with Virtue*

金秋时节霾江遊人問奇
达壶盲滿眼清水象可
数巧造宜絕不蛀蟲丹霞
水雲天芳洲筝鳥國

《七言诗一首》 133cm×69cm　　*A Poem*

王根顺 *Wang Genshun*

王根顺（笔名王大宇），男，1948年生，河南开封人，汉族，现任世界书画家协会加拿大总会理事，美国美洲亚洲艺术学会荣誉博学会士，中国书画家艺术交流协会常务理事，河南省美术家协会会员。

润笔价格：10000/平尺

Wang Genshun, also known as Wang Dayu, male, born in Kaifeng, Henan Province, in 1948, is a council member of Worldwide Calligrapher and Artist Association of Canada, and honorary elite member of America Asian Art Society. He is also a standing council member of Art Exchange Association for Chinese Calligraphers and Painters, and member of Henan Artists Association.

Reference price: RMB 10000 per square feet

《长传民族魂魄》　　138cm×69cm　　*National Soul*

《寿比南山》　138cm×69cm　　Longevity

王珂　　*Wang Ke*

王珂，男，75岁，北京人，汉族。中国书画界联合会会员，中国书法研究院研究员，北京通州区书法家协会理事，长城书画院名誉主席。

润笔价格：3000/平尺

Wang Ke, male, 75-year-old, born in Beijing, is a member of Federation of Chinese Calligraphy and Painting Circles, researcher with China Calligraphy Research Society, council member of Tongzhou Calligraphers Association, and Honorary President of Changcheng (Great Wall) Calligraphy and Painting Gallery.

Reference price: RMB 3000 per square feet

苏东坡　　《念奴娇赤壁怀古》　　132cm×51cm　　*Meditations on the Red Cliff by Su Dongpo*

《沁园春雪》　254cm×33cm　　*Qingyuanchun Snow*

李增雪　*Li Zengxue*

李增雪，男，1949年生，河北省藁城人。系河北省美术家协会会员，河北省中国画研究会会员，三级美术师。

润笔价格：8000/平尺

Li Zengxue, male, born in Gaocheng, Hebei Province, in 1949, is a Class C artist, member of Hebei Artists Association, and of Hebei Chinese Painting Art Research Institute.
Reference price: RMB 8000 per square feet

《骏马图》　69cm×136cm　　*Steeds*

《盛世荷花别样红》　69cm×136cm　　*Blossoming Lotus*

王长金　Wang Changjin

王长金，男，1960年1月生，河南省新乡市人。系河南省书法家协会会员、新乡市凤泉区书法家协会副主席。

润笔价格：7000/平尺

Wang Changjin, male, born in Xinxiang, Henan Province, in the January of 1960, is a member of Henan Calligraphers Association, and Vice President of Fengquan District Calligraphers Association of Xinxiang.

Reference price: RMB 7000 per square feet

《小楷一幅》　　180mm×97mm　　*A Scroll of Regular Script*

李家洪　*Li Jiahong*

李家洪，男，1940年生，江苏省吴江人。现为江苏省吴江市美术家协会会员，中国国际美术家协会会员，江苏南京市金陵书画院一级画师。

润笔价格：2000/平尺

Li Jiahong, male, born in Wujiang, Jiangsu Province, in 1940, is a member of Wujiang Artists Association, of International Artists Association of China, and Class A painter with Jinling Calligraphy and Painting Gallery of Nanjing, Jiangsu.
Reference price: RMB 2000 per square feet

《万重奇峰春晖图》　68cm×136cm　*Multiple Peaks in Bright Spring*

王桢杰　*Wang Zhenjie*

王桢杰，男，1933年生，籍贯河南温县马庄。中国老年书画研究会会员、河南印社社员、北京中东雅菲文化艺术交流中心名誉副主席等。

润笔价格：4000/平尺

Wang Zhenjie, male, born in Mazhuang of Nanwen County, Henan Province, in 1933, is a member of China Calligraphy and Painting Art Research Institute for Seniors, of Henan Society of Seal Arts, and Honorary President of Beijing Mid-East Yafei Exchanges Center of Chinese Culture and Art.

Reference price: RMB 4000 per square feet

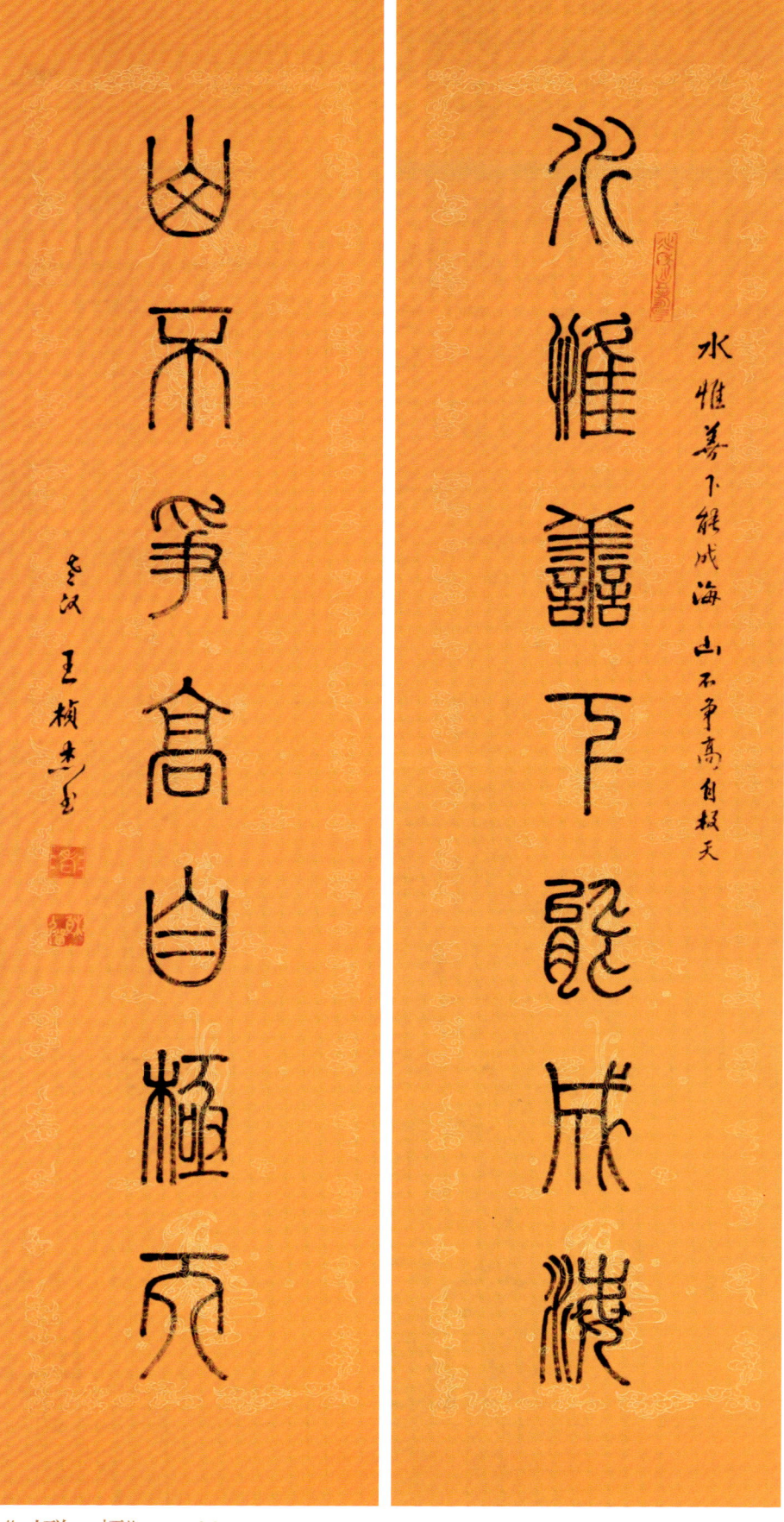

《对联一幅》　　130cm×30cm×2　　*A Couplet*

马福友 *Ma Fuyou*

马福友，男，1953年生，现为中国艺术家协会理事，中国艺术家协会书画研究会秘书长，中国书画家联谊会会员，中国公共关系协会艺术委员会会员。

润笔价格：12000/平尺

Ma Fuyou, male, born in 1953, is a council member of China Artists Association, and Secretary General of Calligraphy and Painting Research Institute. He is also a member of Chinese Calligrapher and Painter Federation, and of Arts Committee of China Public Relations Association.

Reference price: RMB 12000 per square feet

《惠风和畅》　　137cm×68cm　　*Free Breeze*

卫效卿　　*Wei Xiaoqing*

卫效卿，男，山西运城市盐湖区人，1939年12月生。现为中国书协会员，中国书画研究院院士，盐湖区书画家协会会员。

润笔价格：3000/平尺

Wei Xiaoqing, male, born in Yanhu District of Yuncheng, Shanxi Province, in December of 1939, is a member of China Calligraphers Association, painter with China Calligraphy and Painting Research Institute, and member of Yanhu Calligraphers and Painters Association.

Reference price: RMB 3000 per square feet

《松风竹韵》　137cm×35cm　*Charm of Pines and Bamboos*

《爱我中华》　137cm×35cm　　*Love My China*

李景春 *Li Jingchun*

李景春，男，1948年4月生于黑龙江省望奎县，现为绥化市美协会员，绥化市书法家协会会员，中国书画摄影家协会理事。

润笔价格：2000/平尺

Li Jingchun, male, born in Wangkui County, Heilongjiang Province, in the April of 1948, is a member of Suihua Artists Association, of Suihua Calligraphers Association, and council member of Chinese Calligraphers & Painters & Photographers Association.

Reference price: RMB 2000 per square feet

《轻舟短钓平湖好》　　68cm×68cm　　*Fishing in Pinghu*

《花鸟图》 76cm×45cm　　*Flowers and Birds*

文永图　*Wen Yongtu*

文永图，男，湖北省监利县人，中国翰林书画院副院长，中国国家书画院副院长。

润笔价格：3000/平尺

Wen Yongtu, male, born in Jianli County, Hubei Province, is Vice President of Hanlin Calligraphy and Painting Art Academy of China, and of China National Academy of Calligraphy and Painting.

Reference price: RMB 3000 per square feet

《杜甫诗一首》　　138cm×69cm　　*A Poem by Du Fu*

录程颢诗偶句

富贵不淫贫贱乐
男儿到此是豪雄

辛卯冬荣冬文 ... 书

《程颢偶成摘句》　138cm×69cm　*A Poem by Cheng Hao*

吴启祥 *Wu Qixiang*

吴启祥，男，艺名鼓峰，1945年生于黑龙江海伦市，祖籍河北武安，现为中国美协河北分会会员，海内外书画艺术团体会员，中华当代书画研究会名誉教授，中国振鸣书画院名誉院长。

润笔价格：8000/平尺

Wu Qixiang, male, with Gufeng as his literary name, was born in Hailun, Heilongjiang province, in 1945, though his family originated in Wu'an of Hebei Province. He is a member of Hebei Artists Association, and of Worldwide Arts Society for Calligraphy and Painting. Wu is also a honorary professor with Institute for Contemporary Chinese Calligraphy and Painting, and honorary President of Zhenming Calligraphy and Painting Gallery of China.

Reference price: RMB 8000 per square feet

《雍荣华贵翰墨飘香》　　65cm×130cm　　*Elegant Flavor of Painting*

《富贵长寿》　65cm×130cm　　Loftiness and Longevity

沈忠信 *Shen Zhongxin*

沈忠信，男，号思米山翁，1950年生，河北省迁安市人，现为中国书画艺术促进会常务理事，中国书画研究会、翰墨书画院理事、顾问、高级书画师。

润笔价格：4000/平尺

Shen Zhongxin, male, born in Qian'an, Hebei Province, in 1950, and with Simi Shanwen as his literary name, is a standing committee member of China Council of Calligraphy and Painting Art Promotion, consultant, council member and senior calligrapher and painter of China Calligraphy and Painting Research Institute, and of Hanmo Calligraphy and Painting Gallery.

Reference price: RMB 4000 per square feet

《录毛泽东词一首》　68cm×45cm

邓枫 *Deng Feng*

邓枫，男，1960年生于四川洪雅，现为香港东方艺术中心特聘画家、中国美协会员、四川眉山美协副主席、四川眉山画院院长。

润笔价格：18000/平尺

Deng Feng, male, born in Hongya, Sichuan Province, in 1960, is an especially employed painter with Hong Kong Oriental Art Center, member of China Artists Association, and Vice President of Meishan Artists Association. He is also President of Mount Mei Painting Art Gallery.

Reference price: RMB 18000 per square feet

《无处山光不到》　73cm×166cm　　*A Landscape of Mountains*

阎继臣　*Yan Jichen*

阎继臣，男，1935年12月生，安徽萧县人，重庆市老年书画协会会员、硬书会员。
润笔价格：3000/平尺

Yan Jichen, male, born in Xiao County, Anhui Province, in the December of 1935, is a member of Chongqing Calligraphy and Painting Art Research Institute for Seniors, and of Association of Pen Calligraphers.
Reference price: RMB 3000 per square feet

《印章》　100cm×53cm　　*A Seal*

篆宗商周秦漢 楷法魏晉隋唐

壬辰年仲春村山埠阎迷庄書

《篆宗商周秦汉　楷法魏晋隋唐》　136cm×96cm　A Scroll

吴福田 *Wu Futian*

吴福田，男，号墨石，江苏徐州人，1952年生。现为中国国画家协会会员，徐州市美术家协会会员，贾汪区美术家协会秘书长。

润笔价格：8000/平尺

Wu Futian, male, born in Xuzhou, Jiangsu Province, in 1952, and with Moshi as his literary name, is a member of China Association of Traditional Chinese Painting, of Xuzhou Artists Association, and Secretary of Jiawang District Artists Association.
Reference price: RMB 8000 per square feet

《荷塘深处是吾家》　180cm×97cm　　*Home Deep in the Lotus Pond*

《松鹤延年》　180cm×97cm　*Pines and Cranes as Embodiments of Longevity*

尹维忠　*Yin Weizhong*

尹维忠，男，1945年生，甘肃天水人，其作品多次在国内荣获奖项。

润笔价格：4000/平尺

Yin Weizhong, male, was born in Tianshui, Gansu Province, in 1945, and his works won many awards in China.

Reference price: RMB 4000 per square feet

北国风光，千里冰封，万里雪飘。望长城内外，惟余莽莽；大河上下，顿失滔滔。山舞银蛇，原驰蜡象，欲与天公试比高。须晴日，看红装素裹，分外妖娆。江山如此多娇，引无数英雄竞折腰。惜秦皇汉武，略输文采；唐宗宋祖，稍逊风骚。一代天骄，成吉思汗，只识弯弓射大雕。俱往矣，数风流人物，还看今朝。

敬录毛泽东词沁园春雪 壬辰夏 维忠

《沁园春 雪》　　138cm×69cm　　*Qinyuanchun Snow*

半壁東南三楚雄，劉郎死去霸圖空，尚餘遺業艱難誰與斯人慷慨同，塞上秋風悲戰馬，神州落日泣哀鴻，幾時痛飲黃龍酒，橫攬江流一奠公。

孫中山詩抗劉道一 辛卯年荷月 雅興書

《孫中山詩一首》　137cm×35cm　Qinyuanchun Snow

张良田 *Zhang Liangtian*

张良田,男,字寒圣,山西省美术家协会会员、中国书画家协会理事、黄河文化艺术院研究员、中国书画家联谊会艺术交流部理事。

润笔价格:6000/平尺

Zhang Liangtian, male, with Hansheng (Humble Sage) as his courtesy name, is a member of Shanxi Artists Association, and council member of China Calligrapher and Painter Association. He is also a researcher with Yellow River Culture and Art Institute, and council member of Department of Arts Exchange of Chinese Calligrapher and Painter Federation.

Reference price: RMB 6000 per square feet

《金秋》 175cm×95cm *Golden Autumn*

《观瀑图》　178cm×77cm　　Waterfall

袁胜聪 *Yuan Shengcong*

袁胜聪，男，1954年12月生，广西大新县人。现为大新县文化馆美术创作员、广西美术家协会会员、中国书画家协会会员、中国书画研究院研究员、北京清大华文书画院院士。

润笔价格：2000/平尺

Yuan Shengcong, male, born in Daxin County, Guangxi Zhuang Autonomous Region, in the December of 1954, is a painter with Daxin Culture Center, member of Guangxi Artists Association, and of China Calligrapher and Painter Association. He is also a researcher with China Calligraphy and Painting Research Institute, and painter with Beijing Qingda Huawen Calligraphy and Painting Gallery.

Reference price: RMB 2000 per square feet

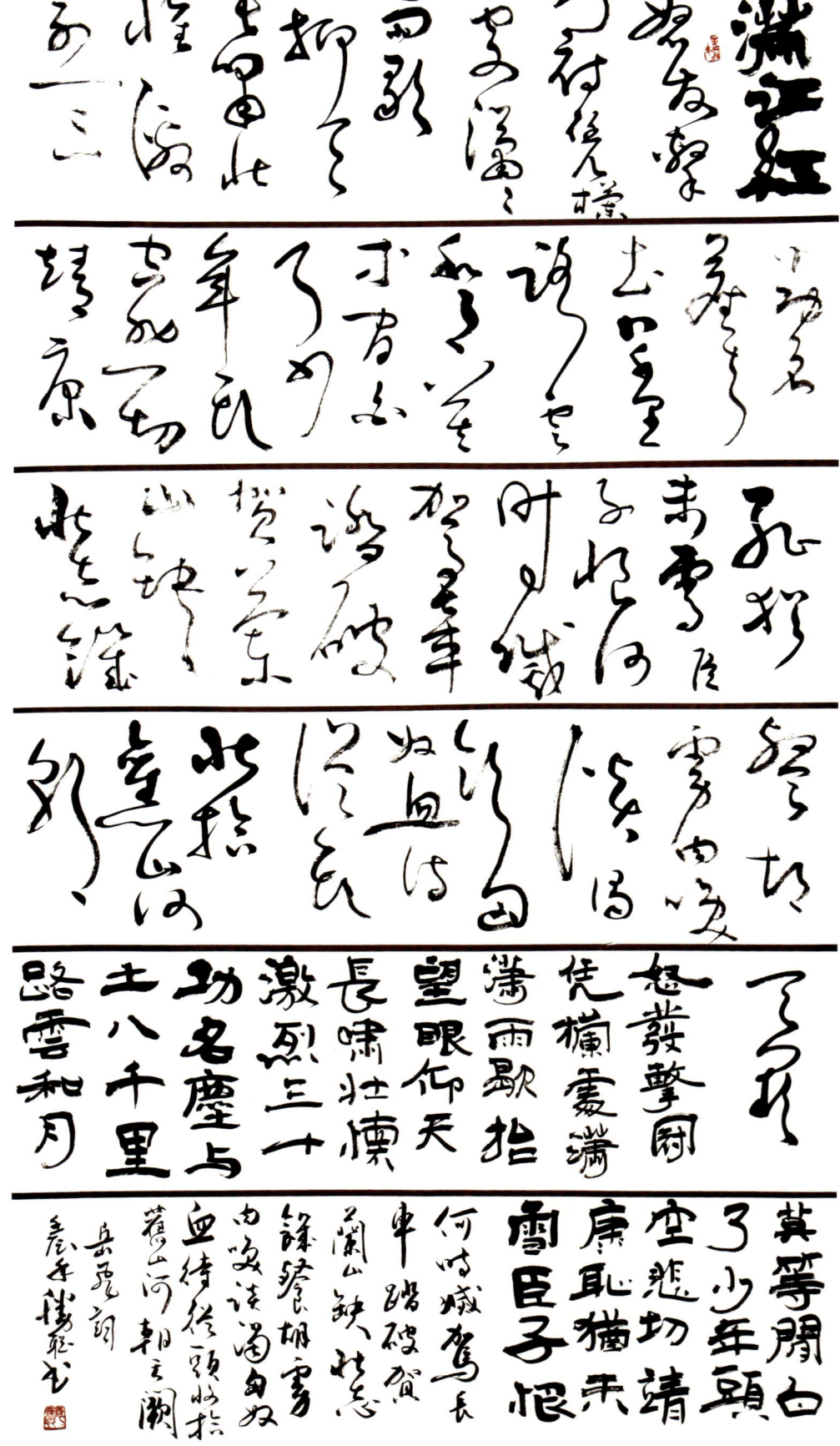

《岳飞词》　　170cm×93cm

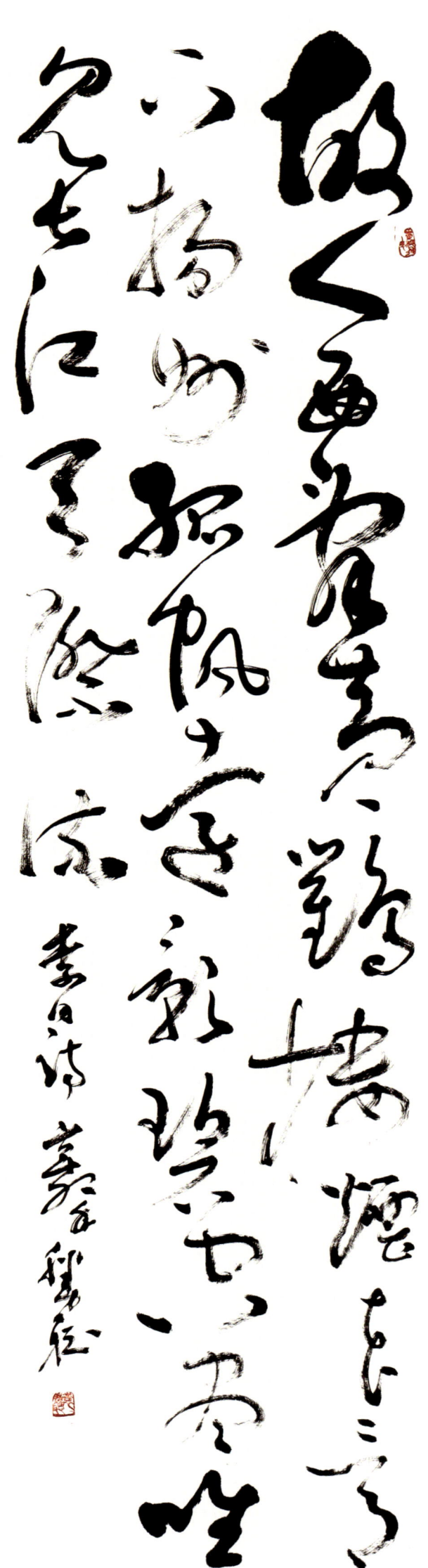

《李白诗一首》 180cm×48cm

陈叔铭　*Chen Shuming*

陈叔铭，男，号马陵山人，又署万寿斋主。1943年出生，山东郯城人。现为山东省美术家协会会员、中国民间文艺家协会会员、中国国画家家协会理事，一级美术师。

润笔价格：4000/平尺

Chen Shuming, male, in 1943, and also with Maling Shanren and Host of Wanshou Study as his literary name, born in Tancheng, Shandong Province, is a Class A artist, and member of Shandong Artists Association. He is also a member of Chinese Folk Artists Association, and council member of China Association of Traditional Chinese Painting.

Reference price: RMB 4000 per square feet

《双寿图》　66cm×66cm　　*Longevity*

《长寿图》　65cm×129cm　　*Longevity*

张伯周　*Zhang Bozhou*

张伯周，男，1967年出生湖南。中国书画创作中心高级理事，画圣吴道子艺术馆顾问。
润笔价格：4000/平尺

Zhang Bozhou, male, born in Hunan Province in 1967, is a senior council member of Creative Center of Chinese Calligraphy and Painting, and art consultant of Wu Dozi (Sage of Painting) Art Museum.
Reference price: RMB 4000 per square feet

王维　《九月九忆山东兄弟》　　100cm×35cm
Thinking of Shandong Brothers on September 9th (Chongyang Festival) by Wang Wei

渭城朝雨浥轻尘，客舍青青柳色新。劝君更进一杯酒，西出阳关无故人。

王维诗一首

《王维诗一首》　95cm×35cm　　*A Poem by Wang Wei*

丁连兴 Ding Lianxing

丁连兴，男，笔名诚丁，号芙渠翁，室署：鱼乐斋。1940年生，山东潍坊人，现为中国书画艺术委员会会员，东方美术馆艺术家协会会员，中国体育高雅艺术活动中心书画创作员，齐鲁书画研究院画家，山东潍坊市老年书画研究会会员。

润笔价格：4000/平尺

Ding Lianxing, male, with Chengding as his pseudonym, with Fuqu Weng (Old Man of Fuqu) as his literary name, and Yule Study as the name of his study, was born in Weifang, Shandong Province, in 1940. He is a member of Arts Committee of China Calligraphy and Painting Research Institute, and of Artists Association of Eastern Gallery. Ding is also a calligrapher and painter with Arts Center of Chinese Sports, painter with Qilu Calligraphy and Painting Research Institute, and member of Weifang Calligraphy and Painting Research Institute for Seniors.

Reference price: RMB 4000 per square feet

《鸟语花香鱼乐春光》　　136cm×69cm　　*Vigorous Spring*

《颂金秋》　136cm×69cm　*Ode to the Autumn*

张坤　*Zhang Kun*

张坤，男，字培龙，笔名家居齐鲁，1960年生，山东省济宁市人，现就职于山东省齐河县人民法院。现为中国书法家协会会员，中国书画名家协会会员，中国书画研究院理事，山东省法官协会书画摄影分会会员。

润笔价格：2000/平尺

Zhang Kun, male, born in Jining, Shandong Province, in 1960, and with Peilong as his courtesy name and Jiaju Qilu (Housing in Qilu) as his pseudonym, works at People's Court of Qihe County, Shandong. He is a member of China Calligraphers Association, and of Chinese Celebrated Calligrapher and Painter Association. Zhang is also a member of China Calligraphy and Painting Research Institute, and of Calligrapher, Painter and Photographer Society of Shandong Association of Judges.

Reference price: RMB 2000 per square feet

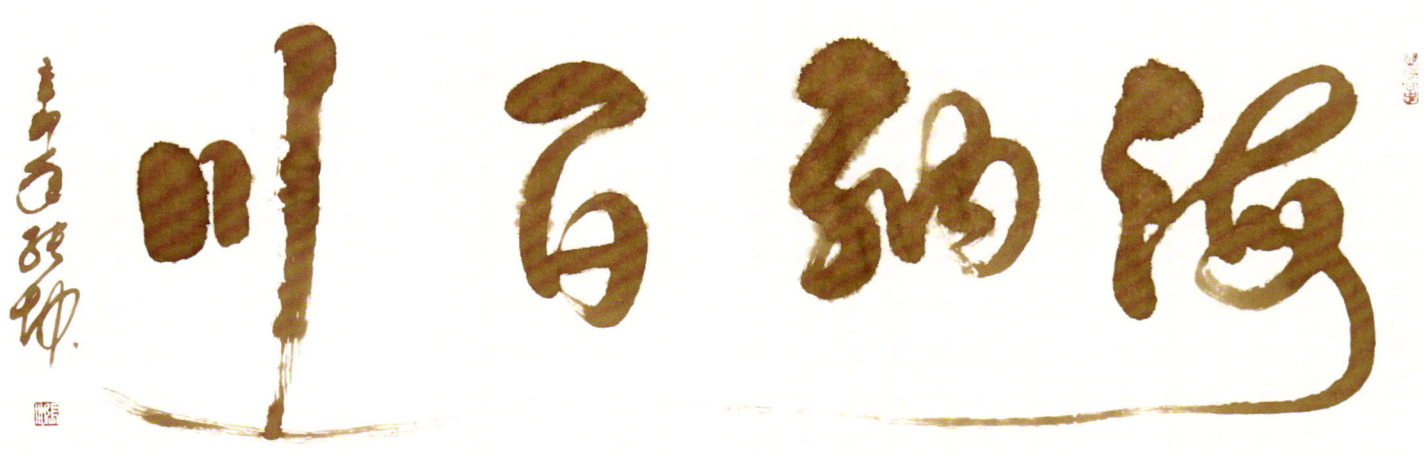

《海纳百川》　133cm×68cm　*All Rivers Run into Sea*

潘国祥 *Pan Guoxiang*

潘国祥,男,1943年生,江苏盐城人,国家一级美术师。现为中国书画研究院理事、中国国家博物馆画廊艺委会委员客座教授、艺术顾问,中国中外名人文化研究会理事、中国书画研究会名誉会长,中国书画艺委会委员。

润笔价格:4000/平尺

Pan Guoxiang, male, born in Yancheng, Jiangsu Province, in 1943, is a National Class A artist, council member of China Calligraphy and Painting Research Institute, and visiting professor and art consultant of Gallery Arts Committee of National Museum of China. He is also a council member of Culture Research Institute for Chinese and Foreign Celebrities, Honorary President and member of Arts Committee of China Calligraphy and Painting Research Institute.

Reference price: RMB 4000 per square feet

《高山流水任瑶弦》　95cm×63cm　*Waterfall*

张连德 *Zhang Liande*

张连德,男,1937年生,北京人。现为中国书画协会理事,世界书法家协会会员,中国硬笔书法家协会会员,九州枫林国际书画艺术院理事。

润笔价格:2000/平尺

Zhang Liande, male, born in Beijing in 1937, is a council member of China Calligrapher and Painter Association, and of International Calligraphies Association. He is also a member of Association of Pen Calligraphers, and council member of Beijing Jiuzhou Fenglin Calligraphy and Painting Gallery.

Reference price: RMB 2000 per square feet

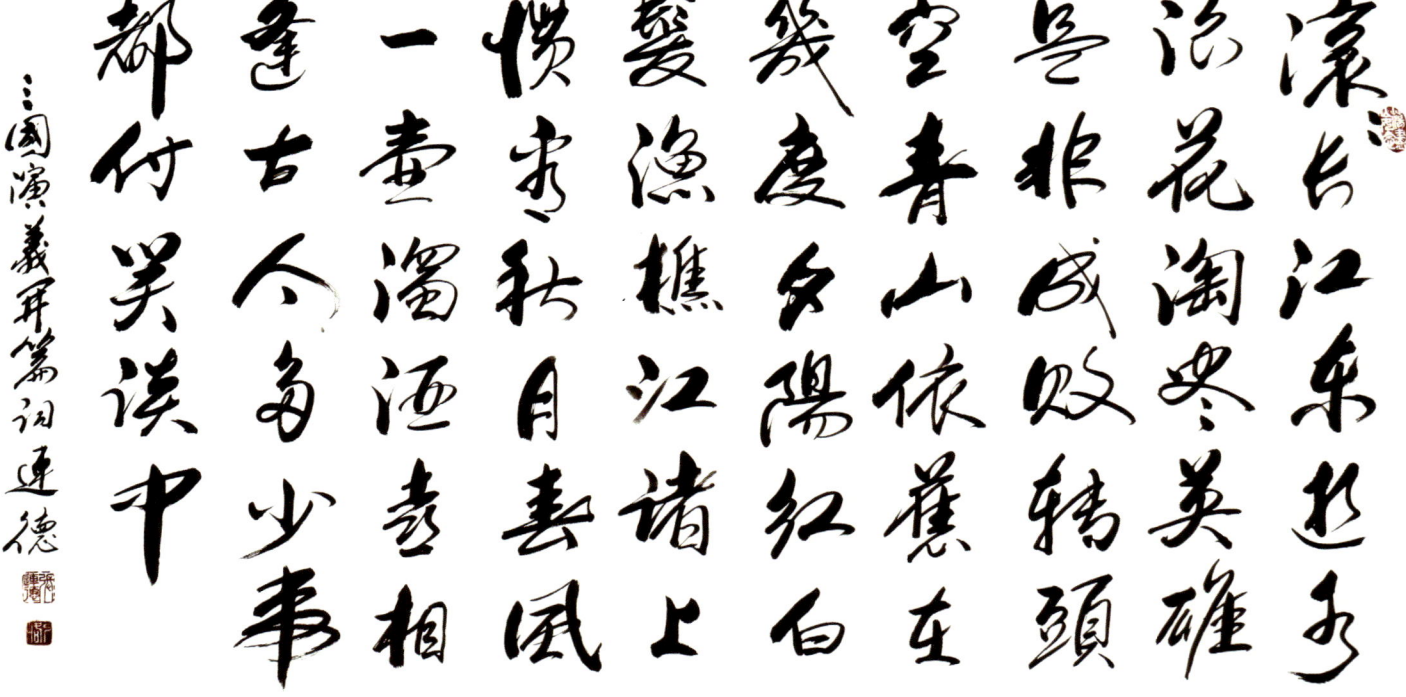

《三国演义开篇词》　138cm×68cm　*The Opening Poem in The Romance of Three Kingdoms*

余展武 *Yu Zhanwu*

余展武，男，1945年生，饶平县人，现为中国书画家协会理事、中国美术家协会敦煌创作中心创作委员，广东省书画家协会、潮州市书画家协会会员。

润笔价格：6000/平尺

Yu Zhanwu, male, born in Raoping County in 1945, is a council member of China Calligrapher and Painter Association, and member of Dunhuang Creative Center of China Calligraphers Association. He is also a member of Guangdong Calligrapher and Painter Association, and member of Chaozhou Calligrapher and Painter Association.

Reference price: 6000 per square feet

《土楼风光》　　178cm×98cm　　*Tulou Scenery*

张明康 *Zhang Mingkang*

张明康,男,笔名张更,现为北京市老年书画研究会会员、北京市楹联学会会员、中国书画家协会会员、北京美术家协会会员。

润笔价格:3000/平尺

Zhang Mingkang, male, with Zhang Geng as his pseudonym, is a member of China Calligraphy and Painting Art Research Institute for Seniors, and of Yinglian Society of China. He is also a member of China Calligrapher and Painter Association, and of Beijing Artists Association.

Reference price: RMB 3000 per square feet

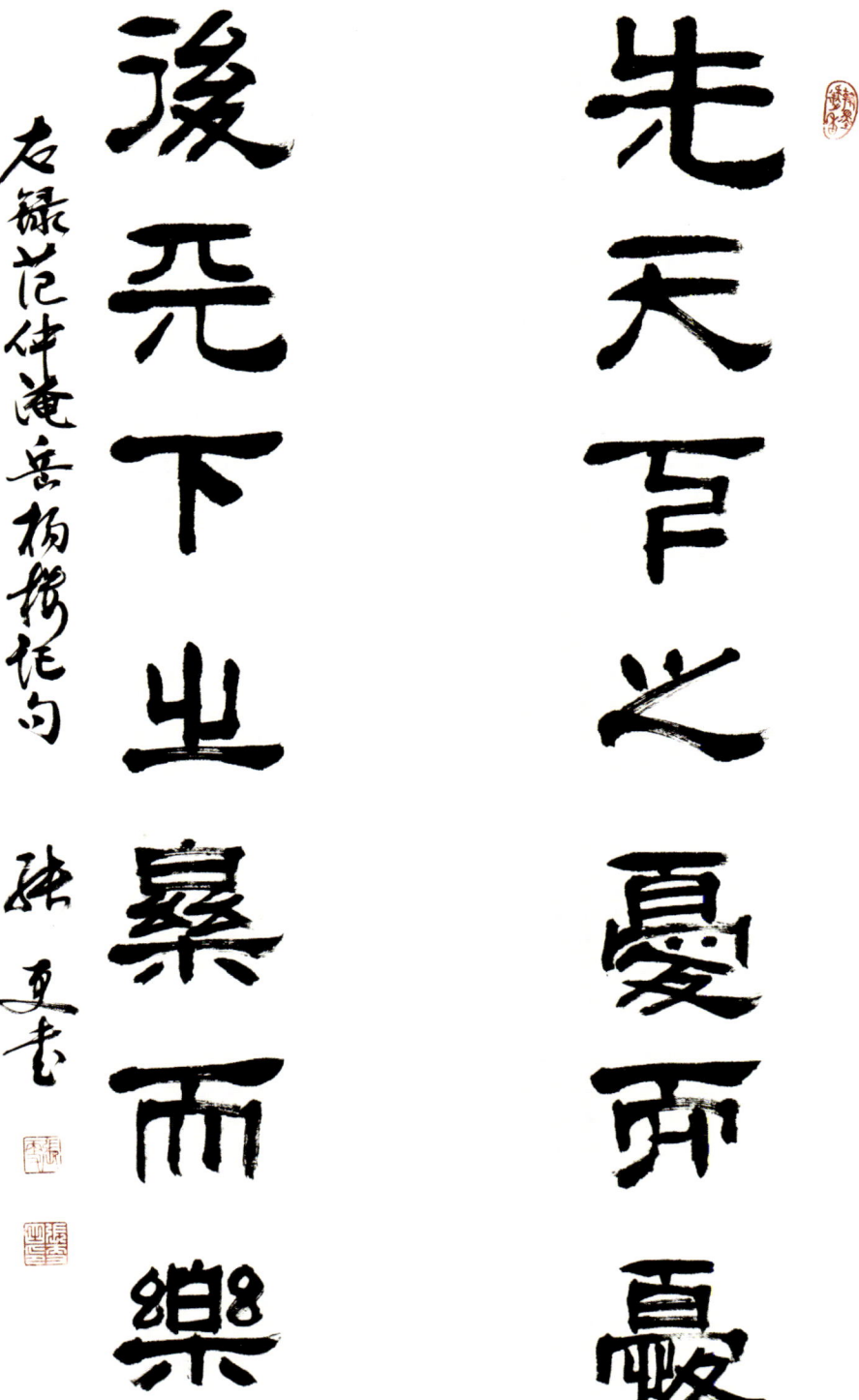

《岳阳楼记句对联》　137cm×35cm×2　*A Couplet of Account of Yueyang Building*

驿外断桥边，寂寞开无主。已是黄昏独自愁，更著风和雨。无意苦争春，一任群芳妒。零落成泥碾作尘，只有香如故。

陆游 卜算子·咏梅

辛卯年初冬 然之书

《陆游诗一首》　136cm×69cm　A Poem by Lu You

胡德保 *Hu Debao*

胡德保，男，1948年生，江西婺源人，中国美术学会会员、中国书画家协会会员、当代中国书画名家协会会员，一级美术家，全球艺术家联盟驻中国办事处主任、江西分会会长；世界黄埔书画文化交流中心常委副主席兼秘书长；神舟书画院名誉院长和高级顾问；北京华夏翰雅书画院校院士、理事等。

润笔价格：4000/平尺

Hu Debao, male, born in Wuyuan, Jiangxi Province, in 1948, is a National Class A artist, member of China Arts Society, of China Calligrapher and Painters Association, and of Chinese Contemporary Celebrated Calligrapher and Painter Association. He is Director of Global Alliance of Artists (GAA) in China, and President of Jiangxi Branch of GAA. Hu is also Vice President and Secretary of Culture Exchange Center of International Huangpu Calligraphy and Painting, honorary President and senior consultant of Shenzhou Calligraphy and Painting Gallery, council member of and painter with China Hanya Calligraphy and Painting Gallery of Beijing, etc..

Reference price: RMB 4000 per square feet

《富贵满堂》　65cm×133cm　*The Hall Full of Wealth and Honour*

《花艳吉祥》 100cm×55cm　　*Propitious Flowers*

张善贵 *Zhang Shangui*

张善贵，男，1947年生，安徽人，现为安徽省书协、美协会员、六安市书协、美协会员、中国书画家联谊会会员，国际美术家协会会员。

润笔价格：3000/平尺

Zhang Shangui, male, born in Anhui in 1947, is a member of Anhui Calligraphers Association, of Anhui Artists Association, of Liu'an Calligraphers Association, and of Liu'an Artists Association. He is also a member of Chinese Calligrapher and Painter Federation, and of International Artists Association.

Reference price: RMB 3000 per square feet

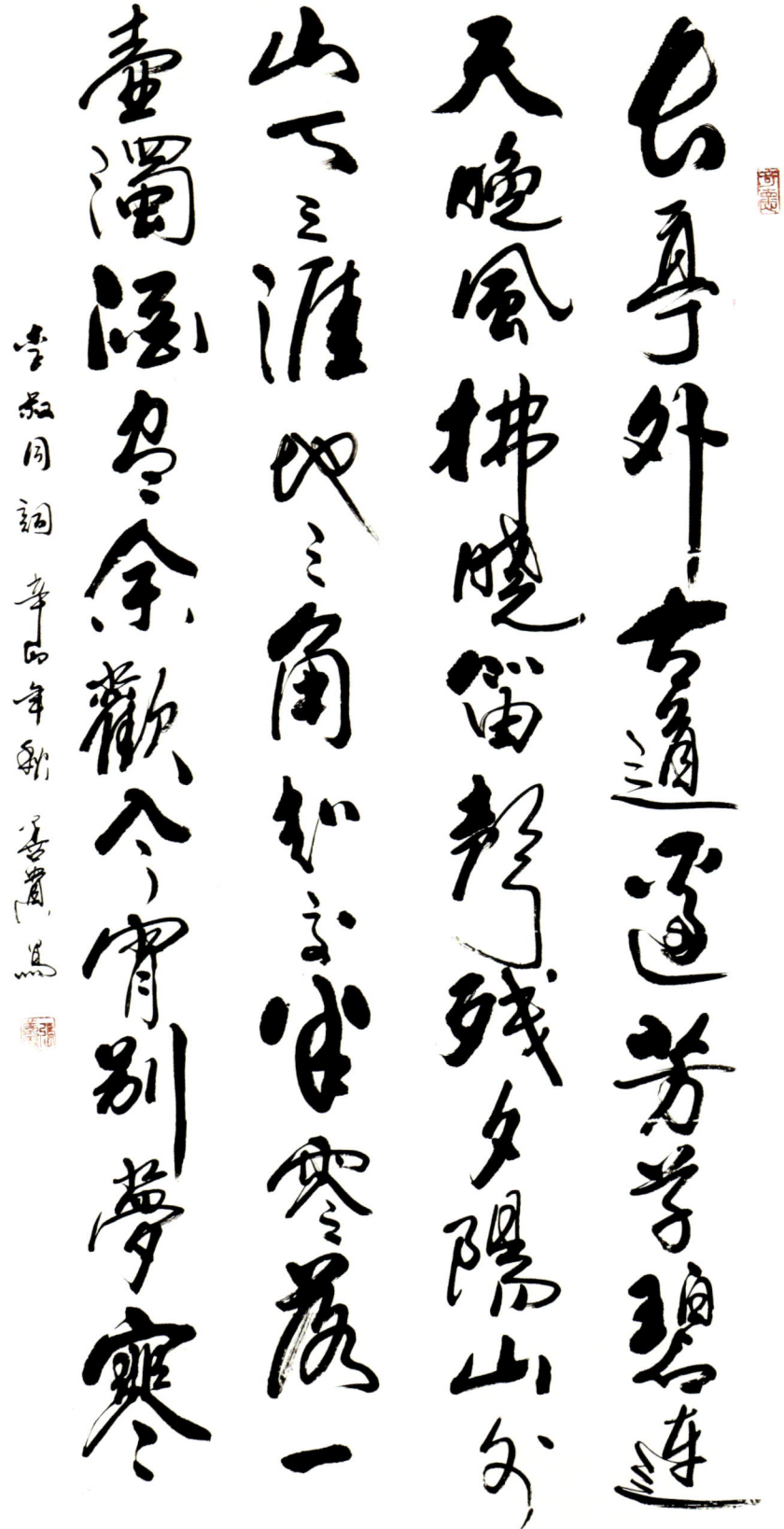

《李叔同诗一首》　　138cm×69cm　　*A Poem by Li Shutong*

我國的書畫藝術是東方的朗珠國寶它不是詩却有詩的韻味它不是畫却有畫的美感它不是舞却有舞的節奏它不是歌却有歌的旋律

鲁迅先生語文

辛卯年冬，慕貴冩於翠峰

李雅鑫 *Li Yaxin*

李雅鑫，女，北京美术家协会会员、北京文联九洲书画艺术研究会理事、北京东城区美术家协会理事、北京丰台区美术家协会会员。

润笔价格：4000/平尺

Li Yaxin, female, is a member of Beijing Artists Association, and council member of Jiuzhou Calligraphy and Painting Art Academy of Beijing Federation of Literary and Art Circles. He is also a council member of Dongcheng Artists Association, and member of Fengtai Artists Association, Beijing.

Reference price: 4000 per square feet

《鲤跃龙门》　137cm×69cm　　*The carp leaps through the dragon's gate. (Big Splash)*

《一展雄姿》　137cm×69cm　*Showing Majestic*

张铁成 *Zhang Tiecheng*

张铁成，男，1965年生，河南新乡人，河南省书法家协会会员，新乡市书法家协会常务理事，新乡市书画研究会副会长，新乡市古雍书画院副院长，深圳市南国书画院副院长。

润笔价格：5000/平尺

Zhang Tiecheng, male, born in Xinxiang, Henan Province, in 1956, is a member of Henan Calligraphers Association, standing council member of Xinxiang Calligraphers Association, and Vice President of Xinxiang Calligraphy and Painting Research Institute. He is also Vice President of Xinxiang Guyong Calligraphy and Painting Association, and of Shenzhen Nanguo Calligraphy and Painting Gallery.

Reference price: RMB 5000 per square feet

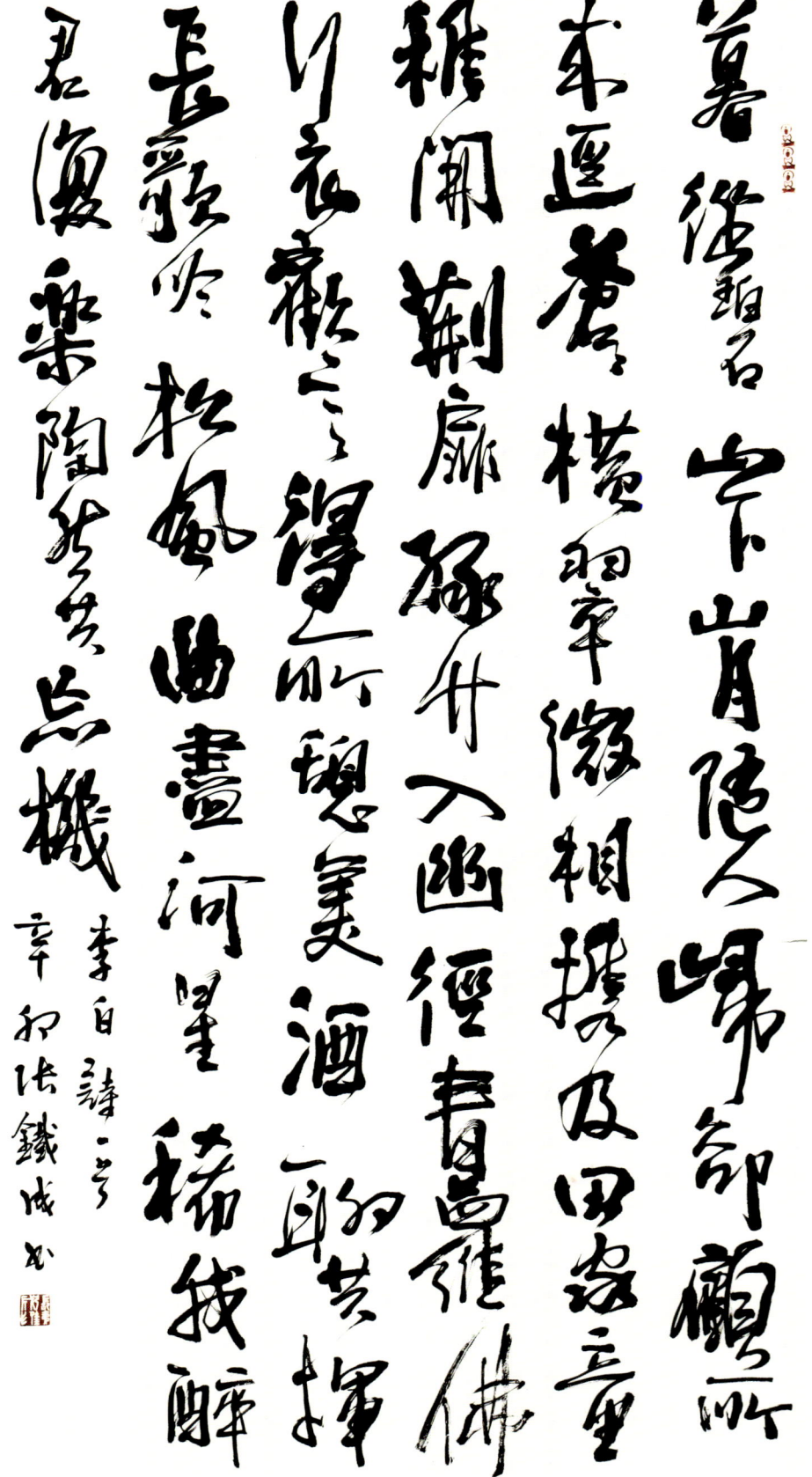

《李白诗一首》　　180cm×97cm　　*A Poem by Li Bai*

顾林祥 *Gu Linxiang*

顾林祥，男，字瑞卿，邳州市陈楼镇大顾村人，1938年生。现为江苏省美术家协会会员，中国老年书画研究会会员，邳州市老年书画协会副会长，邳州市美协顾问。

润笔价格：6000/平尺

Gu Linxiang, male, with Ruiqing as his courtesy name, was born in Dagu of Chenlou Town, Pizhou, Jiangsu province, in 1938. He is a member of Jiangsu Artists Association, of China Calligraphy and Painting Research Institute for Seniors, Vice President of Pizhou Calligraphy and Painting Association for Seniors, and consultant of Pizhou Artists Association.

Reference price: RMB 6000 per square feet

《墨荷》　68cm×68cm　　*Inking Lotus*

张耀宗　*Zhang Yaozong*

张耀宗，男，1939年12月生，江苏太仓人，中国书画家协会理事，华夏夕阳红书画艺术院名誉院长。

润笔价格：3000/平尺

Zhang Yaozong, male, born in Taicang, Jiangsu Province, in the December of 1939, is a council member of China Calligrapher and Painter Association, and Honorary President of China xiyanghong Calligraphy and Painting Art Research Institute.

Reference price: RMB 3000 per square feet

《沁园春 雪》　153cm×83cm　　*Qinyuanchun Snow*

刘绍斌 *Liu Shaobin*

刘绍斌，男，1956年12月生于天津，汉族，天津美术学院毕业。中国美术家协会会员，天津政协书画家研究会会员，大运河书画院理事。

润笔价格：16000/平尺

Liu Shaobin, male, born in Tianjin in the December of 1956, graduated from Tianjin Academy of Fine Arts. Liu is a member of China Artists Association, of Calligraphy and Painting Research Institute of Tianjin CPPCC, and council member of Dayunhe (the Grand Canal) Calligraphy and Painting Gallery.

Reference price: RMB 16000 per square feet

《巴山夜雨》　130cm×125cm　　*Rainy Night in Daba Mountains*

张维　*Zhang Wei*

张维，男，1928年5月生，为天津市书法家协会会员，天津市老年书画院书画师，中国书画研究院研究员，中华书法学会会员等。

润笔价格：3000/平尺

Zhang Wei, male, born in the May of 1928, is a member of Tianjin Calligraphers Association, and painter with Tianjin Calligraphy and Painting Art Research Institute for Seniors. He is also a researcher with China Calligraphy and Painting Research Institute, and member of China Calligraphers Association, etc.

Reference price: RMB 3000 per square feet

文天祥　《过零丁洋》　202cm×71cm　*Crossing the Lingding Ocean by Wen Tianxiang*

夫君子之行，静以修身，俭以养德，非澹泊无以明志，非宁静无以致远。夫学须静也，才须学也，非学无以广才，非志无以成学。淫漫则不能励精，险躁则不能冶性。年与时驰，意与日去，遂成枯落，多不接世，悲守穷庐，将复何及。

诸葛亮诫子篇 壬辰暮春八四叟张维生于津沽

朱国鸿 *Zhu Guohong*

朱国鸿，男，1977年生于山东泰安，书香世家。现为泰安市美术家协会理事，泰安市泰山区美术家协会副主席，湖南长沙欧阳询书法艺术学会会员。

润笔价格：10000/平尺

Zhu Guohong, male, born in scholarly family in Tai'an, Shandong Province, in 1977, is a council member of Tai'an Artists Association, Vice President of Tai'an District Artists Association of Tia'an City, and member of Changsha Ouyang Xun Research Institute.

Reference price: RMB 10000 per square feet

《知己三更夜》　　138cm×68cm　　*Bosom Friends*

《花鸟》　138cm×68cm　Birds and Flowers

赵国俊 Zhao Guojun

赵国俊，男，河南淅川人，1954年生。现为中国书画协会会员，云台书画院特聘高级书画师，中国文化艺术研究中心客座教授，南京神鸟文化传播中心古诗词艺术顾问，世界华人书画艺术家学会名誉副主席。

润笔价格：3000/平尺

Zhao Guojun, male, born in Xichuan, Henan Province, in 1954, is a member of China Calligrapher and Painter Association, senior calligrapher and painter with Yuntai Calligraphy and Painting Gallery, and visiting professor with China Culture Art Research Center. He is also an art consultant of Poetry of Nanjing Shenniao Cultural Communication Center, and Honorary President of Worldwide Chinese Calligraphy and Painting Artists Association.

Reference price: RMB 3000 per square feet

《沁园春 长沙》   53cm×232cm   *Qinyuanchun Snow*

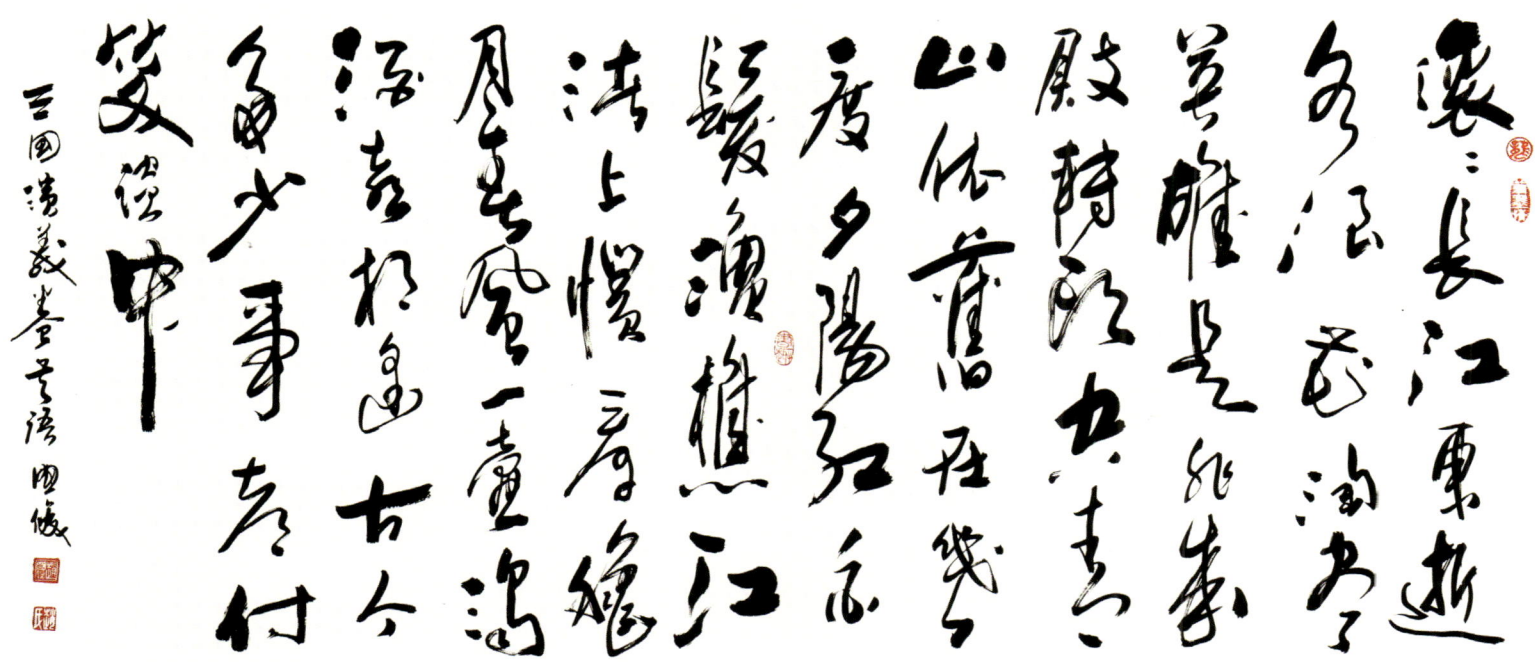

《三国演义开篇词》 66cm×133cm The Opening Poem in The Romance of Three Kingdoms

张映文　Zhang Yingwen

张映文，男，1949年生，湖南宁远人，自幼习画，师从多名油画、国画、雕塑大师，处1969年起一直从事美术工作。1991年开始办学，现任华南工艺美术专科学校校长兼教师。中国国画家协会会员，湖南省老干部书画家协会会员。

润笔价格：6000/平尺

Zhang Yingwen, male, born in Ningyuan, Hunan Province, in 1949, learned with several masters about oil painting, traditional Chinese painting, and sculpturing from his childhood. He has been devoted himself in art since 1969, and been working on art schooling since 1991. Zhang is Principle and teacher of Huanan (South China) Arts and Crafts College, member of China Association of Traditional Chinese Painting, and of Hunan Calligrapher and Painter Association for Retired and Aged Cadres.

Reference price: RMB 6000 per square feet

《九疑山娥皇峰》　97cm×180cm　*Ehuang Peak of Mount Jiuyi*

《疑山深处》　69cm×137cm　As-If Deep in the Mountains

周元蛟　*Zhou Yuanjiao*

周元蛟，男，1933年12月生，安徽人。高级经济师。现任南亚书画研究会理事、山东文艺研究院研究员、国际书画家年鉴博览大观顾问编委、中国风华书协会员、中国书画爱好者联谊会会员、中国新世纪书画研究院名誉院长、画圣吴道子艺术馆特级画师，名誉副馆长。

润笔价格：3000/平尺

Zhou Yuanjiao, male, born in Anhui in the December of 1933, is a senior economist. He is a council member of South Asia Calligraphy and Painting Research Institute, researcher with Shandong Literature and Art Society, and consultant and editor of Yearbook of International Calligraphers and Painters Expo. Zhou is also a member of China Fenghua Calligraphers Association, of Federation of Chinese Calligraphy and Painting Lovers, Honorary President of China New-Millennium Calligraphy and Painting Research Institute, and distinguished painter and honorary curator of Wu Daozi (Sage of Painting) Art Museum.

Reference price: RMB 3000 per square feet

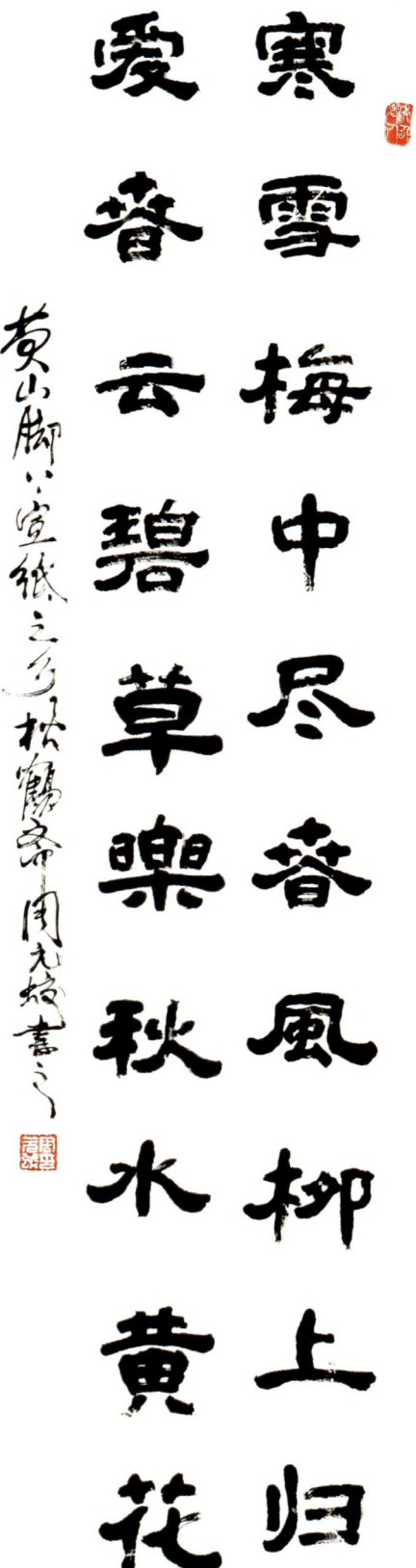

《寒雪梅中尽》　136cm×34cm　*Snowy Winter Ends in Plum Blossoming*

宋存哲 *Song Cunzhe*

宋存哲，男，生于河北省廊坊市，河北美术家协会会员；廊坊市青年书画协会理事；现研修于中国国家画院黄格胜工作室。

润笔价格：14000/平尺

Song Cunzhe, male, born in Langfang, Hebei Province, is a member of Hebei Artists Association, and council member of Langfang Young Artists Association, who now studies at Gesheng Huang Studio in China National Academy of Painting.

Reference price: RMB 14000 per square feet

《厚土情深》　97cm×178cm　　*Feeling for the Soil*

朱长明 *Zhu Changming*

朱长明，男，1934年11月生。笔名墨客、墨痴，辽宁省辽阳县人。现为辽宁省直老年书画协会会员、许昌画圣吴道子艺术馆馆员、中国书画艺术创作中心理事、南京长江书画院和王铎故里书画院名誉院长、环球书画艺术研究院客座教授、福建省盛世开元书画院特聘画家。

润笔价格：2000/平尺

Zhu Changming, male, with Moke and Mochi as his pseudonym, was born in Liaoyang County, Liaoning Province, in the December of 1934. He is a member of Zhongzhi Branch of Liaoning Calligraphy and Painting Art Research Institute for Seniors, librarian with Wu Daozi (Sage of Painting) Art Museum of Xuchang, and council member of Chinese Calligraphy and Painting Creation Center. Zhu is also Honorary President of Nanjing Changjiang (Yangtze River) Calligraphy and Painting Gallery, of Wang Duo Guli (Hometown) Calligraphy and Painting Gallery, visiting professor with Global Calligraphy and Painting Art Research Institute, and especially employed painter with Shengshi Kaiyuan (Prosperous Age) Calligraphy and Painting Gallery of Fujian Province.
Reference price: 2000 per square feet

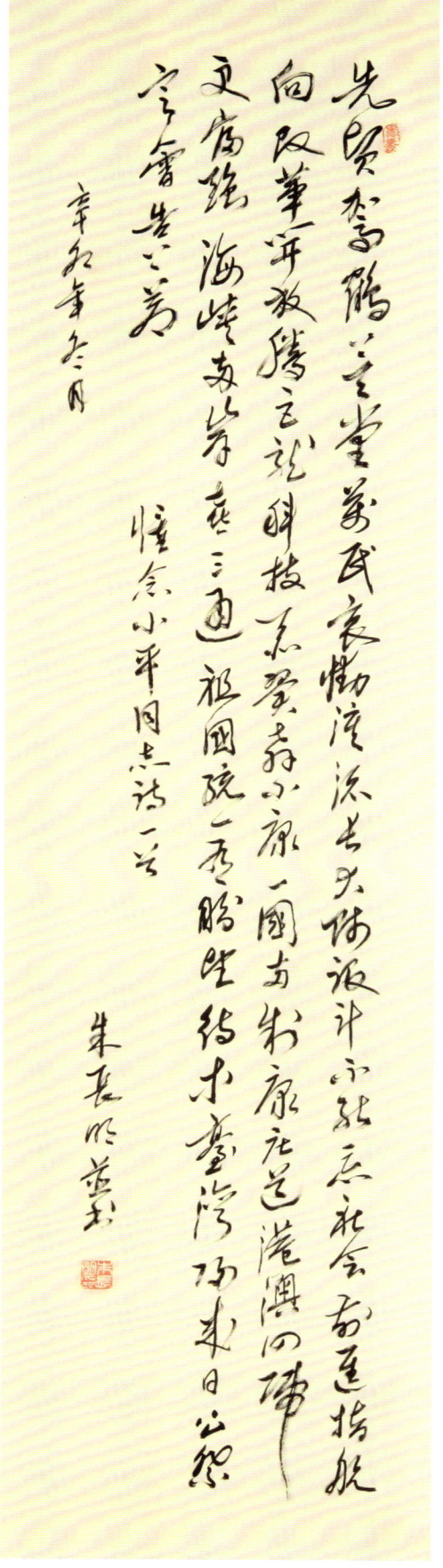

《怀念小平同志诗一首》　137cm×35cm　*A Poem in Memory of Deng Xiaoping*

王明亮 *Wang Mingliang*

王明亮（王馗），男，汉族，毕业于中国国家画院，中国书画青岛创作基地主席，山东省美协、中国书画理事。

润笔价格：8000/平尺

Wang Mingliang, also known as Wang Kui, male, graduated from China National Academy of Painting. Wang is President of Qingdao Creation Base of China Calligraphy and Painting, council member of Shandong Artists Association, and of China Calligraphy and Painting Association.

Reference price: RMB 8000 per square feet

《贺寿》　　70cm×137cm　　*Celebrating Longevity*

李智民　*Li Zhimin*

李智民，男，1952年生，河北曲周县人。现为中国书画家协会会员、河北省美术家协会会员、河北省书法家协会会员。

润笔价格：2000/平尺

Li Zhimin, male, born in Quzhou County, Hebei Province, in 1952, is a member of China Calligrapher and Painter Association, of Hebei Artists Association, and of Hebei Calligraphers Association.
Reference price: RMB 2000 per square feet

《录宋词王祁名句》　　130cm×66cm　　*Famous Lines by Song Qi*

张宝珍 *Zhang Baozhen*

张宝珍,男,1935年生于中国山东潍坊。陆续在国内发表、展出美术作品,并多次获奖。现为山东画院高级画师。

润笔价格:14000/平尺

Zhang Baozhen, male, born in Weifang, Shandong Province, in 1935, is a senior painter with Shandong Painting Art Academy, whose works have been widely published or exhibited, and been granted with various awards.

Reference price: RMB 14000 per square feet

《荷塘小景》 67cm×67cm *A View of a Lotus Pond*

刘中方　*Liu Zhongfang*

刘中方，男，1963年生于山东成武县。中国书画家联谊会会员，中国楹联学会会员，中国楹联书法艺术研究会会员，中国浩瀚书法院理事，中国书画艺术研究院副院长。

润笔价格：4000/平尺

Liu Zhongfang, male, born in Chengwu County, Shandong Province, in 1963, is a member of Chinese Calligrapher and Painter Federation, of Yinglian Society of China, and of Yinglian Calligraphy Art Research Institute of China. He is also a council member of China Haohan (Vastness) Calligraphy Art Gallery, and Vice President of Chinese Calligraphy and Painting Research Institute.

Reference price: RMB 4000 per square feet

《春风满怀》　68cm×138cm　　*Embracing Spring Breeze*

张荣华 *Zhang Ronghua*

张荣华，男，中国美术家协会山东分会会员，山东画院画家，齐鲁书画研究院画家。

润笔价格：4000/平尺

Zhang Ronghua, male, is a member of Shandong Branch of China Artists Association, painter with Shandong Painting Art Academy, and with Qilu Calligraphy and Painting Research Institute.

Reference price: RMB 4000 per square feet

《花鸟》　97cm×180cm　　*Birds and Flowers*

江太生　*Jiang Taisheng*

江太生，男，号云绕斋主，1958年生于安徽太湖，祖籍桐城。现为中国收藏家协会、安徽省书法家协会等近十个单位会员、理事，太湖县书法协会主席。

润笔价格：4000/平尺

Jiang Taisheng, male, born in Taihu, Anhui Province, in 1958, and with Yunrao Zhaizhu (Host of Cloud-Shrouded Study) as his literary name, is a member of China Association of Collectors, President of Taihu Calligraphers Association, and member and council member of more than ten institutions like Anhui Calligraphers Association.

Reference price: RMB 4000 per square feet

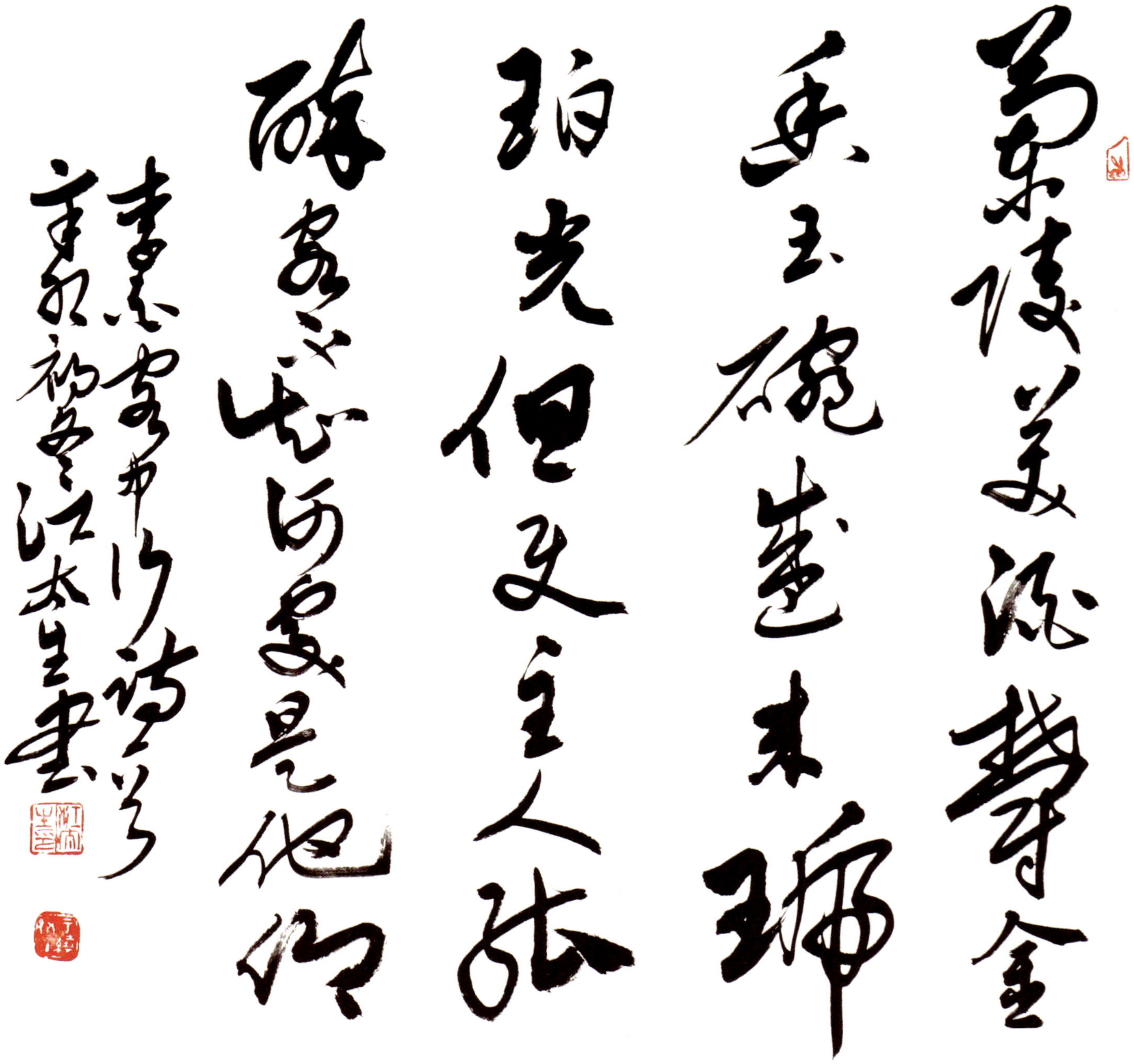

《诗一首》　68cm×68cm　　*A Poem*

张文健 *Zhang Wenjian*

张文健，男，1959年生，四川省合江县人。现为中国美术家协会四川分会会员、泸州市东方艺术研究院研究员、县政协委员。

润笔价格：8000/平尺

Zhang Wenjian, male, born in Hejiang County, Sichuan Province, in 1959, is a member of Sichuan Artists Association, and researcher with Luzhou Oriental Art Research Institute. He is a CPPCC member of Hejiang County.

Reference price: RMB 8000 per square feet

《傲雪斗霜》　　180cm×30cm　　*Frost and Snow*

路建军　*Lu Jianjun*

路建军，男，汉族，山西省平顺县人，1971年生。长治市书协会员，中国书画名家协会会员。
润笔价格：3000/平尺

Lu Jianjun, male, born in Pingshun County, Shanxi Province, in 1971, is a member of Changzhi Calligraphers Association, and of China Association of Celebrity Calligraphers and Painter.
Reference price: RMB 3000 per square feet

《录古诗一首》　　138cm×68cm　　*A Poem*

《对联一副》 138cm×34cm×2　　*A Couplet*

金威昕 *Jin Weixin*

金威昕（爱新觉罗·威昕），男，满族，1956年生，1984年毕业于鲁迅美术学院雕塑系，学士学位，教授，国家持证雕塑家，国家一级画家，现在是中国雕塑家协会会员，中国国画家协会会员，中国美术家协会辽宁省分会会员，抚顺市美术家协会副主席，抚顺市政协常委，辽宁省海外联谊会理事,中国海峡两岸书画家协会会员。

润笔价格：10000/平尺

Jin Weixin, also known as Aisin Gioro Weixin, male, born in 1956, graduated from Department of Sculpture at Lu Xun Academy of Fine Arts, and was conferred a Bachelor Degree. He is a professor, National Licensed Sculpture, National Class a Artist, and a member of Fushun CPPCC. Jin now is a member of China Sculptors Association, of China Association of Traditional Chinese Painting, and of Liaoning Artists Association. Jin is also Vice President of Fushun Artists Association, council member of Liaoning Overseas Friendship Association, and member of China Cross-Strait Research Institute of Calligraphy and Painting.
Reference price: RMB 10000 per square feet

《春风得意》　68cm×138cm　*Complacent Breeze in Spring*

《马》 69cm×69cm　Horses

栾传益 *Luan Chuanyi*

栾传益，男，辽宁大连人，1949年1月生。现为辽宁书法家协会会员，辽宁印社理事，大连印社副秘书长，大连大学师范学院艺术系讲师。

润笔价格：3000/平尺

Luan Chuanyi, male, born in Dalian, Liaoning Province, in the January of 1949, is a member of Liaoning Calligraphers Association, council member of Liaoning Society of Seal Arts, Deputy Secretary General of Dalian Society of Seal Arts, and lecturer with Department of Fine Arts of Teachers College of Dalian University.

Reference price: RMB 3000 per square feet

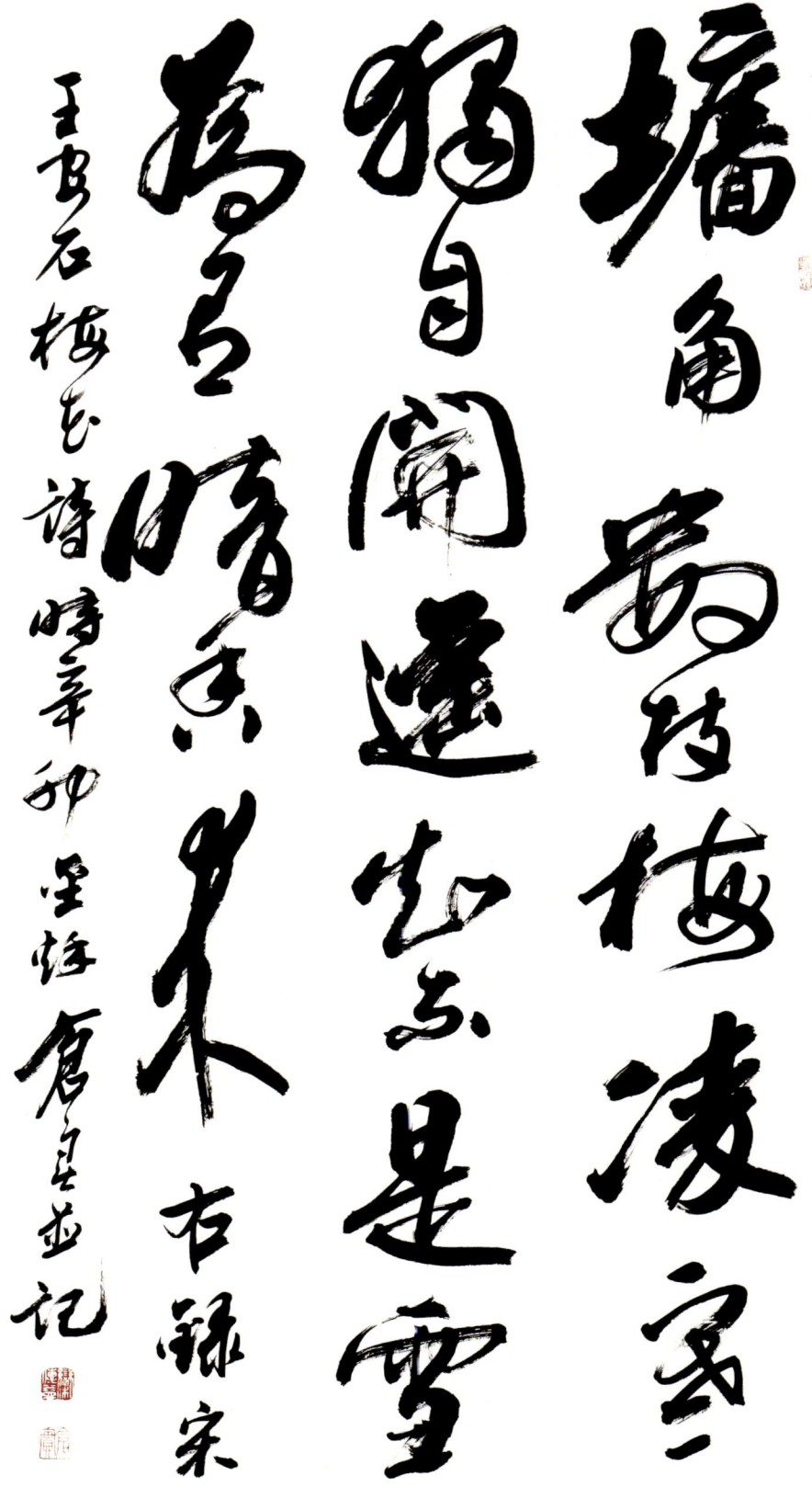

《王安石诗句》　138cm×69cm　*Lines by Wang Anshi*

张馨 Zhang xin

张馨，曾用名张鑫、张立昕，女，得风堂主人，生于河北省，现任中国翰林书画艺术院常务副院长兼秘书长，中国书画院副院长，河北省美术家协会会员，中国书画界联合会会员，中国绘画艺术研究院艺术委员会委员，中国名家书画院副院长，中国书画家协会常务理事。

润笔价格：10000/平尺

Zhang xin, also known as Zhang Lixin, female, with Mistress of Defeng Hall as her literary name, was born in Hebei Province. Zhang is an executive Vice President and Secretary General of Hanlin Calligraphy and Painting Art Academy of China, Vice President of China Painting and Calligraphy Academy, member of Hebei Artists Association, and of Federation of Chinese Calligraphy and Painting Circles. She is also a member of Arts Committee of Chinese Painting Art Research Institute, Vice President of China Celebrity Calligraphy and Painting Gallery, and a standing council member of China Calligrapher and Painter Association.

Reference price: RMB 10000 per square feet

《春风》 96cm×175cm Spring Breeze

罗少模　*Luo Shaomo*

罗少模，男，号山外人，1946年生。四川省兴文县人，现为四川省兴文县书协主席。
润笔价格：4000/平尺

Luo Shaomo, male, born in Wen County, Sichuan Province, in 1946, and with Shanwairen (Mountain Stranger) as his literary name, is President of Xingwen Calligraphers Association, Sichuan.
Reference price: RMB 4000 per square feet

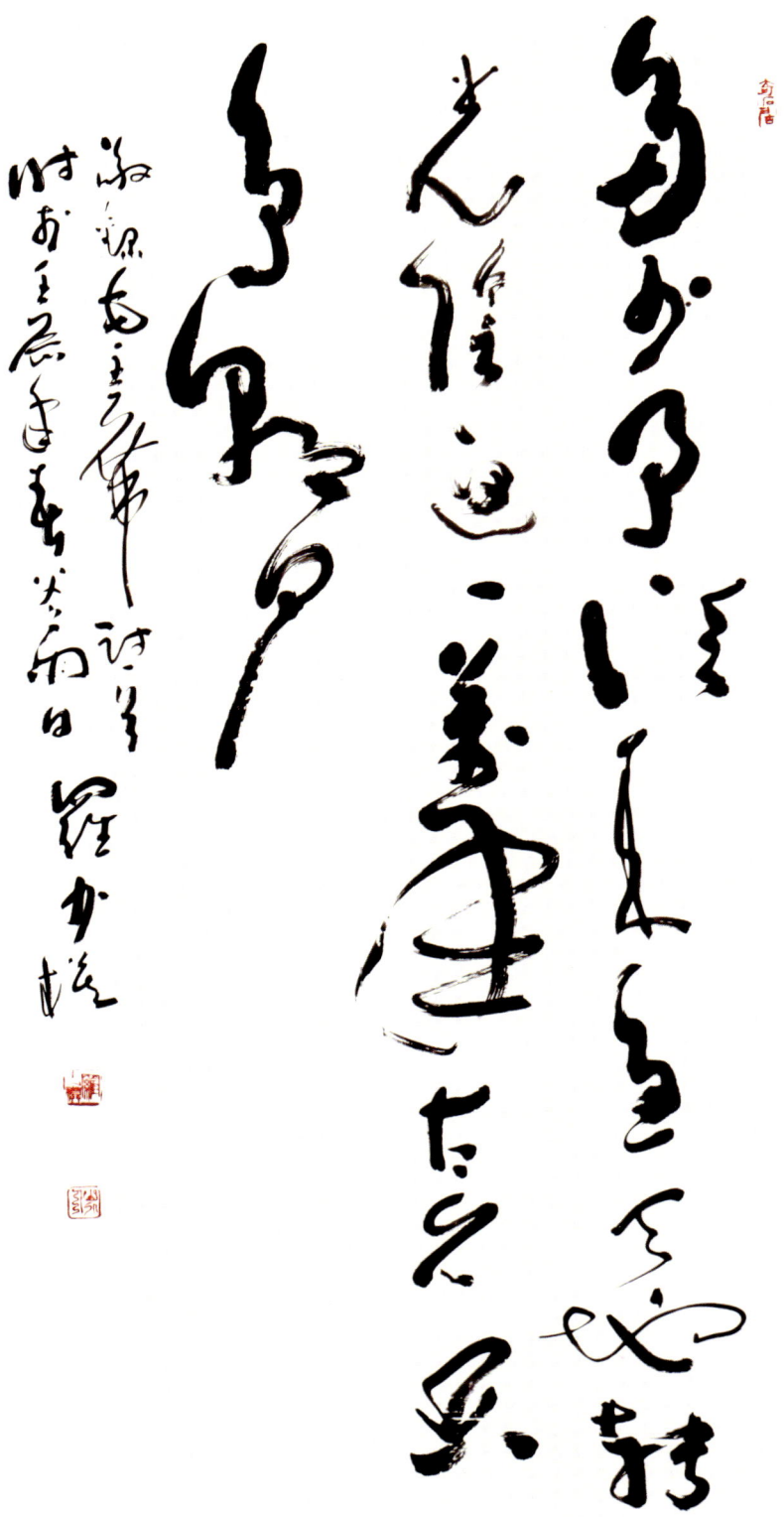

《毛主席诗词》　　136cm×68cm　　*A Poem by Mao Zedong*

甄春明　*Zhen Chunming*

甄春明，男，汉族，1939年生，天津人，现为中国国际书画艺术研究院终身画家、中国文化艺术发展促进会艺术会员、中国书画艺术委员会会员、中国文联书画艺术交流中心会员、中国书画家联谊会会员、中原书画研究院高级画师。

润笔价格：16000/平尺

Zhen Chunming, male, born in Tianjin in 1939, is a lifelong painter with International Calligraphy and Painting Art Research Institute of China, member of Arts Committee of China Calligraphy and Painting Art Promotion Society, and of China Calligraphy and Painting Association. Zhen is also a member of Calligraphy and Painting Art Exchange Center of China Federation of Literary and Art Circles, of Chinese Calligrapher and Painter Federation, and senior painter with Zhongyuan Calligraphy and Painting Gallery.

Reference price: RMB 16000 per square feet

《工笔花鸟》　125cm×81cm　*Flowers and Birds*

马东山　*Ma Dongshan*

马东山，男，1956年1月生，现为中国书法家协会会员，中国当代书画艺术研究会名誉会长，河南省教育书画研究会理事，开封教育书画研究会副会长等。

润笔价格：6000/平尺

Ma Dongshan, male, born in the January of 1956, is a member of China Calligraphers Association, Honorary President of China Contemporary Calligraphy and Painting Art Research Institute, council member of Calligraphy and Painting Education Research Institute of Henan, and Vice President of Kaifeng Calligraphy and Painting Education Research Institute. He also bears some other positions.

Reference price: RMB 6000 per square feet

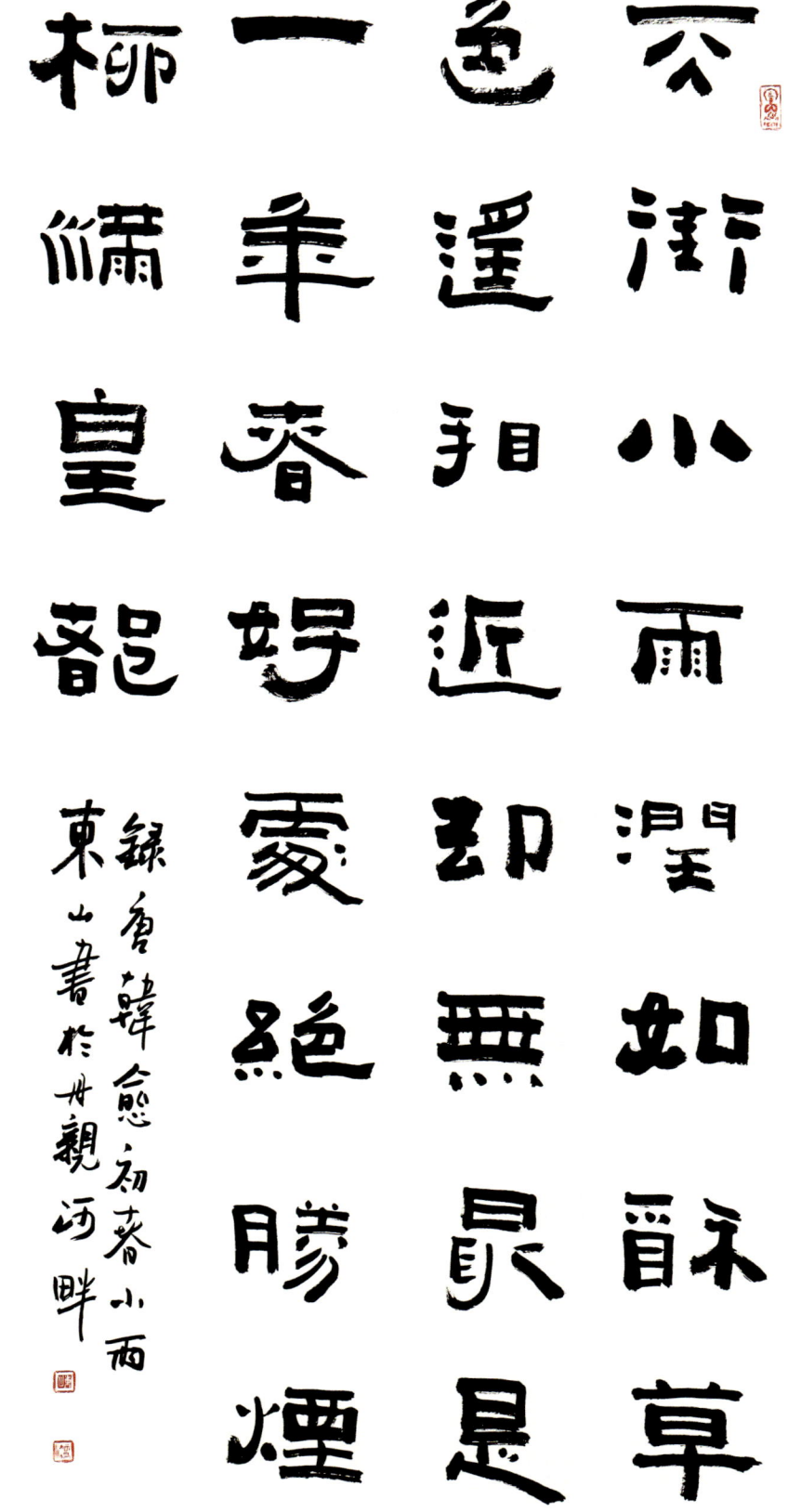

《初春小雨》　138cm×68cm　　*Light Rain in Early Spring by Han Yu*

《毛泽东诗词一首》　　230cm×36cm　　*A Poem by Mao Zedong*

吴俊祥 *Wu Junxiang*

吴俊祥，男，1938年12月生，现为盘锦市老年书画研究会会员，华夏国艺书画院高级书画师。
润笔价格：8000/平尺

Wu Junxiang, male, born in the December of 1938, is a member of Panjin Calligraphy and Painting Research Institute for Seniors, and a senior calligrapher and painter with China Guoyi Calligraphy and Painting Gallery.
Reference price: RMB 8000 per square feet

《贺寿千年》　180cm×97cm　　*Celebrate Longevity*

《花开富贵吉祥如意》　　180cm×97cm　　*Auspicious Blossoming*

马杰 *Ma Jie*

马杰，女，1961年11月22日生于北京，中国书画研究院研究员，中外名人文化研究会会员，北京大学人才研究中心调研员，世界和平女神香港基金会书画艺术委员会理事，东方艺术研究院客座教授，中国桂林炎黄书画艺术研究院院士，世界华人交流协会会员，中国书法研究院会员，（香港）中国文人美术家协会会员。

润笔价格：3000/平尺

Ma Jie, female, born in Beijing on November 22nd, 1961, is a research with China Calligraphy and Painting Research Institute, member of Culture Research Institute for Chinese and Foreign Celebrities, and research with Talents Center of Peking University. She is also a council member of Calligraphy and Painting Art Committee of Worldwide Peace Goddess Foundation of Hong Kong, visiting professor with Oriental Art Research Institute, and painter with Guilin Yanhuang Calligraphy and Painting Research Institute. Ma is a member of Worldwide Chinese Exchange Association, of China Calligraphy Research Institute, and of China Literary Artists Association, Hong Kong.

Reference price: RMB 3000 per square feet

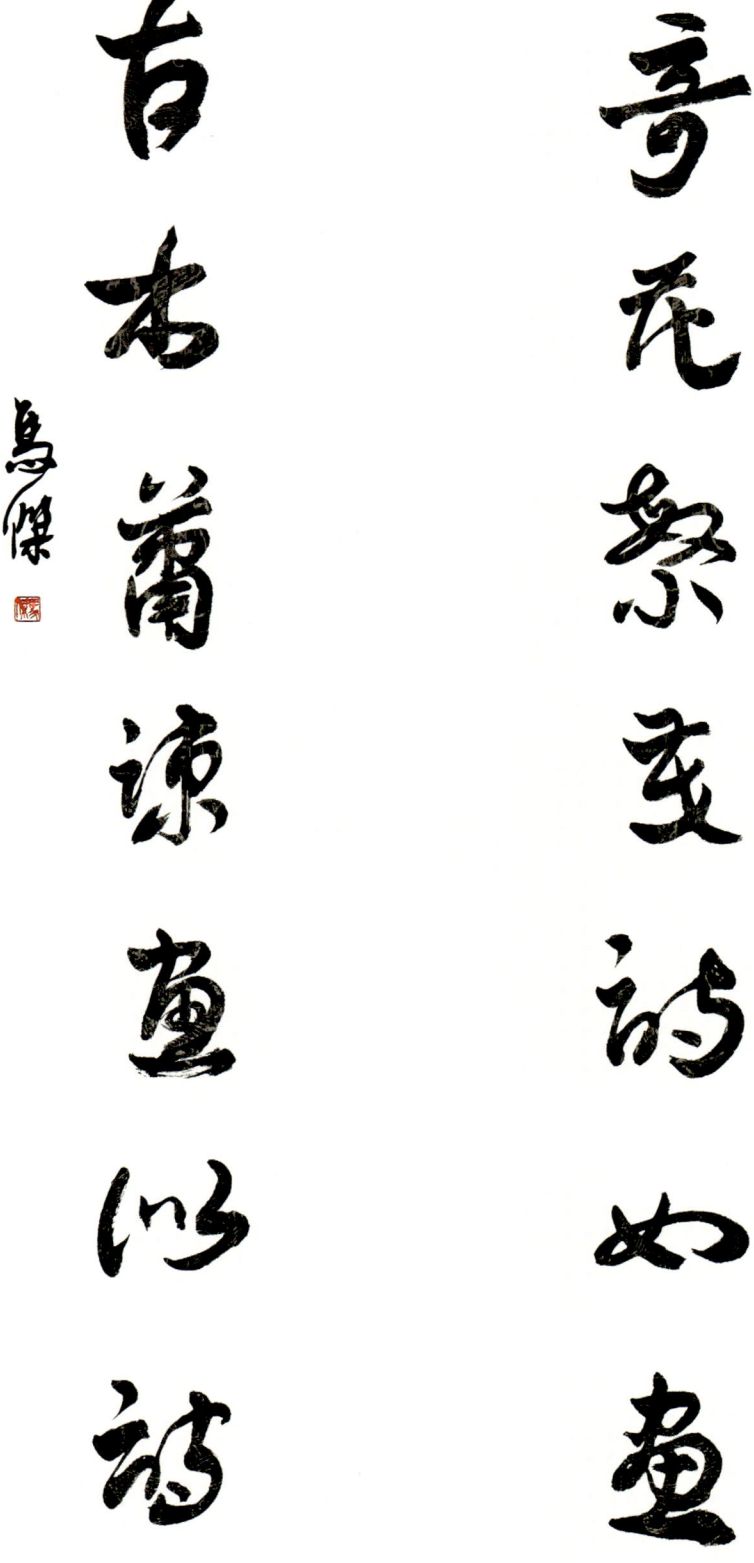

《对联一幅》　　138cm×35cm×2　　*A Couplet*

李恒才 *Li Hengcai*

李恒才，男，1962年12月出生于甘肃，西北师大美术系国画专业，现为甘肃省美协会员，甘肃省国画院山水画创研部主任，武威市美协副主席，武威市画院画家，国家二级美术师。

润笔价格：10000/平尺

Li Hengcai, male, born in Gansu in the December of 1962, majored in Traditional Chinese Painting, graduated from Department of Fine Arts of Northwest Normal University. Li is a member of Gansu Artists Association, and Director of Landscape Painting Department of Gansu Academy for Traditional Chinese Painting. He is also a National Class B artist, Vice President of Wuwei Artists Association, and painter with Wuwei Painting Art Gallery.

Reference price: RMB 10000 per square feet

《龙驼神行》　　68cm×138cm　　*God Flying on Dragon*

毛明强　*Mao Mingqiang*

毛明强，男，号明月清风、惠泉散人、梅花书屋主人，1970年生，毕业于江苏无锡书法艺术专科学校，江苏省无锡市书法家协会会员、楹联学会会员、诗词协会秘书长。

润笔价格：3000/平尺

Mao Mingqiang, male, born in 1970, and with Mingyueqingfeng (Bright Moon and Fresh Air), Huquansanren and Host of Plum Blossom Study, graduated at Wuxi Academy of Calligraphy Art, Jiangsu. Mao is a member of Wuxi Calligraphers Association, of Yinglian Society of China, and Secretary General of Chinese Poetry Association.

Reference price: RMB 3000 per square feet

《自作诗一首》　148cm×47cm　　*A Self-Composted Poem*

樊春华 *Fan Chunhua*

樊春华，男，1964年生，1983年毕业于唐山市二轻工艺美术学校。现为中国书画函授大学书画家协会会员、中国书画艺术研究会会员、唐山市青年书画家学会理事、唐山市收藏鉴赏家协会会员。

润笔价格：8000/平尺

Fan Chunhua, male, born in 1964, graduated from Arts and Crafts College of Tangshan Light Industry in 1983. Fan is a member of Calligrapher and Painter Association of China Painting and Calligraphy Correspondence University, and of Chinese Calligraphy and Painting Research Institute. He is also a council member of Tangshan Young Calligrapher and Painter Association, and member of Tangshan Association of Collectors.

Reference price: RMB 8000 per square feet

《富贵吉祥》　90cm×96cm　*Propitious Nobility*

彭国远　*Peng Guoyuan*

彭国远，男，1939年6月生于江西省吉水县。江西省作家协会会员，中国文人书法家协会终身理事。

润笔价格：5000/平尺

Peng Guoyuan, male, born in Jishui County, Jiangxi Province, in the June of 1939, is a member of Jiangxi Writers Association, and lifelong council member of China Literary Calligraphers Association.

Reference price: RMB 5000 per square feet

《唐诗八首》　180cm×98cm　　*Eight Poems*

唐子西诗云山静似太古日长小年余家深山之中每春夏之交苍藓盈阶落花满径门无剥啄松影参差禽声上下午睡初足旋汲山泉拾松枝煮苦茗啜之随意读周易国风左氏传离骚太史公书及陶杜诗韩苏文数篇从容步山径抚松竹与麛犊共偃息于长林丰草间坐弄流泉漱齿濯足既归竹窗下则山妻稚子作笋蕨供麦饭欣然一饱弄笔窗间随大小作数十字展所藏法帖墨迹画卷纵观之兴到则吟小诗或草玉露一两段再烹苦茗一杯出步溪边邂逅园翁溪友问桑麻说稻粳量晴校雨探节数时相与剧谈一饷归而倚杖柴门之下则夕阳在山紫绿万状变幻顷刻恍可入目牛背笛声两两归来而月印前溪矣味子西此句可谓妙绝然此句妙矣识其妙者盖少彼牛钓马驰尘影中人又乌知此句之妙哉人能真知此妙则东坡所谓无事此静坐一日是两日若活七十年便是百四十所得不已多乎

南宋罗大经《鹤林玉露》而编者以之山静日长 今《鹤林玉露》是一部笔记马名著的南宋笔记之一部其文的笔记影响甚大对后世历史笔著文坛较中为动记载... 但功较大对史料后的小事... 怜忱所述语佳篇山静日长 岁次辛卯春月国杰书于词蕊轩室之鉴 湖畔

《鹤林玉露》 180cm×98cm Helin Jade Crystal Bits

于宏　*Yu Hong*

于宏，男，字永仪，1961年生于辽宁，1988年毕业天津美术学院。现为北京银杏树名人文化艺术发展中心总裁，画山水，花鸟等得名。

润笔价格：14000/平尺

Yu Hong, male, born in Liaoning in 1961, and with Yongyi as his courtesy name, graduated from Tianjin Academy of Fine Arts in 1988. Yu is President of Yinxingshu (Ginkgo Tree) Celebrity Culture Development Center of Beijing, who is famous for painting landscapes, flowers and birds, etc..

Reference price: RMB 14000 per square feet

《波涛起伏水入》　　137cm×68cm　　*Waves Surging toward the Sky*

陈伯龙　*Chen Bailong*

陈伯龙，男，1943年生，山东庆云县大陈村人。现为国家博物馆画廊艺术指导委员会委员、客座教授，东方艺术研究院终身名誉院长。

润笔价格：2000/平尺

Chen Bailong, male, born in Dachen of Qingyun County, Shandong Province, in 1943, is a visiting professor, member of Instruction Committee of Gallery Art of National Museum, and lifelong Honorary President of Oriental Art Research Institute.

Reference price: RMB 2000 per square feet

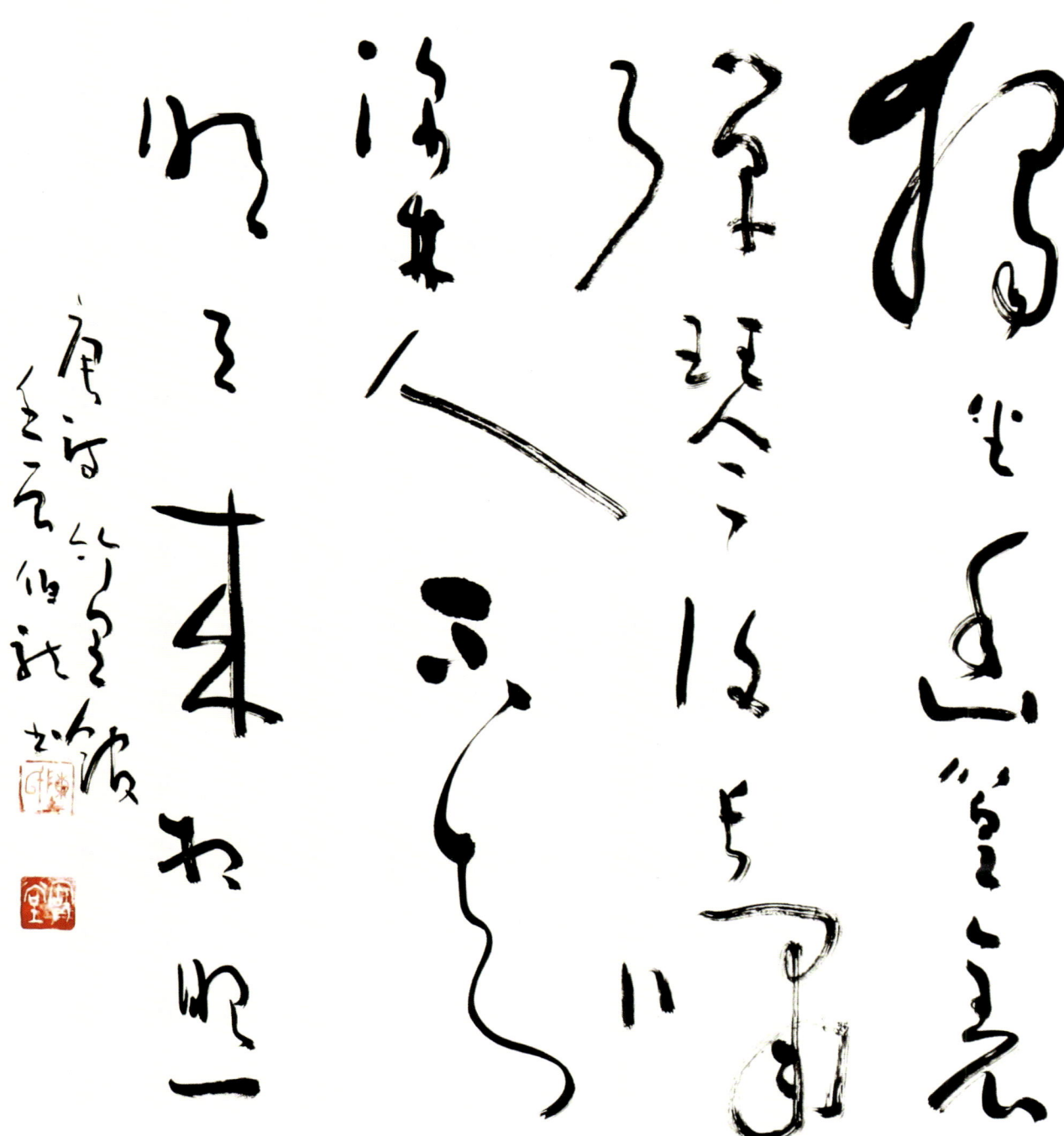

《唐诗一首》　69cm×69cm　　*A Poem*

郭学忠 *Guo Xuezhong*

郭学忠，男，字孝先，1949年3月生，河北唐山人、中共党员。现任河北省唐山石城书画院院长；中国历史博物馆画廊指导委员会委员、客座教授；中国文学界联合会特殊专家、一级画师；中国海峡两岸书画家协会会员。

润笔价格：12000/平尺

Guo Xuezhong, male, with Xiaoxian () as his courtesy name, was born in Tangshan, Hebei Province, in March, 1949. He is a Class A painter, President of Shicheng (City of Stone) Calligraphy and Painting Gallery of Tangshan, and visiting professor and member of Instruction Committee of the Museum of Chinese History. Guo is also a special expert with China Federation of Literature and Art Circles, and member of China Cross-Strait Research Institute of Calligraphy and Painting.

Reference price: RMB 12000 per square feet

《墨凌》　97cm×180cm　*Moling*

蒋徐风 Jiang Xufeng

蒋徐风，男，现年79岁。湖南省书法家协会会员，中华诗词学会会员，中国楹联家学会会员，中国楹联书法艺术委员会委员，中国书画家协会会员，中国国家画院副院长。

润笔价格：6000/平尺

Jiang Xufeng, male, 79-year-old, is a member of Hunan Calligraphers Association, of Chinese Poetry Association, and of Yinglian Society of China and its Art Committee. He is also a member of China Calligrapher and Painter Association, and Vice President of China National Academy of Painting.

Reference price: RMB 6000 per square feet

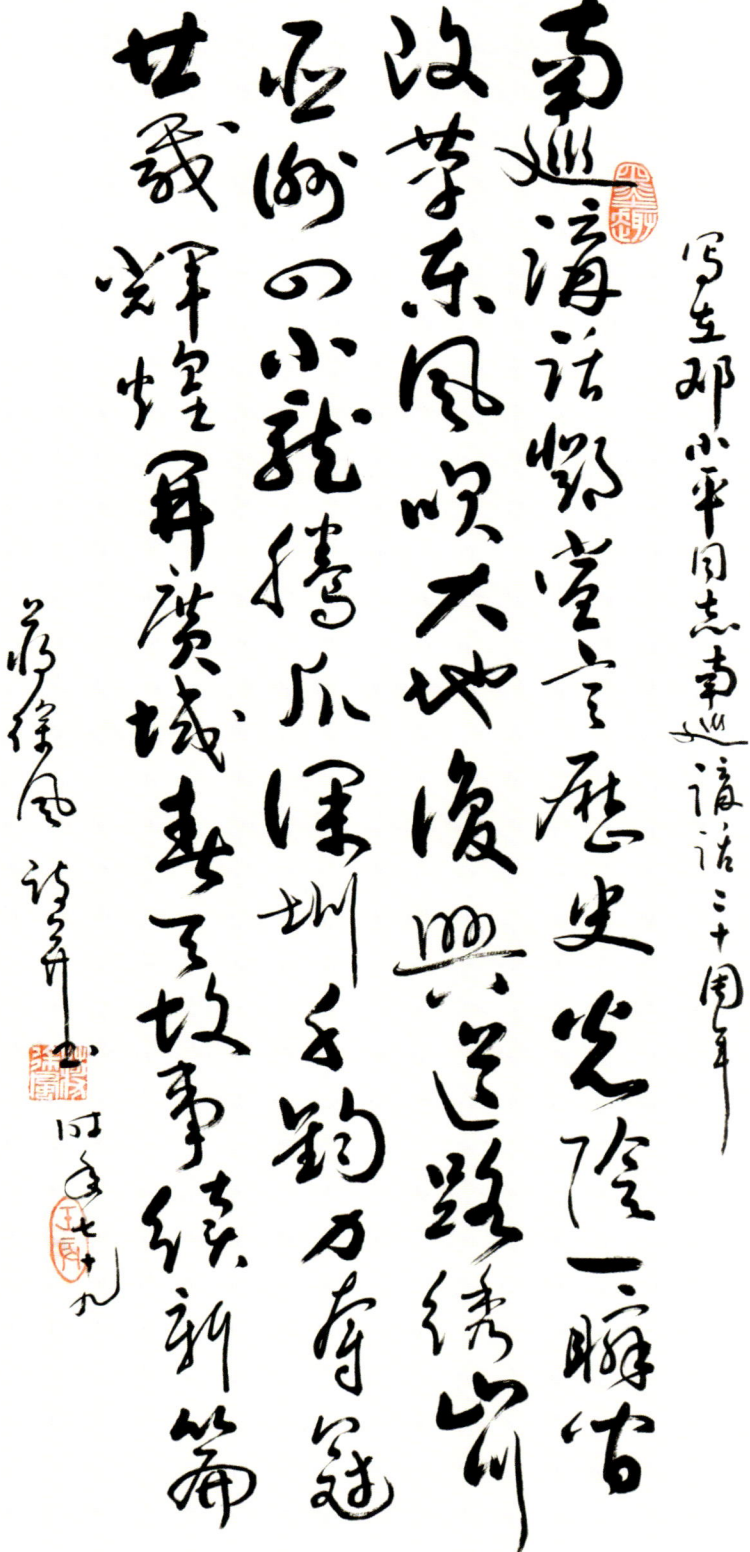

《庆邓小平南巡讲话》　　99cm×50cm　　*Celebrating on Deng Xiaoping's South Tour Speech*

解长河 Xie Changhe

解长河，男，原名解培利，字河子，1964年生于北京。现为北京风雅画院副院长、中国美术艺术家协会理事、燕名书画社社长、北京燕山书画协会副秘书长、北京市房山区美协会员、琉璃河书画协会常务理事、职业画家，中国海峡两岸书画家协会会员。

润笔价格：8000/平尺

Xie Changhe, male, with Xie Peili as his former name, and with Hezi (Son of River) as his courtesy name, was born in Beijing in 1964. Xie is Vice President of Beijing Fengya (Literary Grace) Calligraphy and Painting Gallery, council member of China Artists Association, President of Yanming Calligraphy and Painting Gallery, and Deputy Secretary of Yanshan (Mount Yan) Calligraphy and Painting Association, Beijing. He is also a member of Fangshan District Artists Association, standing council member of and professional painter with Liul River Calligraphy and Painting Association, and member of Beijing Cross-Strait Research Institute of Calligraphy and Painting.

Reference price: RMB 8000 per square feet

《富贵神仙》 80cm×180cm   *The God of Loftiness*

李兴建　*Li Xingjian*

李兴建，男，1938年生于山东临沂，现为中国书画家协会会员，东方艺术研究院名誉院长，文化部侨联文华阁书画院书画师等。

润笔价格：2000/平尺

Li Xingjian, male, born in Linyi, Shandong Province, in 1938, is a member of China Calligrapher and Painter Association, Honorary President of Oriental Art Research Institute, and calligrapher and painter with Wenhuage Calligraphy and Painting for Returned Oversea Chinese under Ministry of Culture.

Reference price: RMB 2000 per square feet

《盛世中华》　　134cm×34cm　　*Prosperous China*

王军 *Wang Jun*

王军，男，字郁之，癸巳冬生于汉上，湖北省美术学院硕士毕业，现为国家一级美术师，中国书画印研究院常务理事，中国剑光书画院高级院士，中国书画名家网艺委会副主席，武汉市道教协会会长,武汉市文史馆馆员，湖北省书法家协会理事,中国工艺学会理事等。

润笔价格：8000/平尺

Wang Jun, male, with Yuzhi as his courtesy name, was born in the winter of 1953, and graduated with an Master Degree from Hubei Institute of Fine Arts. He is a National Class A Artist, council member of Calligraphy, Painting and Seal Research Institute of China, and senior painter with China Jianguang Calligraphy and Painting Gallery. Wang is also Vice President of Art Committee of Chinese Master Calligrapher and Painter Network, President of Wuhan Taoists Association, librarian with Wuhan Institute of Culture and History, council member of Hubei Calligraphers Association, and of China Arts and Crafts Association, etc.

Reference price: RMB 8000 per square feet

《喜报》　　138cm×69cm　　Good News

吴庆瑞 *Wu Qingrui*

吴庆瑞，男，1963年生于中国扬州，现为中国标准草书学社社员、扬州大明寺佛学院书法教师、大明寺鉴真书画院住会常务理事。

润笔价格：3000/平尺

Wu Qingrui, male, born in Yangzhou in 1963, is a member of Chinese Standard Cursive Society, calligraphy teacher with the Buddhist School of Daming Temple of Yangzhou City, and standing council member of Jianzhen Calligraphy and Painting Gallery of Daming Temple.

Reference price: RMB 3000 per square feet

《行草条幅》　　138cm×68cm　　*A Scroll of Semi-cursive Script*

潘振德 *Pan Zhende*

潘振德,男,字述仁,号布衣笔,河北省深州市人,1945年9月生。现为深州市老年书画研究会会员、中国书画家协会会员、中国书画收藏研究院高级院士。

润笔价格: 6000/平尺

Pan Zhende, male, with Shuren as his courtesy name and with Buyibi as his literary name, was born in Shenzhou, Hebei Province, in the September of 1945. Pan is a member of Shenzhou Calligraphy and Painting Art Research Institute for the Seniors, of China Calligrapher and Painter Association, and Senior painter with China Calligraphy and Painting Collection Research Institute.

Reference price: RMB 6000 per square feet

《太行山之景》 138cm×69cm *Scenery of Taihang Mountains*

徐茂 *Xu Mao*

徐茂，男，字干盛、雪飞，号燕山居士。1971年生于河北唐山。自幼受父亲影响，酷爱书法。少时临习柳公权，渐知书法之奥妙情趣，偶得感悟。至青年时，从师著名书法家许乃凤先生，研习清代书法家、学者、教育家张裕剑之书法，自感碑学与帖学融汇之巧妙。老顿悟，每日润墨不辍。现为天津市收藏家协会理事，中国书画研究院研究员，京东书画院院士，曾获"金鼎奖全国书画大展赛"金奖，"仁、义、礼、信全国书画家邀请展"金奖，"福、禄、寿、喜、梅、兰、竹、菊全国书画大赛"银奖，"首届和谐杯全国诗书画摄影作品大赛"一等奖。

润笔价格：4000/平尺

Xu Mao, male, with Gansheng and Xuefei (Flying Snow) as his courtesy name, and with Yanshan Jushi (Yan Mount Hermit) as his literary name, was born in Tangshan, Hebei Province, in 1971. Influenced by his father, he ardently loved calligraphy, and gradually knew its temperament and charm in imitating and practicing Liu Gongquan's works. In his youth, Xu learned with notable calligrapher Mr. Xu Naifeng about the calligraphy art of Zhang Yujian who was a calligrapher, scholar, and educationist in Qing Dynasty, in which he comprehended the artistic combination of Bei-Xue and Tie-Xue. With time goes on, the old Xu achieves the life epiphany and never stopping practicing calligraphy. He is a council member of Tianjin Association of Collectors, researcher with China Calligraphy and Painting Research Institute, and painter with Jingdong Calligraphy and Painting Art Gallery. He won the Gold Award of Jinding National Calligraphy and Painting Exhibition Contest, and of Exhibition for National Calligraphers and Painters of Benevolence, Righteousness, Propriety, & Integrity, Silver Award of National Calligraphy and Painting Contest, and the first prize of the First Harmony Cup of National Poetry & Painting & Calligraphy & Photography Contest.

Reference price: 4000 per square feet

《念奴娇》 47×177 *Meditations on the Red Cliff*

玄一 *Xuan Yi*

玄一，男，现为国家级美术师，中国书画学会副主席，中国艺术家协会会员、中国玄体书法艺术研究院院长，紫龙宾虹（北京）国际书画院院长。

润笔价格：8000/平尺

Xuan Yi, male, is a state-level artist, Vice President of Calligraphy and Painting Society of China, and member of China Artists Association. Xuan is also President of Xuan Calligraphy Art Institute of China, and of Zilong Binhong International Calligraphy and Painting Gallery.

Reference price: RMB 8000 per square feet

《柿来运转鸿运当头》　138cm×69cm　　*Propitious Persimmon*

后 序

文化产业是市场经济条件下繁荣发展社会主义文化的重要载体,党中央、国务院高度重视发展这一产业,为此采取了一系列政策措施,深入推进文化体制改革,加快推动文化产业发展。2009年7月22日,国务院总理温家宝主持召开国务院常务会议,讨论并原则通过了《文化产业振兴规划》。中国书画是我国传统文化的重要组成部分,是我们的国粹,书画产业是我国文化产业的一个重要方面。在当前国内外的新形势下,书画市场的繁荣对于满足人民群众多样化、多层次、多方面精神文化需求,以及扩大内需、推动经济结构调整,都具有十分重要的意义。

总的来看,目前我国的书画产业呈现出健康向上、蓬勃发展的良好态势,正在成为推动社会主义文化大发展、大繁荣的重要引擎和经济发展新的增长点。但同时要看到,我国书画产业的发展水平还不高、书画市场还不太规范,这不但与人民群众日益增长的精神文化需求、日趋完善的社会主义市场经济体制不相适应,而且与我国对外开放不断扩大的新形势也不和谐。

为了适应当前国内外文化市场的新形势,由东方水墨文化有限公司和中央编译出版社联合出版发行的《中国当代书画名家作品收藏指南》系列丛书与大家见面了。编者本着艺术、学术至上的原则来选择书画家和作品,力争把本丛书打造成书画收藏界的经典之作,给广大的书画研究和创作者以及投资者、收藏者以参考借鉴。同时,我们还会给该书所收录的有实力、有潜力的书画家提供一系列的书画经纪服务。我们坚信,通过不懈地努力,本丛书的问世将会为书画市场科学良性产业链的形成大有裨益。

本书的出版发行得到社会各界的帮助和支持,在此一并感谢。囿于各种条件,书中纰漏及不足之处在所难免,恳请读者不吝赐教,以便我们在以后工作中及时改正。

Epilogue

Cultural industry is one of the important carriers of the prosperous development of culture in the socialist market economy; consequently, the CPC Central Committee and State Council have attached great importance to its development, and a series of policy measures have been taken to further promote the reform of cultural system so as to accelerate the development of cultural industries. Premier Wen Jiabao chaired a meeting of standing committee of the State Council on July 22nd, 2009, discussed and approved in principle Promotion Plan of Cultural Industry. Chinese painting and calligraphy is a critical constituent part of our traditional culture, and as one of the most esteemed art, calligraphy and painting industry is an important aspect of China's cultural industry. In the current new situation at home and abroad, the prosperous development of painting and calligraphy market plays an indispensible and important role in satisfying the diverse, multi-level and multi-faceted spiritual and cultural needs of the people, which is also critical in expanding the domestic demand and in the readjustment of economic structure as well.

The painting and calligraphy industry in China appears progressive and flourishing as a whole, which is becoming a major engine to promote the vigorous development and prosperity of socialist culture and a new growth point in economic development as well; however, the development level of Chinese painting and calligraphy is not high and its market management lacks standardization, which is not only incompatible with people's growing spiritual and cultural needs and with the gradually perfecting economic system of socialist market, but also inharmonious with the new stage of our expanding opening-up.

In order to adapt to the new situation of the current domestic and international cultural market, Orient Wash-Painting Art Center in collaboration with Central Compilation & Translation Press issued and published Collection Guide to Contemporary Chinese Painting and Calligraphy Works. Our editors, following the principle of "Art and Academic First", chose some great painting and calligraphy works, so that this book would be classic in painting and calligraphy art, which is bound to benefit most art enthusiasts and creators, and serve for the value reference of investors and collectors. Meanwhile, we also provide a series of painting and calligraphy brokerage services for the talented and promising artists. We firmly believe that through our tireless efforts, the advent of this series of books will be of great benefit for the forming of good industrial chain in art market.

We have received a great deal of assistance and support from various circles in the publishing and distribution of the book. However, owing to a variety of limited conditions, there are flaws and inadequacies in the book, and we appreciate your valuable suggestion for further improvement so that we can promptly improve them.

Yunfei Meng

图书在版编目(CIP)数据

中国当代书画名家作品收藏指南：第二辑/孟云飞主编．
—北京：中央编译出版社，2012.10
ISBN 978-7-5117-1327-8

Ⅰ．①中…
Ⅱ．①孟…
Ⅲ．①中国画－收藏－中国－现代－指南
②汉字－法书－收藏－中国－现代－指南
Ⅳ．①G894-62

中国版本图书馆CIP数据核字(2012)第251063号

中国当代书画名家作品收藏指南（第二辑）

出 版 人	刘明清
出版统筹	谭 洁
责任编辑	杜永明
责任印制	尹 珺
出版发行	中央编译出版社
地　　址	北京西城区车公庄大街乙5号鸿儒大厦B座（100044）
电　　话	（010）52612345（总编室）　（010）52612339（编辑室）
	（010）66161011（团购部）　（010）52612332（网络销售）
	（010）66130345（发行部）　（010）66509618（读者服务部）
网　　址	www.cctpbook.com
经　　销	全国新华书店
印　　刷	廊坊市飞腾彩印制版有限公司
开　　本	787毫米×1092毫米　1/8
字　　数	114千字
印　　张	38.5
版　　次	2012年10月第1版第1次印刷
定　　价	380.00元

本社常年法律顾问：北京市吴栾赵阎律师事务所律师　闫军　梁勤
凡有印装质量问题，本社负责调换，电话：（010）66509618